THE TRAIL OF THE HARE

LIBRARY OF ANTHROPOLOGY

Editor: Anthony L. LaRuffa

Editorial Assistants: Patricial Kaufman and Phyllis Rafti

Advisory Board: Malcolm Arth, Edward Bendix, Marie Clabeaux, May Ebihara, Bert Salwen

Other volumes in preparation

THE TRAIL OF THE HARE
Life and Stress in an Arctic Community

Joel S. Savishinsky
Ithaca College

GORDON AND BREACH SCIENCE PUBLISHERS
NEW YORK   PARIS   LONDON

cc

6002000916

To David, Kate, Ann, Susan and Max

Introduction to the Series

As editor of a new series I am uncomfortably aware of the recent out-pouring of anthropological books, a number of which comprise the "series" genre. Some people may feel that a new anthropology series is simply redundant and can contribute little to our understanding of human behavior. Yet, I would argue, there are enough very talented anthropologists with excellent professional backgrounds and diverse orientations to meet the needs of many more series.

One of the notable objectives of the *Library of Anthropology* is to provide a vehicle for the expression in print of new, controversial, and seemingly "unorthodox" theoretical, methodological, and philosophi-cal approaches to anthropological data. Another objective follows from the multidimensional or holistic approach in anthropology which is the discipline's unique contribution toward understanding human behavior. The books in the series will deal with such fields as archaeology, physical anthropology, linguistics, ethnology and social anthropology. Since no restrictions will be placed on the types of cultures included, a New York or New Delhi setting will be considered as relevant to anthropological theory and method as the highlands of New Guinea.

The *Library* is designed for a wide audience and, whenever possible, technical terminology will be kept to the minimum required. In some instances, however, a book may be unavoidably somewhat esoteric and consequently will appeal only to a small sector of the reading population — advanced undergraduate students and graduate students in addition to professional social scientists.

My hopes for the reader are twofold: first, that he will enjoy learning about man; second, and perhaps more important, that the reader will come to experience a feeling of oneness with his fellow man.

New York City   *Anthony L. LaRuffa*

vii

Table of Contents

List of Maps

List of Figures

List of Tables

List of Plates

Preface

In the year 1841, in the northern forests of the Canadian Arctic, more than twenty Hare Indians starved and froze to death in the gray twilight of winter. It was not the first time that such an event had occurred among these people, and it would not be the last. Below the walls of the fur trading post at Fort Good Hope, and further away, deep among the thick trees and frozen lakes of the spruce woods, men and women died, they killed and ate one another, and they consumed their children.

There is nothing political about such cannibalism when everyone else around you is starving and dying. Nor is it a religious act, or something sanctified by a mystique. It is a response to a threat without quarter, and, as a stab at life, it is pure, and simple, and devastating. If cannibalism and starvation have gradually disappeared from the Arctic in the twentieth century, they have only been replaced by the traumas of change and modernization, and they have left behind them the persistent dangers of an environment which still shows little mercy.

Northern existence amplifies the stresses of life that confront us all, and there is a strain of fatalist wisdom among the people who have survived both the aboriginal and the contemporary worlds of that region. This book is concerned with a small group of such people, and it focuses on a basic set of human problems which face them. It deals with the experience of stress, tension, and anxiety among an isolated band of Hare Indians who continue to live off the land in the Arctic region of Canada's Northwest Territories. The seventy-five individuals whose lives revolve around the tiny village of Colville Lake subsist as hunters, trappers, and fishermen, and in a subtle yet profound way, their collective existence presents us with a microcosm of the human condition. There is much that is richly distinctive and unique about their mode of living, but there are also some universal situations and predicaments which emerge from their way of life. By examining how the people cope with themselves, with their fellow man, and with their environment, we can gain some fundamental insights into both the nature of these experiences, as well as the people's experience of their own nature.

There are a number of ecological and historical features which make the people of the Colville Lake band a very opportune group among whom to examine the problems of stress. They live in one of the harshest environments in the world, and some of the most pervasive dangers and threats confronting them stem from their Arctic ecology. Extreme temperatures, long and severe winters, prolonged periods of isolation, hazardous weather and travel conditions, an often precarious food supply, and the constant need for mobility during the harshest seasons of the year, constitute some of their major problems. Survival has always been a crucial matter in the North, and even in modern times the people have maintained a semi-nomadic life style of hunting, fishing, and trapping which perpetuates these challenges. As a consequence of their subsistence patterns, band members lead a highly mobile existence, travelling thousands of miles each year by dogsled, snowshoe, canoe, and foot. Thus, despite a long history of contact with Western institutions which dates back to the eighteenth century, the people of the Colville region have maintained a deep involvement with their natural environment, and it remains a paradoxical and contradictory source of both richness and challenge to them.

Beyond the severity and the ubiquitous pressures of their ecology, the people of the band are also confronted with a set of social and psychological stresses which are of equally profound significance for them. Their recent history and acculturation, their immediate social environments, their necessary involvement with white persons, their socialization processes, and the conflicting themes and orientations which compose their world-view, all constitute sources of strain and tension. Historically, as well as aboriginally, Indian life styles in the North have continuously presented an array of such difficulties, and these have been met with by native people in both direct and subtle ways. The introduction of trapping and trade goods by Europeans, which occurred at the time of initial contacts in the eighteenth century, led to a restructuring of Indian living patterns and ecological priorities. Over the decades, these changes were intensified by related social factors, including native exposure to European diseases on an epidemic scale, with resultant dramatic population decimation among indigenous groups. The subsequent development, in the nineteenth century, of permanent settlements around fur trading posts, mission stations, and other Western facilities, deepened and expanded the scope of change by introducing new factors of sedentariness and native dependence upon European persons and commodities. More recent developments in the mid-twentieth century, including the post-war economic growth of the North, the region's expanding population, and the increased Euro-Canadian involvement in the Arctic, have all become immediately relevant to both the creation and the understanding of current problems in the community.

In temporal and spatial terms, therefore, the quality of life at Colville Lake has developed as a mélange of historical, social, and ecological factors, all of which impinge upon and color the way in which people relate to one another and their environment. The pronounced physical mobility of the people during the course of every year, which is primarily a response to their traditional survival requirements, has also been developed by band members as a way of coping with these other sources of stress and anxiety. That is, socially, psychologically, and ecologically provocative situations are dealt with, in part, by leaving undesirable environments and shifting to more manageable or familiar ones. The people, in trying to manipulate and control the context of their lives, consequently resort to travel and residence changes as primary coping strategies, and so social as well as ecological tensions contribute to the people's level of movement. It is my purpose in this study to examine the interrelationship of the stress and mobility patterns which are such a basic dimension of Hare existence.

This enquiry seeks to explore the simultaneity of a people's life experiences, and yet it necessarily proceeds in a linear fashion in order to identify and clarify the specific influences which relate to the members of the Colville Lake band. The exploration is thus divided into six sections, the first two of which deal with the ecology and history of the region, focusing upon the aboriginal, post-contact and environmental stresses affecting the people of the area. The second part specifically examines kinship, values, and interpersonal relations within the Colville band, and considers these both as stress sources and as factors which have promoted the continuity and contemporary resurgence of the local community. The range of stresses which have historically and more recently confronted the people is examined, and the primary coping techniques which have been employed by them are outlined. The following section considers in detail the people's relationship with their Arctic environment by taking them through the seasonal dispersals and ingatherings which make up the community's annual cycle. There are six major phases of band movement during the course of every year, half of which the people pass in small, scattered bush camps in the boreal forest, and half of which they spend as an aggregated community at their village. By taking up the specific social and ecological tensions which characterize each season in the same rhythmic manner in which the people experience them, we thus receive a diachronic and existential perspective on stress and mobility.

The fourth section considers how the people relate to the only permanent, non-native residents in their settlement, a white fur trader and a missionary. These two men occupy crucial and dominant statuses on the local scene, and the feud which they have been carrying on with one another for several years has had a deep effect upon stress patterns and village social relations. An equally pervasive presence in the people's lives is the large number of sled dogs which band members maintain, and the relationship between man and dog — a subtle mixture of respect, violence, and interdependence — is explored in the fifth part. The fact that white men and canines are ambiguous and constant sources of both tension and gratification for Indian people, makes the analyses in these two sections especially pertinent for an understanding of community attitudes and coping techniques. The arguments presented in these and preceding parts are summarized in a concluding chapter, in which some hypotheses are suggested concerning the extension of these ideas on stress to other social and cultural settings. The model of stress, mobility, and coping presented here is thus offered as a theoretical approach to comparable problems in other human groups.

This essay, because it is the outcome of both an anthropological and a very personal experience, tries to avoid the pitfalls of impersonality and superficiality into which such accounts can sometimes lapse. An ethnography, in its published form, is by convention and necessity linear, for that is the style and structure of print. And yet a truthful account of a people, beyond isolating the events which influence and derive from that group, ultimately seeks to orchestrate their experiences into a movement which evokes and expresses their way of life. Existence, or rather the experience of it, cannot be strung out like a line and still convey the complexity and perversity of being. Life is too variegated, and it is enriched and mystified by simultaneity. Despite the inherent limits of prose as a medium, there is thus a second purpose to this book, and that is to contribute, in a holistic way, to our knowledge of northern societies in general, and to our understanding of the Hare Indians in particular. We are dealing with the dimensions and ambiguities of a life-way, and with the ambivalences of the people who participate in it. I have tried to convey the essence of that existence by documenting the rhythms and the processes which are the core of this people's experience.

The data and the interpretations presented in my study derive from two field trips to the Canadian Arctic, the first of which was carried out from August of 1967 to August of 1968, while I was a graduate student at Cornell University. This initial trip grew out of an interest in human ecology and the problems of coping with extreme environments, even though I had not originally planned to pursue this particular problem in the North. However, chance and circumstance had drawn my attention to the Indian peoples of northern Canada, and so it was among them that I eventually hoped to discover a group with whom fruitful research could be conducted.

I realized that several conditions would have to be met in order for me to carry out the kind of ecological study that I anticipated. I wanted the group to be small, preferably a band of under one hundred people. This would enable me to get to know each member of the community personally, as well as afford me the opportunity to live and travel with a large percentage of the band's families over a long period of time. Secondly, the people's life style would have to be primarily focused on gaining a livelihood from the forest and the natural environment, rather than from other sources of income or subsistence. In the language of the North, they would have to be a "bush"-oriented band. Finally, I hoped to find a group that was physically isolated from large population centers and Western influences, and whose members were hence relatively less acculturated than most northern Indians and Eskimos.

These conditions were not easy to fulfill because social and economic changes in the Arctic since the Second World War had led to the collapse of many of the region's smaller and more isolated settlements. The native people who had previously lived in such villages were now residing, for the most part, in larger towns, where Western influences had caused them to abandon most of their traditional subsistence pursuits. It was not surprising, therefore — although it certainly was dismaying — that when I wrote to several Arctic experts to ask for advice on choosing a research location, most of the replies indicated that the type of group for which I was looking was now rare if not non-existent.

It was at this point in my research that I was fortunate enough to make the acquaintance of Professor Richard Slobodin of McMaster University, and it was he who first told me of the community of Colville Lake. Although he had never been to the settlement himself, he had heard of it in the course of his own research in the Yukon and Northwest Territories, and an exchange of letters between myself and the local missionary confirmed Slobodin's opinion that this Indian band had maintained the kind of traditional life style in which I was interested. Several months later, with the help of a grant from the

National Science Foundation, and having made the necessary arrangements and purchases of equipment, I travelled from New York to Edmonton, Alberta, and then, in August of 1967, I flew north to the town of Inuvik near the Arctic Ocean. From there, the only way to reach the community at Colville was by privately chartered aircraft, and so I secured a "bush" pilot and a small, single-engine plane equipped with floats, and early on a Sunday morning, we flew the 220 miles into the village and landed on the bay of the lake around which the settlement is located.

Although I did not realize it at the time of my arrival, I was only to spend about half of the next twelve months in the village itself, for the people's nomadic life style would keep me on the move for most of the following winter and spring. By arriving during the summer, however, which is the most sedentary period of the year for the band, I had a good opportunity to first experience the people in a settled and collected condition, and this facilitated my adjustment to them, and, equally important, their adjustment to me. I slowly expanded my circle of acquaintances during the first weeks after my arrival, and I was greatly assisted in this by a voluntary and unwittingly portentous act of some of my closest neighbors. The members of one particular household included two young adult men, Adam and Philip Ratehne, with whom I initially spent a great deal of time hunting, and whose father, Wilfred, first instructed me in basic fishing techniques. One day the father half-jokingly addressed me as *sešile* ("my younger brother"),[1] and the other members of his family followed suit by also using appropriate kinship terms for me.

The consequences of this simple act were immediate, unexpected, and far-reaching, for up until that time, most of the people had been hesitant and reluctant to interact with me — not only because I was still a stranger, but also because there were no standard behavioral patterns that they could legitimately extend to me. Everyone in the village was a close or distant kinsman to everyone else, and kinship was thus the language of interaction which defined community relations. To be without kinsmen was to be in a social limbo. Once I had been given a kinship status within one village family, however, even though it was a mock-serious one, I could then be placed by other band members within their own social networks, for the matrix spread out from Wilfred's household and encompassed all of the band's fourteen families. Thus, I suddenly found myself being accorded a sense of "fit" in the local community, and from then on the process of building rapport proceeded much more rapidly and fluidly.

I spent my first few months in the Colville area both at the settlement proper, and in the neighboring fish camps, where people were putting up supplies of food for the forthcoming winter. I was fortunate to have a small cabin in the "native" part of the community to live in, for this set me apart from the village's missionary and trader, who had physically separated themselves from the people (and one another), and thus established and enforced a "colonial" style of relationship with band members (cf. Map 3). Once the people realized that my attitude towards them differed radically from that of these two other white men, and that I intended to spend a full year in the community (rather than being just another "government white man" passing through), they accepted my presence and my company with surprising readiness, I eventually found myself either welcome, or at least tolerated with amusement, in all of their homes, and the same was true when I visited or lived with people in their bush camps. In turn, many of the villagers came to feel comfortable with me, and curious about me, so much so that after a brief period of residence in the community, I began to receive a constant stream of visitors at my own cabin. As is documented more fully in Part IV, I believe that the feud between the fur trader and the missionary inadvertently benefited me during these initial weeks, because it cast me in the role of a neutral and sympathetic outsider to whom the people could easily express their complaints and dissatisfactions without any fear of reprisal. I thus found myself the recipient of a great deal of personal information and gossip within a brief period after my arrival. The trader and the priest were equally hospitable and informative throughout the year, and they accepted (or, more accurately, learned to cope with) my proclaimed neutrality in their conflict with good grace.

For the Indian people of the community, most of the long Arctic winter is spent in isolated hunting and trapping camps in the boreal forest, and I was able to travel and live with several different families during the course of this season. Initially I stayed with households that contained bilingual members, for I had not had any opportunity, before going to the Arctic, to study any of the dialects of Athabascan — the language spoken by all of the sub-Arctic Indians in the Canadian Northwest. However, by the late winter, my understanding of *deneke* ("the people's language") had progressed enough to permit me to spend several months with a number of monolingual families. I consistently found that I could comprehend much more than I could express in the local dialect, and although my facility with *deneke* never approximated fluency, I found that a substantial vocabulary, combined with a judicious use of non-verbal communication, made it possible to relate to and understand people in a meaningful way.

· Throughout the winter and spring I switched bush camps whenever good opportunities to do so arose. If the people with whom I was staying were shifting their area and travelling through the trapping region of another family, I arranged to live and hunt with the second group. Later in the year, when I obtained my own dogteam, I enjoyed much greater freedom of movement, and was able to camp with many people whom I had previously not been able to keep up with. Altogether I travelled close to 600 miles by dogsled between mid-October and early June. This constant contact with dogs, and the necessity of learning how to drive, train, and handle them, led to my recognition of the social and psychological, as well as the ecological significance of these animals in the lives of the people. These dimensions of life are reflected in the content of this study's fifth section. By staying with both traditional and acculturated families during the various phases of band dispersal, I was also able to observe the people in all of their major economic pursuits, and I was thus in a position to study how they reacted to the many stresses which isolation in the bush presented to them. Experiences in different camps enabled me to check and compare the observations that I had previously made with other families, and it also revealed key differences in individual and family response patterns to the circumstances of bush life.

Ingathering periods at the village were also studied primarily through participant-observation, and paid informants were only utilized sparingly towards the end of my stay in order to collect personal histories and folklore. These were the only times that verbatim statements were directly recorded, as most of the time I relied on an extensively detailed field diary in order to preserve the life of the community. Many of the personal quotes given in the text are consequently reconstructions, or close paraphrases, of conversations that I participated in or witnessed, rather than direct transcriptions of tapes or interviews. The people recognized that I had come to the North to both learn from and study them, because soon after coming to the village, I explained that I was a teacher who wanted to understand the Indian way of life so that I could better communicate it to my students. My true purpose and objective were thus aspects of my presence that most of the band members could comprehend and accept, for they had all had at least some knowledge of the role of teacher and the institution of a school. Thus, when people saw me squatting in the center of the village with a group of women, noting down the details of hide-tanning, or curled up in a corner of a tent after a day of trapping, filling up the pages of my journal, my actions were consistent with my presence, and hence less disruptive or disturbing than they might otherwise have been.

When I lived in the bush with a family, I did so as a full-time, working member of the household, and I shared with the people the responsibilities for hunting, trapping, fishing, cutting wood, and travelling. I found, in fact, that it was impossible to live with a group in the bush and not be a productive member of the camp: the non-participating observer was a drain on already scarce resources, and hence a threat to everyone's well-being. It was with an understanding of my intention to contribute my labor that people agreed to let me stay with them in the bush, and when, eventually, my experience finally superceded my incompetence, the value of my presence in a camp was such that I was actually asked by the heads of several households if I would like to stay and work with them. In the forest as well as at the settlement, I participated in the people's ethic of generosity as best as I could, and rather than use money, I made gifts of meat, fish, wood, and labor to reciprocate the services and favors that I received from others. Though this form of participation was often very time-consuming and exhausting, it greatly enhanced my acceptance by the people, for it helped me to remain outside their stereotype of the exploitative and dependent white man who has little interest or competence in living off the land.

During that first year with the people, many stresses of life were revealed to me as a result of my own exposure and reaction to them. Boredom, isolation, lack of privacy, gossip, hardships of travel, starvation, knife-like cold, pressures for generosity, and drinking, all affected me directly, and in most cases I was first aware of these as personal problems *before* I recognized them as larger issues within the community. When these realizations eventually began to dawn on me, however, I was at first wary of projecting my own tensions and problems onto everyone else in the band: it was quite possible that my own experiences were unique rather than universal, and that the people as a whole were not affected in the same way by the stresses and deprivations that weighed so heavily on my own mind. I therefore deferred any conclusions about the tenor and quality of the people's life style, but I did allow my own reactions to sensitize me to the possible recurrence of these patterns among other band members. I thus became more aware of interaction rates, avoidance patterns, minor complaints, the content of gossip, and the composition of day-to-day and long-term groups. In the months that followed, there were indeed a series of conversations, confessions, confrontations and encounters which confirmed many of my suspicions about stress and response modes, just as these events revealed several stress sources, and an array of coping techniques, that I was initially unaware of. Although the people of Colville Lake can be characterized as an emotionally contained group, the repetitive, daily life of their bush camps was often as dramatic and informative as the more volatile and violent events surrounding their village ingatherings and drinking parties. People unveiled a great deal about themselves under a variety of circumstances and conditions, and verbal, non-verbal, and behavioral clues ultimately revealed a picture of their life that possessed both system and dimension.

The concept of stress, which was central to these understandings, has often been defined operationally in terms of physiological and psychological changes, and, in its most general sense, it is used to denote "a perceived environmental situation which threatens the gratification of needs" or an organism's well-being or integrity (Pascal 1951, p.177; Cofer and Appley 1964, p.453, cited in Appley and Trumbull 1967b, pp.7-8). In applying the concept to the people's life experiences, it became necessary to expand the notion of "environmental situation" to include social and psychological as well as physical dimensions of life, for each of these was equally immediate, and they all contributed significantly to the nature and problems of existence. Well-being also had to be viewed in multiple terms, for people evaluated and responded to their condition on the basis of simultaneously social, psychological, and ecological criteria. In one sense, as Hans Selye (1956) has argued, all of life is stressful, and this necessitated a sensitivity to tensions, threats, and anxieties stemming from a multitude of sources.

Operating on this level of awareness, it became evident that people were being confronted with stresses of varying specificity. Being caught in a "white-out" at -45°F, or finding oneself unarmed in a winter encampment surrounded by hungry, baying wolves, were situations of unambiguous and clear-cut danger. Yet, on the other hand, a general sense of distrust and suspicion directed towards one's kinsmen — a feeling held by many of the people — implied a stress that was less defined and more diffuse; it was, in fact, closer to "free-floating" anxiety rather than being strictly anticipatory or attached to a specific threat in time and space (cf. Slobodin 1960a, p.122).

The people's responses and adaptations to stress were as diverse as the tensions themselves, varying with the nature of the stress source and the particular individuals or families concerned. There were clear differences, within the band, of exposure and susceptibility to stress, and these were manifested in the modes of adaptation which different people employed. Highly acculturated and basically conservative people, for example, responded quite differently to the distinctive stresses of "bush" and village life, the isolation of the former and the concentration of the latter evoking behavioral patterns which marked these two groups off from one another. Men and women similarly exhibited distinctive responses to the particular stresses which derived from the band's sexual division of labor. Yet there were also certain stylistic features which many coping techniques had in common, and so it eventually became possible to characterize as well as simply inventory the people's repertoire of stress reactions. Some of these primary features, including an emphasis upon emotional restraint, an avoidance of direct confrontations, a recourse to movement, and the rechannelling or displacement of affective responses, constituted a behavioral set which the Hare have been found to share with other northern Indians as well.

While most theoretical and common-sense definitions of stress convey the sense in which this concept is used here, it is worthwhile to clarify how situations of stress were actually perceived and evaluated in the course of fieldwork. Operationally, stress has usually been defined by psychologists in terms of either disruptive stimuli or the responses that are made to them. Taking their analogy from physics and engineering, some have viewed stress as the operation of a deforming force upon a body or person, and the outcome of stress as the strain or deformation which that body or person undergoes.

The physical metaphor of stress-and-strain has certain heuristic value, but like all analogies, its uncritical assumption may conceal more than it reveals (cf. Klausner, 1968; McGrath, 1970b). Certain dynamic aspects of the stress process may be obscured by it, such as the way in which the stressful person's responses may alter the actual source of his discomfort. Exposure to certain levels of tension and anxiety has also been found to benefit people by heightening their awareness of circumstances and themselves, and by stimulating them to develop more varied approaches to life. An existence devoid of stress can become flat, unmodulated, and death-like in its monotony and lack of arousal or creativity (May, 1967; Bakan, 1971; Selye, 1956; Bernard, 1968; Marshall, 1968). In addition, stress is not always a threatening or negatively experienced condition. The people of Colville Lake actually sought to involve themselves in certain stresses of life, perceiving some of the conditions of bush existence, for instance, as challenging and exciting. Their lives thus turned on a balance between the seeking and the avoiding of different types of stress, their definition of specific situations often being quite ambiguous and contradictory over time. Furthermore, as experimental and observational work has elsewhere shown, within and between groups there can be considerable individual variation in susceptibility and reactions to given stresses, and this limits the usefulness of operational definitions based on stimuli alone (cf. Langner and Michael, 1963; Appley and Trumbull, 1967b; McGrath, 1970a; Steiner, 1970). At Colville Lake, for example, there were clearly marked differences in personal responses to specific social and physical environments, the outcome depending upon such factors as the sex, personality, age, and acculturation level of the individuals concerned.

Operationally, therefore, I tried to deal with stress in a manner that simultaneously recognized but also went beyond the idiosyncracies of personal reaction patterns. I attempted to derive a model from the villagers' over-all system of response to the wide range of disruptive, challenging, and threatening situations which confronted them. From the types of reactions displayed by the whole community, a basic set of response features emerged which could be distinguished from more individualized adaptations. Positively perceived stresses were often directly evaluated as such by the people in verbal terms: they freely expressed their sense of excitement and anticipation, and they showed their desire to be tested by pitting themselves against persons and circumstances, whether it was within the context of a game or the environment.

I took as a general indicator of negative stress (or distress) the fact that the people's responses to certain situations constituted a disruption of their usual social and psychological equilibrium. Attempts to restore homeostasis, whether it was an equilibrium in terms of psychological states, social relations, or relative physical well-being, were utilized as indices of stressful circumstances. Residence changes, and alterations in the membership of trapping camps, often indicated the presence of social tensions or environmental threats. Outbursts directed at dogs and inanimate objects, or a person's sudden withdrawal from interaction and social visibility, similarly betrayed the experience of psychological stresses. As these few examples indicate, the people's responses were not aimed at a strictly static equilibrium, for coping techniques sought to re-establish a balance at a new level — and often at a new point in time and space. Rather than dealing with the kind of equilibrium model of stress that the medical and material sciences utilize, therefore, I found myself involved in a process that was basically progressive rather than regressive, and essentially dialectical rather than simply integrative. In identifying stressful situations, individuals often noted, in fact, that certain behavioral modes — such as intense affectivity or avoidance — were unusual or remarkable to them, and they pointed this out either generally or with specific instances. Yet people were often unaware, or unwilling to admit of, their own participation in these same coping styles, and so their consciousness of stress-reducing techniques was far from complete. Nevertheless, they were sensitized to the consequences of many of life's threats, and by combining their insights with my own observations, the nature of their adaptive repertoire eventually became clear.

In the field, cues to the presence of disruptive states were noted in verbal, symbolic, and visual aspects of behavior, and these often involved delay or displacement of emotional release in conjunction with cultural patterns of repression and restraint. Verbally, for example, negative comments about a person's generosity or helpfulness would be expressed to myself or a third party, thereby showing both the source of, and the response to, the specific tension at issue. Delayed and displaced responses were often exhibited in a highly public manner during drinking parties, since these events constituted one of the people's few sanctioned outlets for aggressive release. Anger, humor, and vindictiveness were also verbally displayed in the course of gossip sessions, and the content of the people's conversations and jokes often enabled me to link these delayed responses with their ultimate causes. Visually, variations of bodily and facial expression (such as indications of disgust, despair or disapproval), symbolic forms of non-verbal communication (such as the physical separation of persons through avoidance), and the mobility of persons for non-economic or non-medical reasons (such as sudden trips to the village or other hunting camps), were also taken to indicate the presence of stress.

The various psychological states that researchers have included under the stress concept indicate the many forms that this phenomenon can take. These include "anxiety, conflict, emotional distress, extreme environmental conditions, ego-threat, frustration, threat to security, tension, arousal" and others (Appley and Trumbull, 1967b, p.1). While a full psychological or physiological discussion of causes, symptomology, and adaptations is beyond the scope of this study, the people's major sources and means of resolving stress are considered in detail and in context here. Most importantly, an attempt has been made to understand the experience of stress as a process, linking it to other aspects of people's lives, and placing it within the context of their total existence. An extensive account of stresses and coping techniques is given in Tables 7 and 8 of Part VI, which indicate the full range of factors and responses which have been subsumed under the operational use of the concept. These tables summarize many of the insights gained during my first stay with the band, but they also reflect a number of refinements, most of which were made during a return visit to the North several years later.

In the summer of 1971, exactly three years after I had concluded my initial stay in the Arctic, the National Museum of Canada gave me a field grant that enabled me to return to the village at Colville Lake. During the intervening years I had written and thought a great deal about the people of the community, and I had consequently become aware of some of the weaknesses and lacunae in my original work. It is always a good idea, while doing fieldwork, to interrupt one's research for a few weeks in order to think over one's findings, and then return to the community with one's mind refreshed and one's ideas clarified. Unfortunately, I had not been able to do this during my initial stay in the Colville area, for there was no economical way to leave the settlement save by dogsled, nor was there any convenient place to go to except for Fort Good Hope, an Indian town on the Mackenzie River about 110 miles overland from Colville. Good Hope was (and still is) a very important place for the members of the band, not only because it is the closest town of any size for them, but also because they have many friends and kinsmen there whom they visit whenever possible. When a sizable group of the people decided to travel to Good Hope by dogsled during Easter week of my first year, I consequently joined them for the trip. At the time, however, this journey was simply a continuation of my research rather than a break from it, for I was mainly interested in learning first-hand about the people's experiences in this larger, more "urban" environment. Since Easter week was primarily a time of intense sociality and drinking, I was preoccupied with the activities of the season, rather than with a review of my own, previous experiences.

The opportunity to return to the North in 1971 was therefore a very welcome and essential one, for it gave me a chance to re-examine the insights of that earlier trip after a suitable period of thought and reconsideration. I was equally interested in following up the changes that had occurred among the people during the preceding three years, and I had had some indication of these from an intermittent correspondence that I had kept up with several of the local people. I knew from their letters that the fur trader had recently died, as had the band's eldest member, ninety-one year old Joseph Tehgu, who was the community's main repository of folklore and mythology. Some people had also left Colville to go live or work in Good Hope, while others had quit the fort town and shifted their residence back to the settlement. In addition, several children had been born to members of the Behdzi, Yawileh and Bayjere families, and so the size of the village's population had not appreciably altered.

When I returned to the community, I also learned that during the last few years a number of the band's young adult men had obtained seasonal employment from the oil and mineral exploration companies that had become active in the Arctic during the late nineteen-sixties and seventies. Although this work was not carried out in the immediate vicinity of the village, it had nevertheless introduced some subtle influences which affected both the young men involved, as well as — indirectly — the economic conduct of the entire community. However, neither these nor any of the other events which had occurred had radically altered the life style of Colville from what it had been in 1967-1968, and so I have chosen, in this book, to write of the community as it was during those earlier years. The direction and impact of social change in the band are not ignored here, however, for these factors are introduced in the narrative wherever relevant, and they are considered more fully in the book's concluding section.

The main significance of the second trip to Colville lay in the re-evaluation and refinement of my earlier analyses of stress, kinship, mobility, values, and behavioral norms. I was greatly aided in this endeavor by my wife Susan, who had suffered with me through the writing of a doctoral thesis and several articles, and who was therefore able to look at the village with the eyes of a cool, critical, but well-informed newcomer. We spent most of June and July together in the community, and during that time Susan recognized and reformulated several aspects of child-rearing and emotional expression that I had previously either overlooked or misinterpreted. She also helped me to recognize both the limits and the potentialities of our analyses, and so much of what is valuable in this book is attributable to her. I alone am responsible for the final form in which all of this work has been cast.

To the extent that I have succeeded in understanding the nature and significance of the people of Colville Lake, I must express a large debt to the work of certain other scholars from whose insights I have greatly benefited. There has been a long history of anthropological interest in the peoples of northern Canada and Alaska, and this tradition provides a wealth of comparative material on the other

Athabascan-speaking Indian groups who share the sub-Arctic forests with the Hare. Until recently, however, the Hare had actually been one of the least studied of these peoples, and it has only been since the late 1950's that they have been given renewed attention by anthropologists. Professor June Helm visited the Hare settlement of Fort Good Hope in 1957, and she has presented her data in a number of subsequent publications (Helm, 1965a, 1965b, 1968b, 1969a, 1969b; June Helm MacNeish, 1960; Helm and Damas, 1963; Helm and Leacock, 1971). Professor Ronald Cohen conducted an ethnographic survey of the Mackenzie River region in 1960, during which time he also visited Good Hope (cf. Cohen, 1962; Balikci and Cohen, 1963; Cohen and Osterreich, 1967). Six years later, as part of a manpower survey of the Central Mackenzie area conducted by the Department of Indian Affairs and Northern Development, Miss Desmē Villiers again visited the region, and her research (Villiers, 1967) threw important light on the current economic situation of the Hare. The most extensive work in recent years that has focused exclusively on the Hare was conducted by Dr. Hiroko Sue and Janice Hurlbert. The latter two spent the summer of 1961 at Good Hope, and Sue returned for a second field trip that lasted from June, 1962 until January, 1963 (Hurlbert, 1962; Sue, 1964, 1965). Sue spent part of her second trip with the Colville Lake band, and her doctoral dissertation has consequently been a very valuable source for me. Earlier studies of the Hare and neighboring groups were conducted in the late 1920's by Professor Cornelius Osgood at Great Bear Lake (Osgood, 1932) and by Dr. Fang-Kwei Li, some of whose linguistic material has recently been published by Dr. Harry Hoijer (1966). Eighteenth and nineteenth century accounts of the Hare by explorers, missionaries, and early fur traders also offer a great deal of valuable information on aboriginal and post-contact culture, and they have been drawn on for this purpose at various points in the book.

In preparing and researching the present work, I have incurred a great many debts to a great many people, and a few words of thanks will, at the very least, acknowledge those individuals whose help and advice have literally made this book possible. Richard Slobodin and Ann Welsh first introduced me to the possibilities of fieldwork in the North, and their suggestions helped me to plan and organize this study. Discussions with Slobodin, Welsh, June Helm, Annette and Don Clark, Richard Morlan, John Honigmann, Cornelius Osgood, Robert McKennan, J. G. E. Smith, Frederica de Laguna, Catherine McClellan, Beryl Gillespie, Michael Krause, Robert Howren and William Noble have been very fruitful, and Helm has generously loaned me some of her manuscripts and field notes. While en route to and from the field, as well as in the Northwest Territories itself, my wife and I have enjoyed the hospitality of many people, especially Father Adam (O.M.I.), Bernard and Margaret Brown, John and Pat Costellnik, Bill and Daria McNeely, Regna Darnell, and George and Joanne Emery. In Ottawa, we also received the assistance of several people in the Department of Indian Affairs and Northern Development, and I would especially like to thank Dr. Peter Usher and Miss Desmé Villiers.

This book draws upon material which I first presented as part of a doctoral thesis at Cornell University, and hence it has benefited from the advice and teachings of a number of people with whom I have studied. I wish to express my sincerest gratitude to Burt and Ethel Aginsky, Robert Ascher, Thomas Gregor, the late Allan R. Holmberg, Kenneth A. R. Kennedy, Bernd Lambert, and Morris Opler for their time and encouragement over the years, and for the patience with which they have guided me. Other colleagues, kinsmen, and friends, especially Norman Ashcraft, Bernard Bernier, Don and Carrie Brown, Edmund Carpenter, Diane, Frank, Joan, and Marvin Frimmer, Paul and Amy Kaplan, Jeanette Malzone, Sayaka Nagayama, Douglas and Karen Raybeck, David, Kate and Ann Savishinsky, and Yetta Sherman, have discussed certain ideas and concepts utilized in this book, and they have been of great assistance in clarifying their presentation. The National Science Foundation, and the Museum of Man of the National Museums of Canada are to be thanked for sponsoring my field research in the Arctic, and I am also grateful to the Faculty Committee on Research in the Arts and Humanities of Adelphi University for a grant that allowed me the time to finish the manuscript of this work. Portions of the text have appeared or will soon appear in several journals, and so I would like to thank the editors of these publications for permission to utilize materials from the following sources: "Kinship and the expression of values in an Athabascan bush community", *Western Canadian Journal of Anthropology* (1970), **2**, No. 1, pp.31-59; "Mobility as an aspect of stress in an arctic community", *American Anthropologist* (1971), **73**, No. 3, pp.604-618; "Coping with feuding: the missionary, the fur trader, and the ethnographer", *Human Organization* (1972), **31**, No. 3, pp.281-290; "The dog and the Hare: canine culture in an Athabaskan band", *National Museum of Man, Publications in Ethnology, Proceedings of the 1971 Conference on Athabaskan Studies*, Ottawa: National Museum of Canada; "The middle ground: social change in an arctic community, 1967-1971", *National Museum* *of Man, Mercury Publications* (1973), Ottawa: National Museums of Canada.

The people of Colville Lake are the ones who have clearly contributed the most to this book, and I will always be grateful to them for their kindness and understanding. They showed me much of myself as well as of their own ways, and I trust they will appreciate the candor with which I have tried to write of their lives. I also hope that those of the people who may someday read these pages will find here some truths that will enable them to better cope with the problems of their existence. I have used pseudonyms [2] throughout the body of this volume, and so as much as I would like to, I therefore feel that I had best not thank the villagers by name for the hospitality and knowledge that I have received from them. My debt to everyone in the community is nevertheless a very great and conscious one.

Finally, I would like to thank my wife Susan for all of her encouragement and help during every phase of this undertaking. At a material level she has contributed greatly to this book by drawing the figures and illustrations, and by providing the maps and photographs which appear in the text. In addition, however, she has shared with me not only the experience of the North, but also the frustration of trying to recreate that experience in words. Without her support and her companionship, this work would never have been realized.

PART 1

Ecology and Community

1 INTRODUCTION

The first sense is desolation, and the second a stab of unexpectedness. To travel over the northern forests is to be confronted with a landscape so seemingly devoid of animation that one is awed by whatever force or fate it was that first led to the peopling of this world. For the uninformed eye can describe no sign of life, and it sees no trace of passing. Nothing appears to move or be, except maybe the wind, and that stirs the spruce trees and ruffles the waters, but it touches nothing else. If there is any life to be sensed here, then its forms are obscure, and its trails are well-hidden.

Mysteries are a luxury for the uninitiated, but to the involved and the knowledgeable native, their penetration is a secular necessity. The North may be an enigma to the white man, but it is a living, liveable and necessary universe for the Indian and the Eskimo, who have drawn their lives from its substance, spirit, and matter. In the millenia that have passed since the earliest Asian migrations to North America, few continental environments have gone unexplored by these people, and few life-supporting possibilities have been left undeveloped by them. The high Arctic of the Eskimo, with its treeless stretches of northern coast, ice-choked seas, and island tundra, and the sub-Arctic of the Indian, which borders these more barren lands with its lake-studded, forested regions, have been utilized as imaginatively and as creatively by native peoples as any area in the world. If the geography appears to be especially hostile, lifeless, and inhospitable to people of other latitudes, then perhaps this is a measure of our own comfortable inexperience with our physical and natural universe.

In contrast to our own visions and estimates, the Arctic forests can often be rich with life, and in a sometimes erratic, sometimes bountiful fasion, they have supported small bands of hunters, gatherers and fishermen for thousands of years.[1] The Indian people of Colville Lake are one of the few remaining northern groups who

1

continue to live off the resources of this land, and in an era when other Arctic peoples have gradually turned their backs on such a life style, the people of the community continue to be adept, insightful, and expert at coping and surviving. Although they now have access to high-powered rifles, steel axes, metal traps, and other items of Western technology, the members of the Colville band also have a long cultural tradition at their disposal, and they have drawn from it a social and philosophical foundation that underlies and informs all their other adaptive procedures. This ideological framework, which influences their social groups, their movements, and their relations with one another, is foremost an outgrowth of the band's ecology and history, for it has been these latter forces which have molded their approaches to life, and presented them with the major problems of their existence. The ecological and historical dimensions of the people's experience are thus a logical and necessary prelude to any understanding of their contemporary stresses, as well as a basis for comprehending their ways of dealing with them.

2   THE SETTING

The settlement of Colville Lake is situated about fifty miles north of the Arctic Circle, and it is considered, by both northern Indians and whites, to be one of the last "bush" communities in the Northwest Territories. The term "bush" refers not only to a boreal forest of spruce, tamarack, and willow which surrounds the village, but also to the settlement's isolation and small size. It encompasses the fact that the local people derive most of their livelihood from the land, and that they have only limited access to such modern amenities as medical, schooling, transportation, and communication facilities. These and other services are available to the people of the band only at some of the larger communities in the Mackenzie River area, all of which lie from one to several hundred miles distant from the settlement (cf. Map I). The people of the village consequently have only limited and intermittent contacts with a small number of white persons, for beyond the settlement's fur trader and Catholic missionary, there are no government, service, or administrative personnel resident in the community itself.

The permanent log houses of the people, which they have constructed from the spruce trees of the surrounding forest, are located on the shores of a bay whose edge curves in a quarter-moon arc around the southeast end of Colville Lake. Colville is one of several

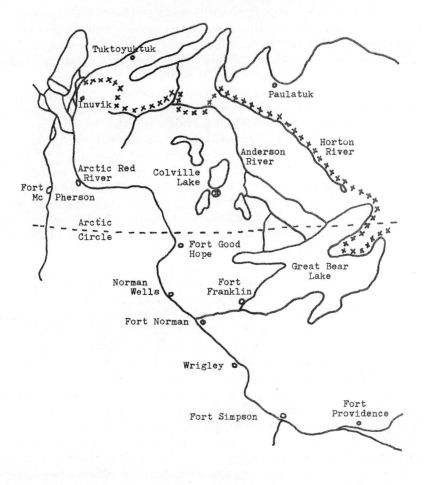

xxx   Tree line

ⓧ   Village site

MAP 1   The Mackenzie river area.

large bodies of water lying between Great Bear Lake and the delta of the Mackenzie River, and the community is only 165 miles south of the coast of the Arctic Ocean. Due east of the settlement, about 140 miles distant, lies the western border of the Barren Grounds, a zone in which the trees of the taiga (or forest) diminish in size and then slowly give way to the open tundra lands which stretch clear to the shores of Hudson's Bay. The edge of the forested region, technically known as the tree-line, generally follows the course of the Horton River, a waterway which traces its route along the very fringe of the Barrens. Far to the east of the village, the tree-line runs from south to north, but then swings in a westward direction as it passes north and northwest of the settlement. The community is thus well within the borders of the sub-Arctic forest, but it is also within reach of other environments as well. These widespread geographic features — the Barren Grounds, the tree-line, Great Bear Lake, and the Mackenzie River — mark the informal borders of the territory that is currently travelled over and utilized by the people. Their domain constitutes the northeastern part of what was once the aboriginal range of the Hare Indians,[2] and the people have, in fact, constructed their settlement upon the site of an old camping ground. There is thus a strong sense of continuity in the life of the village, for its members are not only living "on native ground," but their numbers are also drawn from the descendants of those bands which once lived and roamed in this area in pre- and post-contact times.

While the people have permanent houses and a home village at their disposal, the band is only at the settlement itself for about half of every year. Since most of the winter and spring is spent in dispersed bush camps, the people only experience one another as a community during certain holidays and seasons. When the fourteen Indian households of the band are thus concentrated, the village's population may number sixty-five to seventy-five people, including the priest, the trader, and the latter's family. Such ingatherings are intermittent, however, and the size of the local population often fluctuates for social, economic, and educational as well as environmental considerations. Young children are sometimes sent from the community to pass the winter at residential schools, and there is also a considerable amount of visiting and shifting of residences between Colville and Fort Good Hope. The village's missionary has opened up a fishing lodge which attracts a number of wealthy summer tourists to the settlement, and the men and women of the community are constantly on the move in pursuit of wood, wildlife, and sometimes wage labor in order to further their own subsistence.

The isolation of Colville Lake is a major stress to some of the local people, and this is a prime impetus for some of the travel that they engage in. Band members strive to maintain an extensive network of kinship ties which encompasses not only most of their fellow villagers, but also a wide set of consanguineal and affinal relations that they recognize in Good Hope. Thus during the Christmas and Easter periods especially, there is usually a marked, short-term drop in the community's size because a substantial number of people go by dogsled to visit the fort town. While Colville, in return, receives its share of native, medical, and administrative visitors from Good Hope and other Mackenzie area centers, the community nevertheless remains the most cut-off of all the settlements in the region, and many of the people experience with intensity their feeling of marginality.

One index of Colville's isolation is the village's relative inaccessibility. Most settlements in the Mackenzie valley are located either on the Mackenzie River itself or one of its tributaries, but the people of Colville are without a direct water route to their community. The village can only be reached overland or by small plane, the former being arduous, and the latter both expensive and unpredictable. An overland route to the settlement from Good Hope involves 120 miles of walking and dogpacking in the summer and fall, or the use of a dogsled or automated snowmobile in the winter and spring. The winter route is somewhat shorter than the summer one because the people can cut across the frozen lakes rather than circumvent them, but the 110 mile journey is still a difficult and hazardous one.

Fort Good Hope is the nearest settlement to Colville Lake, and the only one with which the people have regular overland communication. With a population of close to 350 people, the fort boasts a number of facilities and services — including a Hudson's Bay Company store, a nursing station, a Church, a Royal Canadian Mounted Police (RCMP) detachment, a school, an Indian Agent, a game officer, an air-strip, and an electric power station — which give it a much more urban flavor than Colville, and which partially accounts for the force with which it variously attracts and repels certain of the people. [3]

Much of the limited air traffic reaching Colville comes from Good Hope and two other settlements on the Mackenzie River: Norman Wells, the site of the North's only major oil refinery, and Inuvik, a large government administrative center in the Mackenzie delta. The flying distances from these three towns are 88, 124, and 220 air miles, respectively, and the flying times in the small, one and two-engine planes which usually make the journey can vary greatly with weather and travel conditions. Fog, rain, snow, strong winds, and low ceilings or temperatures often lead to the delay or cancellation of flights scheduled for the community. Weather conditions in all seasons often change with dramatic suddenness, and can turn a short, routine flight into a long and precarious one. Pilots departing for Colville Lake have no reliable way of keeping up to date on local flying conditions there. Occasionally an aircraft must turn back in mid-flight, or, having gotten as far as the village and finding the lake too rough to land on, found it necessary to return without depositing its cargo.

Since Colville is such a small and out-of-the-way settlement, it is also one of the few northern communities that does not have its own air-strip.[4] Small aircraft can land at the village during the winter by using hydraulic skis on the lake ice, and by utilizing floats during the summer months on the open water. This situation, however, adds to the unpredictability of flying, because it makes the status of the lake's surface yet another factor to consider in planning and executing a trip.

A further consequence of Colville Lake's size and marginal location is that it is one of the last remaining communities in the Arctic that still does not have a regularly scheduled airplane visit by one of the Territories' commercial airlines. Consequently, all flights into and out of the village have to be paid for as personal charters, and this, because of the great expense involved, effectively puts air travel beyond the means of most Indian families. Such a situation has certain non-economic effects upon the life of the community as well, for it gives the local priest and trader a monopoly over the control of air traffic into and out of the settlement. This control enhances their position of power within the village, and the native people, who are very aware not only of their isolation, but also of their limited ability to overcome it, are often manipulated by the whites through the latter's greater access to aircraft. People who want to leave or return to the village by air experience the dominance of the whites in this area of life, and their resentment is an index of the value which band members place upon mobility and the opportunities which it opens to them.[5]

One gets a very keen sense of the village's isolation when flying out to it from one of the larger communities in the area. Coming from any direction, one passes over vast expanses of apparently lifeless country. Setting out from Inuvik, near the Arctic coast, one first encounters endless stretches of flat muskeg. These are broken only by brush and scrub, lonely stands of isolated spruce or willow, and thousands of small streams, lakes, and ponds, which lay on the surface like drops of water spattered on a polished table. In the North, the table is not the earth's surface, however, but rather the permafrost (i.e., the permanently frozen ground and ice) which lays a few inches or feet just below the earth's surface. The permafrost prevents the water — the rain, and the melted snow and ice of each year — from draining off, and so bodies of water collect in all the depressions and low areas on the land's surface.

As one moves further to the southeast, towards the village, one passes well within the tree-line: the forest becomes thicker and more extensive, and the various coniferous trees stand taller. The landscape also loses much of its flatness and occasionally rolls up into small hills. The topography would continue in this way to the south and southwest of the village if one were to travel on towards Fort Good Hope. The trees continue to get somewhat larger in that direction, and one begins to find stands of birch when passing south of the Arctic Circle.

In the summer there are few signs of life to be seen from the air: a moose or bear may be spotted if one is fortunate and flying low enough, and some waterfowl, or a trout breaking water, can be seen on the lakes. Otherwise, the land seems to sleep in muted tones of brown and green under the long hours of light from the midnight sun. But the whole landscape is really alive with small game and with the countless mosquitoes, gnats and insects which thrive on the wet summer muskegs and bodies of water. The lakes are full of trout, whitefish, crooked-back, loche, and other fresh-water species. Flying over Colville Lake towards the village, one can spot native fish camps along the lake's shore, and follow the wake of the small canoes used by the men to check their gill nets.

In the winter, the colors, the fauna, and the lives of the people become transformed. The country becomes a sea of white, cut by the brown-black shafts of millions of spruce trees. Even in the dark, sunless days of late December, herds of grazing caribou can still be spotted from the air, as can the snaking dogsled trails which cut through the bush and over the frozen lakes. At Christmas and Easter times, sprays of clean, milky funnels of white smoke lift from the ground and announce the village. But during the rest of this period, from the winter's beginning in October to the thawing of the snow and lake ice in June, the people are scattered over a 100 mile radius in trapping and hunting camps of one, two, or three families. Except for the smoke from the missionary and trader's houses, and the tell-tale convergence of dogsled trails, the village is lost in the white ground for most of the year.

The dispersed camps of the people leave their own patterned imprint on the winter taiga. A December domesday chronicle would reveal eight or ten family clusters, far-flung and island-like throughout the forest, each with a satellite ring of smaller tents at over-night trapline stops. Sixty miles to the north of the village one might find Wilfred Ratehne, his wife, and children, camped together with the family of Wilfred's brother-in-law, Maurice Bayjere. Down along the eastern shore of Colville Lake would be a likely place for the household of George Ratehne, Wilfred's brother, along with the family of George's daughter, Paula and her husband, Albert. Farther to the west, forty miles away at *Tueso* (Aubry Lake), Albert's cousin Peter Dehdele frequently camps, and he and his wife Lena are sometimes joined there by the family of Lena's sister, Nora Godanto. South of Colville, along the eastern shore of Lac Belot, Leon and Pierre Behdzi have a favorite trapping area, while their brother Paul usually prefers to go after the marten and fox in the regions just to the east and west of the settlement. Pierre's married step-son Charlie, however, always tries to assure himself and his wife Adele of good hunting during the winter, and so they are most often found to the southwest, either at *Wokatue*, or one of the other small lake districts favored by the caribou. To the northeast are a series of lakes and small hills where two other Behdzi households often camp together, those of Yen (Pierre, Leon and Paul's brother), and Yen's son Yaseh. Finally, far to the east, along the shores of the Anderson River, and sometimes as distant as the western Barrens, old Joseph Tehgu and his descendants can be found, including the families of his daughter Berona, and his married grandson Fred Yawileh.

These fourteen families of the band, alternately dispersed and united, are a strongly independent people, as jealous of their autonomy as they are conscious of their interdependence with one another. André Yawileh, old Berona's husband, a deeply conservative, amiable man, who was born in the Colville bush country and has lived his entire life there, once observed that "the people belong together with this country, and what is best about our life is that it lets us be free." Old Joseph, André's father-in-law, a man with perhaps the deepest sense of tribal history, whose 90-year old face is carved and ridged like the bark of an evergreen, once remarked that "these people have always needed one another," for as much as they may argue or quarrel, "who could survive here alone?"

As Joseph himself perceives, there is a tension in life, a conflict between the ties that bind men, and the impulses that force them apart. People need, like, and look to one another, for they are kinsmen, survivors, and fellow-travellers in this world, and yet the intensity of their gathered existence often divides and drives them from this very company. This is but one of many ambiguities in which the people are caught.

For the band as a whole, there is also the paradox of their autonomy and commitment to the land, on the one hand, and their dependence upon outside goods and services, on the other. The people of Colville continuously experience their reliance upon the facilities of Fort Good Hope, and yet their traditionalist life-way has always kept the band at a social and psychological, as well as a physical distance, from the styles and immediacies of the fort. While they must acknowledge the importance of the town in their lives, the people simultaneously regret and attempt to minimize some of its historical influences. Thus when a mission and trading post were finally established at Colville in the early 1960's, over 100 years after such institutions had been inaugurated at Good Hope, the nature of the community was radically redefined, for these events brought to the settlement the first permanent facilities ever created there. The village suddenly gained a much greater degree of independence than it had ever had from outside centers, and its distinctiveness consequently became more visible and concrete than ever before. Thus, over the decades, the band had preserved and drawn its identity from diverse and ambiguous sources, which included not only the history and physical isolation of the community itself, but also the ways in which the people had related to the social and environmental presences confronting them.

3   THE REGION

The topography, the resources, and the rhythms of the Arctic have provided the framework within which the men and women have played out the drama of their history, and it is imperative to consider the ecology of the people as a background to the other dimensions of their existence. The task is complex because northern Canada is a region that contains within it as many environments as it has seasons. In each locale, every period of the year presents a unique landscape that is rich in nuance and character. This is apparent not only in the feel and color of the earth, but also in the texture and quality of the water, for the North has more of its mass covered by lakes, ponds, swamps, streams and rivers than almost any other land surface in the world. Scholars have estimated that these bodies may account for as much as 25 to 40% of this range, and up to 60% of the surface in some localities. [6] These bodies draw their waters from the glaciers, snows, and rains of each year, and then combine them to form a massive drainage system which eventually carries most of the Northwest Territories' running waters into the Arctic Ocean.

Colville is one of the larger lakes in this drainage system, and its irregularly shaped outline reaches some twenty-five miles from north to south, and about fifteen miles across at its greatest width. Although its surface is frozen for eight months out of every year, the lake is nevertheless continuously gaining and losing water from a number of sources and outlets. It empties out towards the Arctic Ocean at *Duta* ("Among the Islands"), a delta-like stream whose island-filled mouth lies at the lake's extreme northeast corner. Numerous other creeks feed into the lake on all of its shores, including the one that the people call *Coyngeriwelin* ("The Stream That Runs Near the Cabin"), by means of which the waters of Aubry Lake flow into Colville.

The members of the band have an intimate knowledge of the lake because of their daily involvement with it at nearly all seasons. Colville is foremost a source of food for the people and their dogs, providing them with trout, pike, white-fish, loche, grayling and crooked-back. The larger species average between three and four pounds per fish, while trout are sometimes taken in at over forty pounds apiece. People fish the waters of Colville and neighboring bodies throughout the year, relying primarily upon nylon and rope gill nets, which have long since replaced the willow bark fish nets which the "old-timers" once made. The people's ancestors also constructed dams, weirs, fish traps and dip nets to block off the channels of narrow streams, and although none of the families have utilized these techniques for capturing fish in several decades, most of the older people can remember and describe their own youthful experiences with such activities. Leon Behdzi once recounted the excitement of life at a fall fish camp with such vividness, speaking of the shouting people running along the banks, and the scooping up of silver trout in the sprays of water and moonlight, that the young people listening to him induced Leon to build a spruce-and-babiche model of an old dip net, and then used it to capture fish in one of the small streams near the village.

While the people have abandoned much of their ancient fishing technology, they continue to utilize most of the knowledge that accompanied it. Leon and his brothers place their nets in the same locations that have proven most fruitful for generations, and every autumn, during late September and early October, a large group of families can still be found at *Tuesotadelin*, the mouth of *Coyngeriwelin* on Aubry Lake's south shore, awaiting the start of the fall fish run. Working in concert with one another, the people first string gill nets across the stream's narrow passage, and then the men, paddling out in canoes, and illumined at night by the glow of gas-lamps as well as the moon, help drive the swarming shoals of fish into the waiting rope and mesh. In three or four nights work, enough food can sometimes be gathered in this manner to last a household for several weeks.

Fishing is a year-round rather than a seasonal activity, for the people could hardly survive without this major supplement to their other sources of food. Gill nets continue to be used during the winter and spring, being set and then extracted from under the lake ice by a simple but arduous method (cf. Figure 1). Whenever possible, two persons work together on these tasks, helping one another to first position and later check their respective nets, often dividing their total catch between themselves.

In mid-October, shortly after the lake had frozen and the ice was thick enough to support people, Leon Behdzi and *beša*, "his brother's son" Yašeh, showed me the standard way in which band members go about this work. Having first fixed their nets with sprucewood floats and rock sinkers at their camp, the men hauled the netting and the tools that they needed out to their fishing location by dogsled. Then they began by chopping a line of holes in the lake ice, spacing the openings about twelve feet apart from one another. When this series of holes stretched out over a distance that equalled the length of one of their nets, Leon tied one end of a long rope to the base of a fifteen-foot pole. He then introduced this stick into the first opening, and shoved

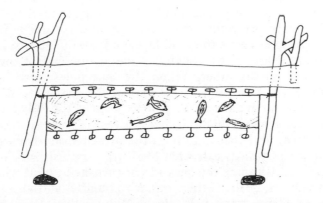

FIGURE 1   Winter fishing under the ice.

it towards the second hole. Yašeh stood over the second opening with a carved *tehⁿehdiwoⁿ*, a large forked stick, which he used to catch and guide the pole under the ice when it reached this opening. The two men continued to guide the pole in this manner until it reached the final hole in the series, and they then pulled it out onto the frozen lake.

All this time, the pole had been simultaneously trailing the long rope in its wake, and so the latter now reached from the first opening, where several feet of it still remained unravelled on the ice surface, all the way to the last hole, where Leon held the rope's other end in his hand. Yašeh then got the prepared and folded fish net out of the sled, and attached to one end of it a large stick which had been stripped clean, except for a single, downward-pointing branch. Yašeh carried the net over to the first opening, and having firmly tied its other end to the remaining portion of rope, he signalled to Leon. Leon then began to haul on the rope end that was in his hands, and as he did, his pulling slowly unfolded the net at Yašeh's feet and carried it through the first hole and into the water. A minute later, Leon having literally come to the end of his rope, the entire net was under the ice, neatly suspended in the water between the first and last openings. Leon then attached a branched stick to his end of the net, just as Yašeh had done, and both of them fixed anchor stones to their respective ends. Then they each knocked a final, upright forked stick into the ice near their respective openings. They poured ice chips and water around the bases of these last poles, and thus froze them solidly into place within a few moments. Finally, the branched sticks at either end of the net, which reached down far into the water, were hooked at their upper ends onto the notches of the stationary, forked poles, thus securing the net in place until it was time to check it for fish.

Two days later we returned to the site, and set about freeing the branched end-poles from the solid layer of ice which has since formed around them. Yašeh cut through the ice at one end of the net, and Leon worked on the other. When the end poles were free of the surrounding ice, Yašeh untied his end of the net from its stick and anchor stone, and in place of the pole he secured the tail of a long rope to the netting. When he had finished this task, Leon pulled out his end pole, and then slowly began to haul the attached net from the water. As he did so, he quickly extracted the thirty-one fish which had been caught, and by stunning the ones which thrashed about with a sharp blow on the head, he made them easier to handle, and also spared the net from excessive tearing. While he did all this, Leon folded the emptied portions of the net into a careful pile at his side. In the process of checking the net, he had also been pulling along behind it — under the ice — the long rope which Yašeh had attached to the far end. This cord was the means by which the men now reset the net.

To do this, Yašeh simply picked up the free end of the rope which lay at his feet, and by hauling out the submerged section of it, he simultaneously pulled the net at the other hole back under the ice. With Leon carefully feeding the netting back into the water, its entire length was soon back in position under the ice. Yašeh then untied his end of the net from the rope and retied it to its original end-pole and anchor stone. Finally, he and Leon re-hooked their respective end-poles onto the stationary forks, which held everything in place until the ice was reformed around the end sticks themselves. The net was thus secure and in position to trap fish again, and throughout the rest of the winter it could be rechecked in this manner as often as necessity, the weather, and the men's inclinations would dictate.

The waters of Colville and the surrounding lakes are highways as well as food sources for the people. Frozen and criss-crossed by sled trails during the winter, and plowed by paddles and outboards during the summer, the people take advantage of these more direct and unobstructed water routes whenever they are on the move. After the October freeze-up, they travel across them with dogs on their way to traplines and hunting camps, and between the break-up of the spring ice and the following winter, they utilize boats to check their summer fish nets, as well as to haul in logs and hunt waterfowl and moose.

There is actually a technological split within the community which reflects some key differences in how the people utilize the resources and advantages of the lake. The main division is between men and women, for females almost never handle or make use of boats on their own. This sex-defined realm of involvement and expertise is quite rigid: women do not make or paddle canoes, they do not operate or repair outboard motors, they never go hunting by boat, and they never check their family's fish nets from a watercraft. These separate areas of experience are not only an outcome of the band's sexual division of labor, they they also stem from some deeply-held beliefs that the older people still articulate. One afternoon, while I was helping André and Berona clean their fish nets in the village, André explained to me that:

Women can do a lot of work with nets and boats on the land. They help us mend the old nets, and Berona sewed and patched the canvas cover on my hunting canoe. Certainly, they clean all the fish when they are brought in. But for a woman to paddle out on the lake to empty the nets would never happen. They just wouldn't do it. It's bad luck for fishing — very bad, the old-timers say. The boat would then be no good and the fish would leave the nets and not come back.

André smiled and threw a quick, rhetorical glance over at Berona, who just nodded her head in agreement. But I asked her anyway, and she raised her chin, pursed her lips, and laughed out a quiet "no, I wouldn't do it."

Yet some women do visit their family's nets during the winter when their men are gone on the trapline, but that does not involve their use of watercraft. Fishing spots can then be reached via dogsled and snowshoe, thus maintaining the separation between women and boats. The only time that females can be found in watercraft is when an entire household is moving out to, or returning from a bush camp during a season of open water. Even during the winter, females in the more tradition-minded families, such as Berona's, avoid crossing directly over a net which has been set under the ice. They stop their dogsleds just short of the net, grab the lead dog, and guide the entire team around the area in order to avoid violating the taboo.

The limited access which women have to water transport is actually a key to a larger set of differences between the respective life styles of men and women. Males enjoy a much greater amount of mobility than females, and this pertains to a number of travelling modes, watercraft being just one case in point. The visiting patterns, dogsled trips, short-term residence changes, and day-to-day subsistence pursuits of the men all involve styles and degrees of sex-defined movement which amplify their differences from the women. Since the capacity for movement is often translated by the people into a means of avoiding stressful situations, this differential access to mobility becomes a basic dimension of coping and personal adaptation for the two sexes (cf. Part III).

There is not only a stylistic and technological difference between the movements of males and females, but also a *de facto* division among the men themselves. The younger adults make frequent and heavy use of larger, home-made scows powered by "kickers" or *klason* (outboard motors), while the older, more conservative men rely primarily on the smaller, spruce-framed *alaiya* ("hunting" or "rat", i.e., muskrat, canoes), which are the traditional form of water transport in the area. While these latter craft are now covered with canvas rather than bark, the village's elder and abler craftsmen, such as Leon, André, and their age-mates, continue to construct their own hulls entirely from local materials. They feel safer and more comfortable in these canoes, for as Leon once expressed it:

I don't know anything about using motors like that . . . I can't fix one of them. If it stopped or broke, I couldn't do anything to it and I'd be stuck out on the lake. So all I know real good is my "rat" canoe. I'll leave those *klaso^n* to Yašeh, Adam and those boys.

The scows are, indeed, more complex, as well as larger, faster, and actually much more stable than the narrow *alaiya*. The younger men who operate the larger boats, and who in many cases pursue their winter trapping more assiduously than their fathers and uncles, are able to afford the necessary motors, tools, and equipment for these craft from their annual fur money. Like so many other Western items, however, their motors also have some inherent — one is tempted to say purposely built-in — disadvantages. Not only is their obsolescence apparently planned, but — as far as the people can see — so are their constant breakdowns. Thus, beyond being expensive to buy and fuel, motors are also unreliable and often frustrating. Since there are no supplies available locally, any needed materials, like the engines themselves, have to be ordered by the people from the "outside" (i.e., outside of the Territories), which can leave a motor idle for weeks or months, and its owner dependent upon the equipment of others. Outboards, as well as the gas-powered chain-saws which some young men have bought, consequently create a community of interest among their owners, who share their parts and expertise with one another, and who often seem to spend more time fixing their engines than actually running them.

There are a similar set of concerns which bind the elder canoe-users together. Their fragile, exposed, and unstable craft require careful handling and decision-making, and a constant awareness of wind and water conditions on the lake. The men consequently set their fish nets within the bay which borders the village, for its surface tends to be calmer than the more open waters, and it is protected from strong north winds by the projecting tip of land at its northeast entrance. Singly and in groups, one can often see the men studying the condition of the bay as they relax or go about their daily tasks, and much of their casual conversation turns upon the hazards and possibilities of that day's fishing.

Throughout the summer and fall, the older men usually check their nets twice a day. Because they only like to go out on the lake when the wind is at its lowest, their trips are most often made in the morning and evening. Furthermore, just as the people of the band camp together in family clusters because they do not like to be alone in the winter bush, these elderly men similarly gain security by paddling out to their nets in groups of two, three, or as many as six canoes at a time. Since the approximate time of day at which they go out is known to all of them, as soon as one man is seen heading towards his canoe, two or three others may also take up their paddles and join him. And since the men's nets are usually set in the same area of the bay, they can all travel out and back together. If the weather and the condition of the lake look threatening, a group of them may stand on the shore where their boats are beached, and then discuss the advisability of going out before they come to a decision. It is rare to see one man travelling out on the lake when the others have decided it is too dangerous to do so.

The stresses and hazards which lake fishing present for elderly men are thus handled by them in a number of ways. In the first place, they seek to minimize the dangers they face by fishing in the safest, most sheltered areas. Secondly, they visit their nets at the calmest times of the day, first conferring with one another when conditions on the lake are doubtful. They also keep from their nets and boats the only persons — their wives, sisters, and daughters — whose presence could conceivably bring bad luck and misfortune upon them. Finally, the men enhance their security (and, more importantly, their *sense* of security) by visiting their nets in groups rather than going out individually. Taken together, these simple strategies illustrate the kind of complementary repertoire by means of which the people cope with so many of the stresses and anxieties confronting them.

All the men of the village, regardless of their age, have an encyclopedic knowledge of the lake and its properties. The younger men, whose boats enable them to travel extensively, have each developed a detailed, mental map of shoals, sandbars, and shallow spots, and they share with their fathers and elder kinsmen an intimate familiarity with the lake's resources, their seasonal availability, and the dimensions and significance of the shoreline. This cognitive control of the environment, this internalization of its surfaces and content, is a hallmark not only of the people's spatial orientation, but also of their existential approach to the qualities of ecological survival. Their knowledge derives from relationship, be it with people, places, or their properties, and experience is thus invested with an intense consciousness.

Young Philip Ratehne, Wilfred's seventeen year-old son, first acquainted me with the richness and subtlety of the lake's contours by taking me with him on a hunting trip along its eastern shore. Every landmark that we passed drew forth some comment from him — "good duck hunting," "muskrats in the spring," "pools of grayling in the fall" — and, featured or unmarked, there was an Indian name for every point where land and water met. Back at the village, the lake's identity continued to unfold, for Philip took the pen and paper that I offered him, and in one smooth motion, he outlined the entire shoreline shown in Map 2, and then proceeded to dot its borders with a score of Indian place-names (Table 1). As we read over and translated these words, and as Philip — squinting through his one good eye — explained what he knew of their origin, a keen sense of

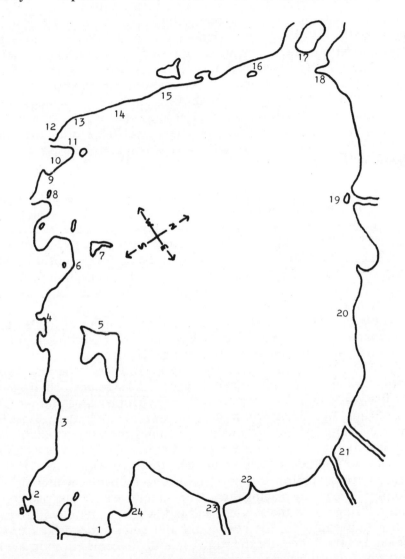

MAP 2   Colville Lake native place names (based on a drawing by Philip Ratehne).

history as well as geography emerged. Hunts, haunts, battles, deaths, the nature of the beasts and their seasons, encounters, and the real and more-than-real persons who have known this land were all evoked, turning Philip's map into an environmental almanac which recalled time while it described space.

K'apamitue is the Indian name by which the people identify both Colville Lake and their own community. The word is an ecological statement in its own right, for its literal translation, "ptarmigan-net-lake," denotes a traditional food harvesting technique still employed by the band's older women. Ptarmigan are a species of grouse whose members remain in the Arctic throughout the year, rather than migrate south like the area's more seasonal waterfowl. They are thus a constant, if somewhat meagre, resource for the people during times of shortages and hardship. During the winter, one of the few food sources left to the ptarmigan themselves are the green buds of the dwarf willows, which grow along the shores of lakes and rivers. The southeast rim of Colville Lake is one of the most bountiful locations for this food, and so here, as well as at their bush camps, Philip's mother Bertha, and the other elderly women, stretch out their old fish nets among the willows in order to trap the ptarmigan. When the birds fly in among the shoots to eat the buds, they tangle their bodies and wings up in the netting, and they remain suspended there until the women come to gather in their daily harvest. Plucked, gutted and roasted, the ptarmigan make for a welcome variety in the sometimes monotonous mid-winter diet.

The people actually have access to a large number of foods during the course of every year, but their meals are nevertheless focused around a small number of basic items, particularly caribou meat and fish. Along with ptarmigan and the snowshoe (or "varying") hare, both of which the people trap and snare at all seasons, fish are one of the few year-round food resources that the people can count on. They are of equal significance for feeding the several hundred sled dogs that the band supports, for without these canines the winter mobility and survival of the people would now be impossible. When families are able to accumulate a surplus of fish, they consequently store and preserve these against a time of future need. In the winter fish can simply be frozen by placing them atop an outdoor storage platform or *alahfi* ("stage"). In the summer and fall, when the temperature is too warm to permit this, the people dry and smoke the fish, a process which preserves them for the winter months to come. Even in the late autumn, when sub-freezing conditions have not yet begun, people will take long willow branches, ram them laterally through the gills of ten fish, and then store several of these racks on an *alahfi*. While these "stickfish," as the people call them, will turn slightly rotten before the winter sets in, they nevertheless make excellent and convenient dog food.

One other storage and preservation technique that the people use for fish has a double purpose. The men in several families including André Yawileh, Maurice Bayjere, and their grown sons, have dug deep pits near their homes, going down seven or more feet into the permafrost layer. These holes, with their walls of perpetually frozen material, thus constitute underground ice-houses with excellent storage potential. The tops of the pits are covered over with moss and brush, and just a small opening is left at ground level. Fish are thrown into these holes in the fall and early winter, and although a certain amount of decay occurs, the coldness of the pits slows and retards the

TABLE 1

Colville Lake native place names

1. *Sanefīga* . . . "White Hair of an Old Man"
2. *Mits'airmošon̄tin* . . . "Mits'air's Mother is Buried There"
3. *Ala'inurat'adu* . . . "Airplane Point"
4. *Ōndahwadon* . . . "Sitting Jackfish"
5. *Dugā* . . . "White Island"
6. *Nofayfīwehon* . . . "Loche Skull Point" (actually a hill)
7. *Fōlehdūway* . . . "Sawbill Duck Island"
8. *Duehtsēhgay* . . . "Between the Island" (an inlet)
9. *Ehgon̄erīwelin* . . . "Fish Scale Stream"
10. *Behguhulēhson̄ti* . . . "Toothless Old Lady Buried There"
11. *Gok'ayēh* . . . "Blackbird Eddy"
12. *Coyn̄gerīwelin* . . . "The Stream That Runs by The Cabin" (the stream that connects Colville and Aubry Lakes)
13. *Bayrehhohējin* . . . "Hooked a Big Trout"
14. *Ehjirihofīwehnewehun* . . . "Musk Ox Skull"
15. *Wonraglin* . . . "Alone Again"
16. *Fiziahdā* . . . "Spruce Gum Point"
17. *Duta* . . . "(The Stream) Among the Islands"
18. *Ahdahdahwēlay* . . . "The Island at The End of a Point" (this is actually part of the point, being connected to it by a thin strip of land)
19. *Behkahdūweh* . . . "Sea Gull Island"
20. *Behk'āhrehedah* . . . "Sea Gull Point"
21. *Dedēlilin* . . . "Sucker Creek"
22. *Sehlēhrahdah* . . . "Sehlehr's Point"
23. *Sehlēhrriwelin* "Sehlehr's Creek"
24. *K'apamī* . . . "Ptarmigan Net" (the village itself)

process of putrefaction so that the fish do not fall apart or lose their nutritive value. While their powerful stench prevents the people from eating these fish, no such inhibition affects the dogs, who thrive on such food during the winter. Their penetrating odor also lends the fish added value, for the long distances over which their stench is broadcast makes them excellent bait for winter traps. Marten, fox, and other animals are attracted by their smell, and so when the people move out into the bush to pursue furs, they try to take a supply of this "pitfish" with them for use on their traplines.

The main source of meat in the people's diet are the large, migratory herds of caribou which move into the Colville area from the Barren Grounds each November. The herds break up into smaller, roving units of several dozen animals once they reach the Colville vicinity, and they remain in the region until late May or early June, at which time they reform into larger groups and begin migrating back to the Barrens for the summer months. The people hunt the caribou throughout the winter and spring, and preserve their meat for the summer either in underground ice-houses or in the form of drymeat, smoked meat, or pemmican.

The snaring and spearing of caribou, the use of bows, arrows, and deadfalls, the construction of pounds, pits, surrounds, and drift fences, and the utilization of large communal drives to take great quantities of game, were all once prime hunting techniques in the region, but they have long since disappeared from the band's repertoire. Instead, men now take the animals with high-powered rifles, pursuing them either individually or in cooperation with the other hunters in their encampments. The extreme dispersal of the caribou during their winter stay, and the people's intense dependence upon them for their own survival, are factors which necessitate the band's corresponding fragmentation during much of ever year. Since the caribou are only present in large herds during the late spring, the people try to coordinate their winter moves and camps to coincide with the scattered availability of caribou and other key resources. And since the fish, fur, and fuel upon which the people also depend are similarly dispersed, the band's families experience their yearly· isolation as a stressful but necessary concomitant of their life style and ecology.

The importance of the caribou in the people's lives includes the utility of the animals' hides and bones as well as the edibility of their meat. An adult caribou, depending upon its age and sex, and the season in which it is killed, not only weighs some 150 to 400 pounds (Burt and Grossenheider, 1952, p.234; Kelsall, 1968, p.29), but its skin , hair, antlers, and skeleton continue to provide the people with materials which are essential for their survival and well-being. The hides which the women laboriously clean, scrape, soak, stretch and tan are made into moccasins, mukluks, and mittens, the untanned skins are cut into cord-like strands of babiche, the sinews become thread, and the softened hides whose hair is left on are utilized as sleeping rugs. The pelage of the caribou provides excellent warmth, not only because of the thickness and length of the coat, but also because each caribou hair is hollow inside, and thus carries within it a highly insulative pocket of air. Some of the more assiduous and utilitarian women in the band, such as Peter Dehdele's wife Lena, Bertha Ratehne, and old Berona, also sew winter socks and slippers out of the caribou hides. The pieces of footwear are made with the hair turned inwards against the wearer's skin, and when worn under a pair of well-sewn mukluks, they enable a person to withstand some of the coldest weather that the Arctic winter offers. In the midst of a seventy-degree-below-zero spell one February, Peter Dehdele and I were camped out on his trapline, and he held up a pair of hide slippers that his wife had made him:

I don't think I could take it for long out there without these. Two weeks ago all I had were those lousy woolen ones from the store, but they weren't worth a damn. It was forty or fifty below and my feet were freezing. Then I had Lena make me these. That's some difference I'll tell you. I put these on and I don't care if it's sixty below — it's like I don't feel anything and my feet never hurt.

There are thus some native materials from the people's traditional culture for which there are still no adequate Western substitutes. The babiche which the people make from caribou hides is one of the most versatile of these resources. It is essential for constructing the webbing of snowshoes, and is also used to make and repair a wide variety of other items, including ice-scoops, sleds, dog harnesses, snares, and whips. I have seen men who could not secure parts for their chain-saws and kickers make ingenious use of babiche and spruce wood in order to repair these engines.

The people have, of course, abandoned a great many aspects of their old life style. Caribou are hunted quite differently from aboriginal ways, and the animals are not utilized as fully as they once were. In the band's low carbohydrate diet, however, the large quantities of back-fat that caribou provide still allow the people to generate the body heat that they need to withstand the winter cold (Symington, 1965, pp.49-50; Kelsall, 1968, pp.41, 209-211). The women continue to smash and boil the bones of caribou to get the fat and tallow, and they also split open the larger leg bones and use their sharpened edges — as well as scapulae — for hide scrapers. But neither bone nor stone are utilized now as needles or knife blades, nor are antlers employed as ice chisels any more. Iron and steel have superceded these latter uses of caribou, just as modern containers have replaced the intestines and stomachs of caribou as convenient storage pouches for fat and liquids. Similarly, curved and frozen caribou leg skins, which were once loaded up with food, and then dragged from camp to camp like toboggans, have given way to the bent wooden planks, backboards, and canvas sides of the modern cariole or dogsled (cf. Figure 2).

The people's ancestors also made much more use of caribou and hare skins for clothing, by making parkas, ponchos, capes, leggings, moccasins, mittens, pants, hoods, and entire head-to-toe outfits from these materials. Hare pelts were cut spirally to form a single, continuous strip, and then several of them were woven together by the women to make a garment. Caribou skins, generally with the hair left on, were sewn together with babiche and sinew, and, as was true of neighboring groups like the Chipewyan, perhaps eight or ten pelts were needed to make each person's winter outfit in the old days (Oswalt, 1966, p.25). [7]

A commitment to these types of apparel actually affected the mobility and territoriality of these early Indians, for the winter pelts of caribou, despite their long hair, are really not suitable for large items of clothing. Rather, it is the late summer and early fall hides which are in optimum condition, and this necessitated that the people pursue

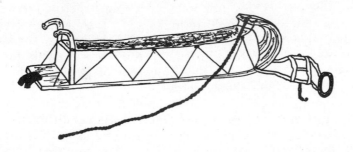

FIGURE 2   Native dogsled with wrapper (cariole), backboard, braker, head-line and first or "wheel" harness.

the large herds out onto the Barren Grounds each year in order to obtain these pelts. The seasonal quality of the caribou hides has to do not only with the fact that their long winter hairs easily break and fall out after continuous use — thus requiring their annual replacement — but, more importantly, with the large number of warble fly larvae which infest and pockmark the underside of almost every living caribou's skin. This infestation, from which the caribou are never really free, follows an annual cycle in which the flies pupate in early summer, and then reinfest the caribou before the onset of winter. The flies burrow down to the underside of the pelt on the animal's legs or rump, migrate to the back area, and then, after cutting breathing holes, utilize the surrounding skin as food during the coming months. Such infested hides can be decimated by the following spring, making these animals of very limited utility for clothing.[8]

It was consequently the newborn caribou calves of each summer — who accompanied their mothers to the Barrens, but whose hides had not yet been populated with the warble flies — who presented the people with some of the best clothing pelts available. Adult hides were also in optimum condition now because the breathing holes of the larvae had healed over with scars (Kelsall, 1968, p.274). In the late summer and autumn, the hairs of both calves and adults were short but firmly rooted, and their skins were thin, relatively unmarked, and very pliable. Members of the Indian bands which bordered the Barrens therefore made an annual trek to the summer grounds of the caribou, and hunted these animals on the tundra. The Hare and neighboring groups — especially the Chipewyans, Yellowknives, and Dogribs — were literally "edge of the woods people," as much at home on the tundra as they were in the taiga.[9] The people dried and smoked the meat they obtained for easier transport back to the forest, and also brought with them enough hides to make new sets of winter clothing. In the Colville area, these summer hunting expeditions actually persisted into the first decades of this century, for although the people now rely heavily upon the commercially made clothing found at the local trading post, the elder Yawilehs, Behdzis, Ratehnes and Bayjeres can all remember these trips to the Barrens in their own youth, as well as the caribou hide clothing which they once wore.[10] Their memories and experiences are thus a direct link with the band's past, and a reminder of the vast geographic areas over which the people have always wandered.

The earlier travels of the people out onto the Barren Grounds also brought with them within reach of the musk-ox herds, which were once a significant part of the food supply and trading economy of the northeasterly Hare Indians. Unfortunately, under the impetus of the fur trade in musk-ox pelts in the latter part of the nineteenth century, the herds to the north of Great Bear Lake became severely depleted, and so musk-oxen have not figured importantly in the people's economy since the early 1900's (Kelsall, Hawley and Thomas, 1971). Besides the caribou, then, there are only two other large animals from which the people now obtain meat and hides, and neither of these — the moose or the bear — is as plentiful for them as the caribou have been. Bears are actually feared by many of the villagers, and everyone in the community knows the stories of the close encounters which André Yawileh and other men have had with these animals. The browns, blacks, and grizzlies of the region are therefore hunted only infrequently, and more have been killed in the last few years because of chance and circumstance than by design or tracking.

Moose, however, despite their scarcity, are regarded in a totally different manner by the people. They are unquestionably the most highly valued animal in the area, not only for the great amount of meat that they supply, but — most important of all —for their tough, thick hides, which provide the people with the best possible material for mittens and mukluks. In the depth of winter, these pieces of foot and hand gear protect the most vulnerable parts of the people's bodies from frostbite, and so their quality and manufacture are a prime local concern. No other material available to the band can compare with moose hide for these purposes, and so there is considerable — and understandable — excitement whenever one of these animals is shot, and its meat and hide divided up among the hunter's kinsmen and friends.

Moose hide is so scarce — and so valuable — to the people of Colville, that they carry on a very active trade in it with the families of Good Hope. Due to its distinctive forest ecosystem of willow, poplar, and birch, the vicinity of the fort still abounds with moose, and the members of the band receive several hides each year from their friends and relatives there. The relationship is one of reciprocity, however, for there are also some key resources to which the villagers, in their turn, enjoy greater access. The caribou herds, for example, restrict their winter movements to the climax spruce-lichen forest characteristic of the Colville area, and because they therefore do not migrate as far to the southwest as Good Hope each winter, the townspeople often look to their more isolated northeastern kinsmen for seasonal gifts of meat.[11] The fishing around Colville also surpasses that found in the Good Hope area, and it is a rare dogsled or plane that leaves for the fort without several bundles of smoked trout, as well as a pile of caribou quarters. There is thus a regional trade network, operating along kinship lines, which redresses certain ecological imbalances, and gives people access to natural foods and materials that would be otherwise scarce commodities for them.

The large array of Western foods which are now available to band members still accounts for only some thirty percent of their overall diet, for people continue to utilize small as well as large game for their subsistence. Consequently, a constant occupation of women throughout the year is setting and checking hare snares, which provides a small but steady supplement to family diets. Aboriginally, and throughout the nineteenth century, the hare were a very important source of food and clothing for the people, and their pronounced dependence upon this animal in some areas led to the tribal name by which they are now collectively known. Other English, French and Athabascan terms for regional groups also reflect this fact by incorporating rabbit, *lièvre*, and *g'a* or *ka* ("hare") in their designations, such as in Hareskins, Rabbitskins, Peaux-de-Lièvres, and Kawchodinne ("People of the Great Hares"). [12] This historical dependence was so pronounced for most bands, that when the cyclic hare population reached a low point, as it did every six to ten years, the Indians were struck with widespread starvation and cannibalism because other food sources were usually not sufficient to make up for the decrease in their diet (cf. Rand, 1945, p.74, cited by Sue, 1946, p.21). [13] Even nowadays, when the people are still faced with periodic hunger in the heart of winter, they survey the land and its seasonal poverty, and tell one another, in Wilfred Ratehne's words, "Well, it's back to choking rabbits."

Like hunger, waterfowl are also a seasonal phenomenon for the people, for their area swarms with a variety of ducks, geese, and swan, who come north to breed every year during the late spring, summer, and autumn. The people hunt them and gather their eggs without much concern for the "open" and "closed" seasons now set by the government, for there are no game officers in the immediate vicinity to enforce these laws. Thus, as soon as the shallower ponds begin to thaw in mid-May, hunters can be found among the shoreline brush and willows, waiting in these natural "blinds" for the birds to land. As the open waters expand and spread to the larger lakes, the waterfowl eventually become more dispersed, but the people still continue to hunt them by boat during the few ice-free months of their stay.

Coinciding with the appearance of the waterfowl, the open waters of spring also allow the people to hunt the beaver and muskrats which now emerge from their winter lodges to swim on the surface of the region's ponds and lakes. The meat of these animals is considered a delicacy, but they are primarily sought for the value of their furs. The northern forests of the Eastern and Western Hemispheres are rich with fur-bearing animals, and at Colville Lake, a major part of the people's income derives from trapping them. The most plentiful local species is marten, but the people also take red, cross and white fox, squirrel, ermine (weasel), mink, wolverine, wolf, and lynx, as well as the seasonal muskrat and beaver. While the latter two animals are mainly hunted with small gauge rifles, all the other fur-bearers are taken with variously sized steel traps during the winter. Their pelts are in optimum condition during these months, and so from October until early June of every year, the search for fur keeps the people of the community in the bush. The band's traplines extend over an area of thousands of square miles, and they disperse and spread the people to the limits of the forest. Fur trapping thus structures a major part of their annual cycle, and the sparse, scattered distribution of the animals pursued has concomitant effects upon the nature — and stresses — of band social organization.

While fur is thus central to the economy and life style of the people, the importance and pursuit of trapping is actually a modern consequence of early Western contact. Aboriginally, fur was primarily of value for clothing and insulation, and people still use wolverine, beaver, and other pelts for their parkas, mittens, and foot gear, However, after its introduction to the Hare in the late eighteenth century, the fur trade became the natives' main means of access to the European goods upon which they became so quickly dependent. At present, for example, a wide variety of Western commodities, including fish nets, traps, ropes, pots, tents, stoves, axes, ammunition, clothing, canned goods, flour, sugar, matches, packaged fruit (for making homebrew), lard, and tea, are all available at the settlement's fur trading post, as well as at a small store maintained by the local priest. While these facilities, and the village's Catholic mission, have developed into focal places for the band, their presence in the settlement is actually quite recent, and they only alleviated the people's long-standing reliance upon Fort Good Hope in the early 1960's. Until that time, the people had been travelling to the fort each year for trading, religious, and medical services, for Fort Good Hope had been the only convenient, permanent community and fur outlet available to them since the early 1800's. While trapping has thus involved a necessary dependence upon the outside, the fur trade has also kept the people involved with the land over the centuries, for by fostering a type of autonomy and identity for them, it has enabled the band to maintain a life style which still draws its substance and spirit from the forest.

The trees of the taiga have, in fact, supplied much of the material out of which the people have literally built their lives. Their ancient shelters consisted of moss and hide-covered poles, and nowadays, snowshoes, dogsleds, caches, fur stretchers, tent floors, axe handles, ice scoops, canoes, and paddles are just some of the handmade items which the people continue to manufacture from local wood. Their homes are constructed from spruce trees — the dominant conifer of the boreal forest — and they also make use of tamarack (larch) and willow, as well as moss and lichens for insulation, and summer berries for food. Although birch trees can rarely be found as far north as Colville, the people can still obtain this wood when they travel further to the south and west near Good Hope. As is typical of the northern forests, with their thin soils, harsh temperatures, and short growing seasons, the local trees do not attain as great a height as they would in more southerly regions, which makes their utilization that much more precious. Spruce trees in the Colville region rarely exceed forty feet, and the thickness of the forest cover is itself highly variable. Numerous lakes and wide stretches of swampy muskeg break up the wooded areas, and wherever fire has destroyed the climax forest of spruce and softwoods, thick enclaves of willow and brush have succeeded them.

The high pitch content of coniferous trees makes them very susceptible to destruction by fire (James, 1951, p.334), and this, combined with the extremely dry conditions which prevail during the long, hot days of constant summer sunlight, makes forest fires a constant threat during this time of year. In snowshoeing through the bush with Peter Dehdele one winter, we travelled over a wide radius from the village, and saw the evidence of many such blazes. There have been a few fires within the vicinity of the village itself in recent years, but, as Peter observed, since these have left behind them a good supply of firewood, especially in the form of dead standing and fallen timber, the people have not been particularly worried about them.

Of greater importance than this firewood, however, are the large swathes of ground cover and foliage which these fires destroy. The spongy, tufted growth of moss and lichens, which lays and rolls like a carpet across the forest floor, is the prime winter food of the caribou herds, and an area denuded of lichens soon becomes an area bereft of caribou. The herds divert their migration and wintering habits to avoid these barren tracts, and the situation is a long-range proposition, for the slow pace of growth and re-growth in the northern taiga may require from several decades to a century or more to replenish the supply of forage (cf. Kelsall, 1968, pp.263-268; Symington, 1965, pp.45-46). Fires thus affect the carrying capacity of the environment, and this, in turn, limits the places and possibilities within which the people can survive and live.

The village site at Colville Lake has been cut and hacked out of the wooded growth which once covered its ground, and although there are no trees left within the community itself, a quarter of a mile away one is already deep within the forest. From the shores of the bay where the settlement stands, the land rises abruptly to the east and southeast, and then presents a level surface which overlooks the water. This parcel, upon which Wilfred Ratehne and Maurice Bayjere built the first cabins back in the 1930's, parallels the curve of the bay, and extends inland to a distance of fifty to eighty yards. The tract slopes downward towards its north end, and it is on this abrupt plateau — reaching from its northern extremity to the deep curve at its southern belly — that all of the people have since erected their log homes (cf. Map 3).

Over the years, band members have cleared away the trees and brush from the vicinity, although some willows have been left between the houses and the shoreline. Several paths now cut through this brush to the waterfront area, where people draw their drinking water, beach their boats, and sometimes tie up their dogs during the summer. At other seasons, canines are kept chained up to stakes behind the people's houses, leaving the central part of the village free for walking, playing, communicating, and travelling into and out of the community by dogsled.

There are many well-worn trails which wind out of the village in various directions, their routes either a path to resources, or a road of escape from the pressures of communal life. Some are used for getting to firewood, others lead to hunting, trapping, and fishing camps. In winter the people cut across the frozen bodies of water, as well as the tree-less, marsh-like region of scrub, willows, and streams which lies to the east and southeast of their homes. Directly behind the community, the land immediately drops, and because the settlement's plateau blocks this lowland from draining into the lake, this plain provides a large breeding ground for mosquitoes and insects in the summer. However, its shallow ponds also thaw out earlier than the surrounding lakes in the spring, and thus furnish an excellent duck hunting area for the band as well. Beyond this marsh, the land rises once again, and the boreal world of hills, lakes, muskegs, forests and streams emerges, which is the people's true living environment, as well as the earthly heritage of their ancestors.

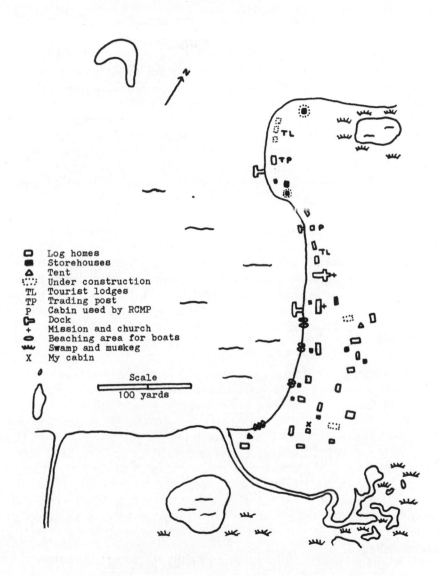

Log homes
Storehouses
Tent
Under construction
TL Tourist lodges
TP Trading post
P   Cabin used by RCMP
Dock
+   Mission and church
Beaching area for boats
Swamp and muskeg
X   My cabin

Scale
100 yards

MAP 3   Colville Lake in 1967.

The Trail of the Hare

4 THE YEAR

Although the force of history is rarely an immediate presence in the North, the rhythm of time is. Historical events have indeed altered the lives of the people and their institutions, and yet if change is not direct and pressing, its effects are more often assumed than experienced. Ecological time, however, the flow of forces in life's immediate context, is unavoidable; it is, perh'aps, the key dimension of relation and being in the Arctic. No one escapes or ignores the seasons, for too much is at stake, and literally everything is involved. Food, fur, and fuel, shelter and movement, man's relationships and moods, they each change and transform with every phase of the year. Their cycles punctuate the the rhythm of existence, and they provide a sense of continuity and depth that linear time so often deprives us of.

In the pulse of every year, the people of Colville confront dramatic extremes of temperature, and stark variations in the relative length of day and night. The annual temperature range often covers a span of over 160 degrees, and during the first seven months of one year (1968) it went from a low of -75°F in early February to a high of +88° F in mid-July. [14] Snowfall and subfreezing temperatures begin in late September, and the southern bays of Colville are completely frozen over by the second or third week of October. This "freeze-up" marks the beginning of real dogsled travel and the commencement of winter trapping. The heaviest accumulations of snow usually occur in November, December, and January, and while smaller amounts continue to fall through May, the sub-Arctic actually has a much lower level of winter precipitation than more southerly regions. Winter snow fall averages forty to fifty inches, and the total annual amount of water, in fact, "is within the limits usually associated with deserts" (Kelsall, 1968, p.47). Although there are no statistics available for Colville Lake itself, total yearly precipitation, if "calculated on the basis of ten inches of snow equalling one inch of rain" (Phillips, 1967, p.14), amounts to ten to fourteen inches for most of the boreal forest (Kelsall, 1968, p.47). It is the poor drainage of the permafrost, and the meager evaporation of the summer, which keeps most of this water at, or just below, the surface of the land, and produces a situation in which up to forty percent of some regions are covered by water bodies and muskeg.

During the long winter in the Colville area, temperatures are usually between -20°F and -50°F. The coldest months of the year are January and February, during which readings in the -50°F's and -60°F's are frequent. Between January 28th and February 7th of 1968, for example, the approximate mean daily temperature was -53° F. Yet temperature is also highly variable during this severest part of the winter. Following a week of -38°F to -75°F readings, there were six days of -5°F to +10°F. After that the temperature dropped back into the -20°F to -50°F range, only to rise again after two weeks to an unseasonable high of +45°F on February 29th. No temperature that high was recorded again until April 28th.

It was remarkable to witness the sense of relativity with which people responded to some of the more precipitous temperature reversals during this period. On days when it was -50°F or colder, most activities in the bush camps were curtailed. No long hunting or trapping trips were taken, and fish nets were rarely checked. Some wood might be cut, and of course the dogs would be fed and cared for, but otherwise people stayed inside their tents and skinned pelts, sewed clothing, and repaired equipment. Once, when the temperature shot up to -30° F a few days after a cold spell, everybody resumed outdoor work, commenting on how warm (*goweleh*) it had become. About a week afterwards, my outdoor thermometer rose to -10°F, and everyone in our camp ran outdoors in the morning, dressed only in thin pants and shirts. We squinted into the feeble sunlight of mid-February, and, observing to one another how much like spring it seemed, we all worked outside for the rest of the day without putting on any additional clothes. Yet three mornings later, when the reading again fell to a more seasonable -30°F, we were all shivering and complaining, despite the fact that exactly one week previously we had greeted the identical temperature with expressions of warmth and gratitude. Regardless of what biological resistance the people have developed to cold through diet, training, and heredity, then, they still must obviously readjust themselves to the constant changes of every season.

Wind can be an even more crucial weather factor than temperature in the Arctic, and a consideration of one feature without the other — as Peter Dehdele once said — would be like trying to walk cross-country with just one snowshoe. One observer of the North has written that:

For human — or animal — comfort, temperature is of far less consequence than the wind. An intensely cold, calm day is infinitely more tolerable than a moderate one with winds of gale force. The effect of wind-chill, the rapid loss of the body's warmth through radiation, is keenly felt (Phillips, 1967, pp.13-14).[15]

I can remember the time when Leon Behdzi once set out with perfect equanimity on a calm, -40° F day, whereas four mornings previously, he and Yašeh had been immobilized at Aubry Lake by a -5°F temperature with a thirty mile per hour headwind.

Leon and all the people showed an exquisite sensitivity to subtle changes in both wind and temperature, and without any reference to thermometers, they could, from day to day, recognize drops or rises of five degrees. Their consciousness of wind conditions — including strength, direction, and consistency — was pervasive, and so was their constant awareness of the quality, depth, and compactness of snow and ice. Like a computer digesting a dozen sources of raw data, the people could process the environment with simultaneity, precision, and a flexible view to multiple outcomes. When living in the bush with them and confronting these forces every day, one could not help but sense and respect the experience, balance, and judgment that went into every hunting and travelling decision. Yet it was all done by the people with an outward quietude — a few words, silence, a nod or two — and the men had reached a concensus on a good route, a worthwhile trail, and a fruitful objective. Within the limits of their knowledge, people tried to maximize the safety and utility of their efforts by sharing their knowledge and by respecting the dangers that they were up against. Peter Dehdele once expressed this attitude to me by using one of the people's favorite — and most oblique and understated — aphorisms:

"Elegu go^n raehtseh dloleh," he said, "don't ever laugh at the cold." If you try to ignore it or take it for granted, if you don't dress right and stay alert when you travel, then you're headed for trouble. The cold gets angry when people laugh at it, and so it strikes out at them. It can remind you by killing you.

The stresses and anxieties of the winter are very real and intense for the people, and while they do not exaggerate them, neither in their thoughts and words do they try to minimize them. Too many of their own kin and friends have frozen or starved to death in the last fifty years — the Behdzi brothers' elderly father, Wilfred and George Ratehne's younger siblings — for people to experience their anxieties as historical artifacts. The environment and its rhythms are still too immediate for that. And yet seasonal stresses have their own rhythms as well, and there is a perceptible lightening of mood when the harshness and solitude of winter have passed. To the people, the end of February marks the finish of the most difficult part of their year, and they were careful to point this out to me. "If you can make it past the end of February," Maurice Bayjere once confided, "you can stop worrying. You'll be okay after that. That's the end of *'xai'*, the real Indian winter."

True to Maurice's words, March did witness a number of important transformations. Daily temperatures gradually rose, sunlight and day length increased, and by the end of the month, readings above 0° F were fairly common. Each of these changes had been in process for several weeks. Back in December, the sun had dipped below the horizon one day, and then had not been seen again for several weeks. There was a pale gray light, dim and weak, which lasted but a few hours. That was all that one could travel or work by in early January, although there had been a few nights of moonlight, as well as the milky, colored ribbons of the aurora borealis. But the mid-winter dark had been mercifully brief, for Colville is not too far north of the Arctic Circle, and the rainbow waves of northern lights were soon diluted by the growing daytime hours of February. Light brought warmth and glare as well, for the reflection of the sun off the snow and ice — crystalline, sharp and dazzling — brought the ever-present danger of snowblindness, and people took to sunglasses and smudging the rims of their eyes with soot. By late April, there were no more "minus" degree days, and afternoon temperatures were around or above the freezing mark. When, in early May, the people dispersed once again for the final weeks of spring caribou and beaver hunting, the days were consistently sunny and warm, and the snow was fast disappearing from the land.

The heat of the long and lengthening days was also melting and rotting the lake ice, and waterfowl were reappearing on the open ponds. As the thaw continued into June, the "break-up" of the ice on the larger lakes occurred, ending the frozen period begun by the mid-October "freeze-up." The people returned to the village from their hunting camps, and settling in for a summer of relative ease and communality, they once more set their fish nets in the open waters of the bay. The warm, unending days of midnight sun continued through July, providing an uninterrupted backdrop for the people's affairs and pursuits. But in August the temperature started to drop, and brief periods of rain and nighttime began to invade the daylight. By September, the air was chilled around the freezing point, and a foretaste of winter was again in everyone's mouth.

These rhythms in the people's lives — their swings between seasonal extremes, their cyclic movements from village to bush, warm to cold, light to dark — create an annual cycle alive with tension, ambiguity, and the particular satisfactions that competence and community can bring. Experience alternates between intensities of people and textures of environment, demanding a protean ability to cope with both physical and social nature. If people are sometimes ambivalent about the dimensions of their existence, then it is these stark contrasts in life which intensify their unease, while simultaneously affording them a necessary variety, release, and stimulation.

Existence is quintessentially mobile, for movement characterizes every phase and transition in the band's experience. The annual cycle falls into six alternating periods of community dispersal and social ingathering (Figure 3), creating a life style of semi-nomadism. The lengthy winter and spring, demarcated by the yearly freeze-up and break-up, encompass three major separations, during which time the people live in canvas tents, and move through the forest in small hunting and trapping groups. These three periods, in which all travelling is done by dogsled and snowshoe, are in the early winter

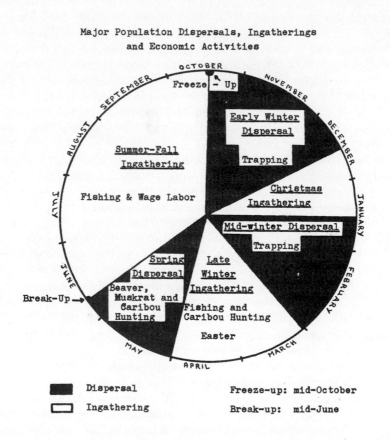

Major Population Dispersals, Ingatherings and Economic Activities

FIGURE 3   The annual cycle.

(from mid-October to mid-December), in the mid-winter months (of early January to early March), and in the early spring (from late April to mid-June). Between these dispersals, the people aggregate at the community for brief holidays, but they must pass most of their year in the scattered encampments of the bush in order to subsist. Altogether, a contemporary family which is conscientiously trying to live off the land will actually spend at least half of every year in the bush, and experience — during these dispersals — the company of only two or three other households for much of their lives.

The settlement at Colville Lake is the scene of three major band reunions each year, counterpointing these phases of social atomism in the forest. One ingathering is in late December, during the Christmas period, and a second comes in the late winter months of March and April. The latter follows the close of the area's main fur season, the dates for which are regulated by the government, and includes the Easter holiday. A third ingathering covers the summer and fall months from mid-June until late September or early October, during which time the people often spend several weeks in nearby fish camps and make their preparations for the coming winter. There is usually some wage labor available from the village's fur trader and missionary then, and at this time the settlement also receives its seasonal visits from the police, tourists, medical personnel, and local administrative officers. The village's size is further increased by the arrival of the children who were sent away to residential schools the previous fall, and so both families, and the entire band, are now reunited for the lengthiest communal period of the year.

In its totality, the current annual cycle of the people is a mixture of ecological, governmental, and religious time schedules, and these diverse features reflect the combination of traditional and Western elements which affect band members. People are simultaneously oriented to a range of expectations and timings, including Church holidays, trapping regulations, and school terms, and yet the environmental dimension takes precedence over these for it is the one most intimately connected with the dangers and possibilities of survival. While the people have taken on some of the external trappings of Western time-keeping, such as clocks, watches, and calendars, in a more fundamental sense they continue to operate on an ecological rather than an artificial model of life and scheduling. They still think of the year in terms of *xai, golu, uyalele, i^{n}pe*, and *k'ata^n*, the five seasonal divisions that their ancestors recognized. These were explained to me by André Yawileh and some of the other people, who defined these periods in terms of their environmental features, as well as their calendrical equivalents.

xai: "winter"; the period following the freeze-up of the lakes in mid-October and lasting until early May. The people also speak of a period towards the end of the winter called *golu* or "crust." Andrē described it as follows:

This starts in March when the sun really comes back strong. When it's warm during the day and the snow on the lake melts, then in the evening it gets cool and it freezes into a hard crust on the snow. That makes it real good for travelling.

Yen Behdzi explained:

It's the strong winds in March that make the snow on the lakes so hard on top. They blow it hard like it was ice.

uyalele: "the melting of the ice." Andrē's son Martin described it as "the time when ducks fly north and water starts to come on top of the lakes; this is the Indians' 'spring'." It begins in early or mid-May and ends with the break-up of the ice in mid-June.

iⁿpe: "summer" or "the time when it gets warmer" (Sue 1964:98). This begins with the break-up of the lake ice in mid-June and lasts until mid-August, when the temperature starts to drop once again.

k'at'aⁿ: "autumn"; this begins in mid-August and concludes with the freeze-up of the lakes in mid-October. As Yen Behdzi explained it: "Then bush life and real winter starts again for us."

Freeze-up and break-up, the presence or absence of snow and ice, and the types of mobility that are feasible, clearly dominate the people's vision of the year. Their persistent concern with ecology rather than clocks is indicated not only by their seasonal scheme, but also by some finer distinctions that they make within the annual cycle. While they are familiar with the names of Western months, many of the people continue to conceive of time as a series of "moon" divisions, thus perpetuating a type of aboriginal lunar calendar which was once ubiquitous in the sub-Arctic.[16] Yen and Yašeh Behdzi once named and translated for me the following *sa* or "months," which demonstrate how deeply the events and migrations of every year enter into the people's vocabulary of time (Table 2).

TABLE 2
Native terms for lunar months

Approximate Gregorian equivalent	
January	*Delederahodedele* . . . "The Month of the Sun Coming Back"
January-February	*Li^{n}šayduwesa* . . . "It Is So Cold that When The Dogs Piss, They Piss On Themselves"
February	*Akaradetsisa* . . . "The Month of The Wind"
March	*Raxo^{n}raselsa* . . . "The Month of a Slight Touch of Snowblindness"
April	*Raxo^{n}radesa* . . . "The Month of Very Bad Snowblindness"
May	*Li^{n}yatisa* . . . "The Month of The Barking Dog"
June	*Bemetegoxay* . . . "The Month of The Ice Melting"
July	*Ehgaygo^{n}sa* . . . "The Month of Eggs"
August	*Ehšuwego^{n}sa* . . . "The Month of Ducklings"
September	*Bekaraheh^{n}deri^{n}daygo^{n}sa* . . . "The Month of Ducks Going Back
October	*Tayaahgo^{n}sa* . . . "The Month of The Caribou Migration Back From The Barrens"
November	*Ehseh^{n}go^{n}sa* . . . "The Month of Caribou Rutting"
December	*Begetei^{n}aisa* . . . "The Month When The Sun Disappears Below The Horizon"

5   CONCLUSION

The fact that the people's calendar is a description rather than simply a demarcation of time reflects their concern with the natural world, and serves as a mirror of their own participation in it. Their ecology embodies some of the most visible threats and anxieties with which they have to contend, and these dangers are more consciously perceived of by the people than are the subtler stresses of their social life. In a community where death by starvation and freezing have occurred within living memory, survival is a challenge rather than an assumption. When one adds to this the hazards of hunting and dogsled travel; the dangers from bears and wolves; the possibility of accidents with guns, axes and knives; and the frustrations of perverse weather and unpredictable caribou migrations, then one begins to sense the full dimensions of human ecology in the North.

The Arctic is often considered to be the harshest environment in the world, but few people get beyond temperature, ice, and wind when they think of it in these terms. They forget that there are hunting-fishing-and-gathering groups in other regions who have also occupied, into modern times, equally "marginal" ecologies, such as deserts, jungles, and rugged coastlines. Having been pushed or kept from seemingly richer areas on their continents by the expansion of agricultural and herding societies, hunters and gatherers in most parts of the world have nevertheless been able to maintain a viable lifeway. In fact, recent studies of extant hunting-gathering populations have revealed how secure and often leisurely their lives can be, despite the apparent severity of their surroundings (cf. Lee, 1968, 1969; Lee and Devore, 1968; Service, 1966; Sahlins, 1968).

What underlies the security of most of these groups is the access that they enjoy to abundant, wild, and edible plants or shellfish, with the result that, in their cases, the "gathering" of these resources supercedes "hunting" and "fishing" as a means of acquiring food (Netting, 1971, p.5). In this respect, the Arctic and the sub-Arctic are doubly damned in an ecological sense, for not only do northern natives have to deal with extremities of weather, but they are also faced with a paucity of edible vegetation. Berries, certain boiled mosses, and rose hips are the only wild plants which the people of Colville employ as food, and these make up a very small and very seasonal component of their diet (cf. Sue, 1964, pp.212-225). [17] Their subsistence thus turns predominantly upon the availability of meat, fowl, and fish, and survival becomes a function of their ability to understand, stalk, and keep up with animal movements — a much harder task than collecting sedentary foodstuffs.

Certain behavioral characteristics of the animals upon which the people depend make it difficult for them to lead a secure and predictable life during the winter. Caribou are in the area for only seven months out of the year, and they remain nomadic throughout their stay in the forest zone. Hunting them necessitates a comparable level of mobility, but perhaps the most stressful aspect of the caribou is the unpredictability of some of their seasonal moves. Caribou are notorious for the erratic nature of their migration habits, and herds which have regularly come to a particular region for many years may suddenly fail to turn up one winter. The forest fires of the preceding summer — many of which were caused by lightning — may be responsible in some cases, but more often there is no discernible reason for the change, and both Indian hunters and Western scientists remain baffled by the perverseness of the herds. [18]

Hunting possibilities within a given locale can also change radically from week to week as the caribou shift their grazing range, forcing families to either move, or rely upon fish and hare for their food. There is evidence to indicate that many sections of the aboriginal range of the Hare were periodically devoid of caribou, necessitating the people's dependence upon smaller game in earlier times as well. The writings of early explorers graphically described starvation among Indians and Eskimos deprived of their usual supply of caribou. [19] Since aboriginal families would have needed 100 to 200 caribou per year to maintain themselves and their dogs, this fluctuating situation intensified their reliance upon their other sources of food and clothing. [20]

Fish also present a problem of movement to the people because they change their primary locations during the winter as a result of varying temperature and ice conditions. Nets which have been coming up full may suddenly yield a very small harvest, impelling either a change in fishing sites, or perhaps the move of an entire camp to a new lake. If such a move must be made in the latter part of the winter, there is the added hardship (and occasional impossibility) of having to re-set one's net under a six to seven foot layer of ice.

Waterfowl and moose embody some of the same dynamic problems as caribou and fish, being in one case migratory and seasonal, and in the other both sparse and dispersed. The variously scattered, mobile, or erratic nature of these food sources is complemented by the cyclical nature of other important species. Snowshoe hare, mice, and lemmings go through population cycles every few years, which affects the people in a dual manner. The hare is still an important food resource for the band, and as a reminder of earlier centuries of starvation and cannibalism, the years in which its numbers reach a low point continue to mean winters of exceptional hardship. Furthermore, a decline in the population of hares, mice, and related small mammals leads to a corresponding decrease among the marten, fox, lynx, and other carnivorous fur-bearers which feed off these smaller species. The people may thus find not only their food supply threatened, but also experience a simultaneous decline in their trapping income. There is even observational evidence indicating that caribou herds may go through a thirty-five year population cycle, and while this is far from conclusive, their drastically declining numbers in the mid-twentieth century — a result primarily of fire and over-kill throughout the North — has certainly sharpened the people's problem of survival, and heightened their contemporary chances of starvation. [21]

Over the centuries, the fur trade — besides giving people access to many Western goods — has also, with characteristic ambiguity, both altered and intensified certain ecological patterns. While it has made available a more sophisticated technology, steel traps, rifles, and commercial fish-netting have not changed the nature or habits of the fur and food-producing species which the people pursue. It is true that these may all be taken now with greater efficiency and more individualized effort, but one can still only live off the animals that are immediately at hand: if game is scattered in time and space, if migrations and cycles continue to create seasons of plenty and winters of discontent, then all the steel, rope, and fire-power in the world will not produce food.

The presence of Western foods has, of course, alleviated some of the insecurity in life, but here again there are some ecological dimensions to so mundane a matter as shopping. There is food — and netting, traps, and weaponry — at the trading post, but one can obtain them only in exchange for furs, and so the people must look again to the forest for their subsistence. If sources of food are scattered in the environment, then fur species are even more dispersed, and trapping thus involves an even greater separation of the people than was probably true under aboriginal conditions. Successful trapping involves prolonged stays at distant encampments, and since the people can transport only a limited amount of supplies with them in their small sleds, they inevitably have to turn to fish and game to support themselves in the bush. Trapping thus perpetuates some of the band's classical survival anxieties, and, by making isolation more pronounced and prolonged than ever, it intensifies some of their primary social stresses as well.

The consequences of these various stresses forms the substance of the following chapters, but we have already seen some of the responses which the people have developed to them. While band dispersal is a necessity of life, the people are able to temper this with alternating periods of seasonal aggregation at the village. The annual cycle engenders extremes of population density, and taxes the people's ability to deal with social milieus of greatly varying intensity. A keen sense of interdependence and interrelatedness within the community facilitates the people's adaptation to these conditions, but stresses often strain some of the closest of social bonds. Mobility and emotional restraint provide means of controlling and channeling the disruptive expression of some of these tensions, but there are also situations in which stress responses are openly acted out. Relations with whites and dogs, as well as with kinsmen, are similarly ambiguous, alternating between affective extremes, and again being aggravated by the types of mutual reliance which bind Indians and whites, and people and canines.

An examination of the band's ecology has also revealed some of the people's strategies for meeting the physical hazards of their environment. In carrying out canoe fishing, for example, a complementary concern with taboos, togetherness, and consensus, provides the fishermen with psychological as well as survival security. As illustrated in place names, "calendars," and levels of knowledge and awareness, responses to dangers are invested with a cognitive control over the environment, which heightens and deepens people's sensitivity to the animate, the inanimate, and the animated in their world.

The band's division of labor also has functional dimensions because it allows for the formation of sex and age-defined levels of competence and interest: these extend to the use of canoes, chain-saws and outboard motors; the tanning of hides, the sewing of clothing, and the driving of dogs; and the pursuit of hunting, trapping and fishing. While these tasks and responsibilities are not strictly differentiated along sex and age lines, they do lead to distinctive living patterns for men, women, and older and younger people. One concomitant of this is that band members participate in different types and amounts of mobility, which underlies some of their main stylistic differences, as well as their varied adaptive approaches to stress and tension.

The community as a whole also maintains certain relationships with the outside which fosters the people's collective well-being. The regional trade between Colville and Good Hope redistributes ecological resources beyond their normal range, giving the members of the two settlements access to what they need and want, but would otherwise lack. Kinship is the facilitating medium here, and it also enables people from both communities to find hospitality whenever they visit the other band. It is possible that the current situation may represent the continuation of older, inter-band trade networks, in which aboriginal groups, who may have "specialized" to some extent in utilizing local ecologies, were also able to share, in times of plenty, in the resources of neighboring areas. The nomadism, the fluid membership, and the patterns of intermarriage among these bands, which are explored in the following section, would have made such contacts frequent, and would have promoted the viability of just such an exchange system.

It is clear that, over time, the people have developed many ways to meet the particular challenges of their existence. Social, cognitive, psychological, and material techniques are all involved. What is perhaps most striking to the Western observer is that the people deal with the ambiguities of experience by accepting and participating in them, rather than by trying to reconcile or eliminate life's contradictions. This is an element of what the poet Keats called man's "Negative Capability," which emerges "when man is capable of being in uncertainties, Mysteries, doubts, without any irritable reaching after fact and reason" (1817, p.261). By rhythmically moving between poles of existence and styles of experience, the people of Colville Lake share in qualities that a more restrictive, narrowly-defined, and consistency-oriented lifeway would deprive them of. Life is indeed stressful because of the extremes to which the people are subjected, but stress *per se* is not necessarily or entirely negative in its implications, for it also operates as a stimulant which invests life with motion, motive and awareness. The people actively seek to experience some of the most challenging circumstances of their existence, and they derive some of their deepest satisfactions from the sense of competence, ability and harmony which these social and environmental involvements provide. It is these contrasting and ultimately creative qualities of life and stress which impart a uniqueness to the people's existence, and it is to an exploration of these dimensions that the remainder of this book is devoted.

PART 2

Kinship and History

1 INTRODUCTION

The idea that man is a social animal is a reflection on human nature, but in the North, necessity is even more immediate than propensity. There is too much to be contended with for a man to exist without a wife, or for a family to survive without kinsmen. Lone persons are actually pitied and feared, and if isolated, they may become the freakish and mysterious *lariyin* ("bush men") who, when cut off from people, lose their humanity, and take to roaming the forests with cannibalistic intent. For the native person, isolation *in extremis* is dehumanization in earnest, for people need one another to insure their survival and preserve their nature. As the band's "bush man" implies, life is indeed *with* people and *within* nature, and necessity — if not history — becomes the mother of kinship.

Relationships bind the Colville Lake community into an intricate fabric, but since kinsmen can conflict as well as cooperate with one another, social life crystallizes some prime sources of ambiguity. People can cope with their ambivalences about one another in many ways, however, and by shifting between intimacy and avoidance with difference relatives at different times, people enjoy a degree of latitude which lends life some of its flexibility and distinctiveness. The manner in which kinship relations are derived and dealt with is but one of many dimensions of existence in which fluidity and alternation characterize the people's existence.

Kinship patterns in the band involve an individual with both his maternal and his paternal kinsmen, for Colville Lake is characterized by what anthropologists call a "bilateral" social system. That is, in an individual's social life, there is a complementary or "bilateral" emphasis in which a person considers all his kinsmen to be of potential significance, regardless of whether they are related to him on his mother's or his father's side. This local pattern differs from the social organization of certain Lapp, Siberian, Alaskan and Yukon groups, for some of the latter people are organized into more complex clans, sibs, moieties and unilineal kinship groups in which either the

43

mother's *or* the father's kin may take precedence over the other group. When one compares these various patterns with the bilateral structure of Colville Lake, they demonstrate the great range of social diversity that can be found within the circumpolar regions. [1]

Beyond the distinctiveness of these local groups and their particular environments, however, one can also make a strong case for some basic similarities which cut across the taiga and tundra zones, and give to the various northern peoples a set of common cultural denominators. Specifically, there are four dominant cultural orientations which are shared by many northern groups, and these involve a strong emphasis upon (1) kinship ties, (2), generosity, (3) emotional restraint, and (4) behavioral flexibility. It can be suggested that these four themes have great adaptive value for the rigorous environments in which they are found because, in combination, they bring elements of security, stability, and adaptability to life. This argument is a simple but nevertheless compelling one, especially for those persons who have experienced at first-hand the exigencies of an existence which is devoted to living off the land in the Arctic or sub-Arctic regions. Though these four themes are combined and modified in a variety of ways by the different groups that adhere to them, their ubiquity, including their presence at Colville Lake, underlines their significance for a wide range of northern life styles.

Recent workers in large northern settlements have pointed out that these traditional social values have persisted into many areas of contemporary community life. In some instances these themes have been modified by native people to suit new institutions and conditions, while in other cases their continuance has produced stress because of their inconsistency with certain demands of modern "urbanized" life in the North. These themes have a considerable historical depth to them, and as they are participated in by the people of Colville Lake, they show an elaboration and integration with many aspects of existence. It is consequently both illuminating and essential to focus on kinship as a basic social dimension, and to examine how, in historical and contemporary terms, communal attitudes and behavior have exhibited the complementary themes of generosity, emotional restraint, and flexibility.

In sum, then, this chapter is an attempt to realize the historical significance of values and kinship in the lives of the people: it examines how kinship has promoted the survival of the band in the face of ecological disasters and social change, and it explores how the people's concern with reciprocity, restraint and adaptability have bound them into a community possessed of its own consistencies and contradictions.

The relevance of Colville Lake for such an analysis is manifest because, in many regards, the members of the band represent a transitional stage between an aboriginal style of life and the more settled existence of present-day towns. The small size and isolation of their village, their "bush" orientation, and their limited contacts with white outsiders, resemble the living conditions that most Indians and Eskimos experienced during the bulk of the post-contact era. The current life style at Colville Lake was widespread in the North as recently as twenty-five years ago, and most native people abandoned it only in the post-World War II period. An analysis of this community can thus provide us with insights into the past and the future, as well as the present, of the Athabascan Indians of this region, for by emphasizing the cultural values noted above, we will be highlighting a key aspect of the social transformations that these people are currently undergoing.

2 HISTORY AND IDENTITY

A crucial dimension of life in the band is the complex, bilateral network of social ties that links the native people of the village. The Indian members of the settlement comprise fourteen separate families, and the people of every household can trace blood and marital relationships to persons in several of the community's other residential units. This type of ramifying and overlapping kinship pattern gives cohesion and unity to the band, and it has operated, over the years, as an important force in maintaining and strengthening the existence of the community.

This is significant because Colville Lake is, as we have seen, something of a satellite of Fort Good Hope, a settlement which has been the regional economic and social focus for the Indians since its founding in the early nineteenth century. This area of the northwest was first opened up to the European fur industry by Alexander Mackenzie, who, in 1789, explored the river that now bears his name. Prior to this, trapping and trading activities had been steadily expanding westward from the southern Hudson's Bay region since the early eighteenth century. During this period, Cree, and eventually Chipewyan, Yellowknife and Dogrib Indians had operated as intermediaries between the traders and the northwesterly groups of the Arctic drainage; but after Mackenzie's explorations, more direct contact was begun with these interior peoples by the opening up of forts in their own territories.

Fort Good Hope was initially begun in 1806 as a fur trading post by Mackenzie's nephew for his employers, the Northwest Company. After the commercial interests there were taken over by the Hudson's Bay Company, which absorbed the Northwest Company in 1821, the fort's location was changed several times in order to increase trade with Kutchin and Eskimo groups, as well as with Hare Indians. The present site of the town was settled on in 1836. For over 150 years after Good Hope's founding, the various Hare groups that lived in the forested regions to the northeast of the fort travelled there periodically to trade, socialize, arrange marriages, seek medical assistance, and, after the establishment of a Catholic mission in 1859, to participate in religious holidays and observances there. The Catholic priests inaugurated an annual religious cycle in which three major holidays were emphasized — Christmas, Easter, and the Feast of the Assumption in mid-August — and these have influenced the timing of community ingatherings right down to the present day.

The Canadian government finally concluded treaties with the Mackenzie area groups in 1921, and at that time all of the Hare were administratively joined together as "Band Number 5." The people who now make up the Colville Lake community are drawn from the various groups that traded into Good Hope during the last century and a half — a time period that has witnessed many intermarriages and migrations among the native people from these two locales. The people of the Colville area thus have a long-standing set of social and economic relationships with the town of Good Hope, and, until recently, the smaller settlement lacked even a semblance of self-sufficiency. It had thus persisted over many years as a "contact-traditional all-native community," viz., a village without white personnel or institutions, but one which was

itself oriented toward a focal center of White institutions in the region, a settlement that may be characterized as a "Point of Trade" (Helm and Damas, 1963, p.10).

Prior to the European presence in the Northwest, aboriginal groups lacked the kind of unity that is implied by the tribal names (such as "Hare") which Westerners later applied to them. Most of the groups simply identified themselves as *dene* or *t'ine* ("people"), and they referred to themselves and their neighbors by terms which described bands as "the people of . . ." (i.e., . . . *godene*, or . . . *got'ine*) a given place or area (such as *dutagot'ine*, "among the islands people").

Social structure was fluid, and it was based upon a multiplicity of kinship ties which individuals could utilize as circumstances warranted. For the "Hare," as for other Athabascan peoples in the region, intermarriage, trade, and economic interdependence during times of scarcity, were factors which linked local groups with one another. The flexible nature of social organization thus allowed people to shift their group membership as social and economic conditions necessitated (Helm and Leacock, 1971, p.347).

Kinship was the basis for membership in both large and small groups, and each household joined larger groupings on the basis of wider kinship connections, personal relationships between male household heads, and other haphazard factors. In spring and summer most of the Hare were on the Mackenzie River, but in winter and late fall they broke up into small camp groups of not more than two or three family units which were spread throughout the bush. There were no family hunting territories (Cohen and Osterreich, 1967, p.4).

While there were cultural, linguistic, and geographic differences which gave identity to regional bands, there was no formalized leadership to bind different groups together in the aboriginal period, nor were there any "tribes" to explicitly distinguish larger groupings from one another. Social organization, in many respects, was thus not political in nature. Nevertheless, the regional bands who were collectively designed by the term "Hare" did gather several times a year for ceremonial purposes, for arranging marriages, for cooperative fishing during the summer and fall, and for joint hunting expeditions during the caribou migrations. [2] In small and large aggregations, they were in contact with many neighboring peoples, including Kutchin (Loucheux) groups to the west, Eskimos to the north, Dogribs to the south, Satudene (Great Bear Lake Indians) to the east, and Mountain Indians to the southwest. [3]

Folklore and historical accounts reveal contacts with the more southerly Cree, Slaves, Chipewyans and Yellowknives as well. Hostilities and contacts with many of these groups may have been augmented in the eighteenth and early nineteenth centuries as a result of the "middleman" position in the fur trade that some of the latter people occupied (Rich, 1967, pp.97-98). Their geographic position placed them between the most advanced European outposts of the time and the more isolated, interior groups like the Hare, giving them a trading and material advantage over the latter. [4] They thus involved these Indians in the fur trade long before there was direct white contact with them, and may in fact have pushed certain groups, including the Hare, into more northerly regions than they previously inhabited. Although it may not be historically definitive, André Yawileh can remember his grandparents telling him how the Cree (*a'da*, "the enemies") and the Chipewyans (*gasehlet'iⁿ*) used to raid and cheat the people for their furs "long ago." As André expressed it:

There used to be lots of marten around here. Some guys were taking them with deadfalls and they were getting so much fur they just kept them. And the Chipewyans knew about the white men to the south, the whites were already down there. The Chipewyans used to come up here (to raid the people) for the furs. The Chipewyans didn't tell these people there were whites to the south. [5]

The nomadic, aboriginal life style of the Hare periodically brought them into touch with neighboring groups in other contexts as well: to the east and northeast, for example, the seasonal pursuit of caribou by Satudene, Dogribs, Hare and Eskimos brought all of these peoples into touch with one another on the Barren Grounds. In their own oral traditions, the people of Colville Lake portray their ancestors as being defensive and fearful about these encounters. Many of their tales involve the powerful medicine man and shaman *Asoneh* ("Caribou Dung"), who is usually called upon in the narrative to save the people from their enemies, or to avenge them upon some raiding group. Old Joseph Tehgu recounted some of these stories to me, and Philip Ratehne translated them in the following way:

Asoneh was travelling with these people down by the Anderson River (*seholiliⁿne*, "Connie River"). They were always afraid of meeting Eskimos so they told everyone not to go too far. Asoneh was walking along the shore, and while he was walking there, he saw three Eskimos coming towards him in kayaks. Asoneh walked poorly, trying to make himself look like he was weak.

Then the three Eskimos came to the shore and went to Asoneh. They never know him. The Eskimos chased him and Asoneh ran crying: heee yeeeeee, heee yeeeeee! Just like that. They were chasing him and hitting him with mud. And Asoneh was running a little faster than they were running. Then Asoneh jumped right to the top of a cliff and these Eskimos were running back for their kayaks. Asoneh ran after them and knocked them on the head. He killed them and threw them in the river. He threw their kayaks in the water too.

The people were still on the Anderson River. Asoneh went back again. He had seen real lots of Eskimo camps. The Eskimo saw him and said: "There's a little kid coming." There were four boys who ran faster than the other ones. They were running just behind Asoneh and throwing mud at him. They kept on throwing mud at Asoneh and Asoneh kept running. Asoneh jumped to the top of a cliff again. Then these Eskimos remembered about Asoneh and started running back. But Asoneh was faster. He knocked their heads off. Asoneh threw them in the river and then went to their camp. There were still lots of Eskimos yet and they were saying that there's a kid coming. They were telling each other to kill him just with mud. Four big boys ran after him and Asoneh was crying while he was running away. Then he did the same thing again. He turned back and killed them all. He killed all the Eskimos that were there in the camp, and after that he went back to the people.

Some Eskimos were staying along the Anderson River. Once in a while caribou came across the river and the Eskimos killed some of them. These people and the Loucheux couldn't go near there because the Eskimos always killed them. Asoneh was travelling with the people from around here. These people travelled way down and they didn't want to get closer to the Eskimos. Then Asoneh told them he would walk and hunt around and so he was gone.

When Asoneh came back, they asked him, "Where were you?" And Asoneh said: "Walking by the sand." They asked where the Eskimos were and Asoneh said that there were no Eskimos around. These people decided to go across the Anderson River because there were no Eskimos there.

Before, when Asoneh went around, he saw Eskimos and he came to the Anderson River just near them. They chased Asoneh and he started crying. They kept on chasing Asoneh, and then he turned back and started fighting. The Eskimos were sorry because they didn't know it was Asoneh. After he killed them all he went to their camp. When he went into it he saw an old lady who was blind. This old woman told him that the Eskimos said there was one boy around and they all went to chase him. Asoneh said: "Yes, I know."

Asoneh didn't want to kill the old lady: he only wanted to take the tobacco and the flint which she used to make fire with.

After that he left the old lady alone and went back to the people and told them that there were no Eskimos. The people wanted to see what Asoneh did, so they went on a hill and saw the camp and it was empty. They thought the Eskimos had gone some place. Asoneh was walking way behind. When the people went around the camp, the old lady was still alive. This old woman told the people that her people had gone away: there probably were some caribou that they were hunting. These people never told her anything. She said they might be back any time.

But they were all lying outside dead. Asoneh had killed them all. These people left that old lady alone and they never said anything to her. The old lady finally died: she was blind and just crawling around and just finally died.

Warfare and trading were not carried on by the Hare in an organized manner, for, like other Northern Athabascan peoples, the Hare lacked any political centralization and did not "consider themselves as composing neat political or cultural units" (Osgood, 1936a, p.3; cf. also Keith, 1890, p.123). There was, in fact, a general cultural uniformity among all the Arctic drainage groups (MacNeish, 1956), with the main distinguishing features of the Hare being their heavy reliance upon hare-skin clothing and their widespread reputation for timidity (Richardson, 1851i, pp.211-212, 1851ii, pp.3-32; Mackenzie, 1801, pp.44, 50; Jenness, 1967, pp.392-395). Mackenzie compared them with other Athabascan peoples he had encountered on his journey in 1789, and remarked that: "Several of them were clad in hare-skins, but in every other circumstance they

resembled those whom we had already seen" (1801, p.44). Half a
century later, the explorer John Richardson made a similar comment
based on his own experiences:

> Various tribes have been distinguished by peculiar names, but there is little variety in
> their general appearance, and few discrepancies in their dress, customs or moral
> character. The Hare Indians (*Ka-cho-'dtinne*) inhabit the banks of the Mackenzie,
> from Slave Lake downwards, and the Dog-ribs (*Thling-e-ha-'dtinne*) the inland
> country on the east, from Marten Lake to the Coppermine. There is no perceptible
> difference in the aspect of these two tribes. They meet in the same hunting grounds at
> the north end of Great Bear Lake, intermarry, and their speech scarcely differs in
> accent. The Hare Indians, frequenting a thickly wooded district in which the
> American Hare abounds, feed much on that animal, and clothe themselves with its
> skins, while the Dog-ribs depend more upon the rein-deer (caribou) for a supply of
> winter dresses, but in all essential respects, they are the same people . . . (1851ii,
> pp.3-4).

Jenness noted that the nearest neighbors of the Hare, i.e.,

> the Kutchin, Eskimo, and Yellowknife, rather despised them on account of their
> timidity, for they often concealed their camps under fallen trees some distance back
> from the river and fled at the slightest indication of strangers (1967, p.394).[6]

In most other regards, however, including technology, social
organization, shamanistic practices, and ritual, there was little to
differentiate the Hare from surrounding peoples (Jenness, 1967,
pp.394-395). In historical perspective, therefore, the term "Hare" has
been used to designate a number of bands which shared linguistic,
cultural, kinship, and territorial ties that only partially distinguished
them from other such loose groupings in the Mackenzie area.[7]

It is probable that whites (including anthropologists) have imposed
a much greater sense of tribal identity upon the Northern
Athabascans than they themselves possessed aboriginally. This stems
not only from ethnographic and administrative convenience, but also
from the Western penchant for thinking of peoples in political and
corporate terms. In more recent times these modes of identification
have actually gained some historical validity, however, as a result of
the collection of large and increasingly sedentary native populations
around the trading forts (cf. Osgood, 1936a, pp.3-5; MacNeish, 1956).
This increased sedentariness, along with the native peoples' growing
identification with a "home town," and their restricted travel over a
more limited territory than was used aboriginally, have all intensified
the sense of separateness among formerly contiguous and
geographically overlapping groups.

In the historical period since the beginning of European contact, several observers have tried to describe the number and location of native bands among the Hare. The Oblate missionary and explorer Emile Petitot, who lived and travelled in the Fort Good Hope area in the latter half of the nineteenth century, published several band lists during that era. In the twentieth century, several recent scholars have performed a similar service (Osgood, 1932; Hurlbert, 1962; Sue, 1964). What is most striking about these band inventories is the repeated inconsistencies that they display, a feature which suggests some corresponding attributes of Hare social organization and fluidity. Petitot, for example, gave differing band designations on each of three occasions in the nineteenth century (1876, 1889, 1891), and these, in turn, differ considerably from those offered by Osgood in 1932. These discrepancies led Osgood to remark that:

The frequent lack of correspondence in lists which designate divisions sometimes called bands, such as exists between mine and Petitot's, or the inconsistencies of Petitot's several lists, or the inconsistencies of my own informants, all these lead me to suspect that the reason lies in the *mutability* of these so-called bands (1936a, p.12; emphasis added).

There is considerable evidence from recent studies of Fort Good Hope (Hurlbert, 1962; Sue, 1964), and from the personal histories of the people of Colville Lake, to support and clarify Osgood's contentions on the fluidity of Hare social structure. Part of the confusion stems from the native custom of designating people in terms of the area in which they camp and hunt. Although people develop preferences for camping in certain areas and so become identified in terms of these locales, the descriptions so used to identify people can vary in their geographic precision (Sue, 1964, pp.32-33). A family, for instance, may be identified simultaneously in three different spatial contexts, including (a) the general region they are in, (b) the particular lake they camp at in that region, or (c) their specific camping site on that lake.

Thus, Antoine can be described as *dala-go-t'ine*, showing the audience that he migrates and camps mostly in the eastern half of the present Hare Hunting Area; as *tu-šo-go-t'ine* (Man of Aubry Lake), Aubry Lake being his most favorite region; or *tu-ho-ta-deli[n]-go-t'ine* (man of the spot called tu-ho-tadeli[n] on Aubry Lake where he is currently camping) (Sue, 1964, pp.32-33).

This pattern of identifying and grouping people geographically can give the impression that there are many more "bands" than actually exist. That is, the number of terms for geographical groupings becomes very large since actual groups can be referred to in a number of contexts. [8]

Furthermore, although specific people tend to frequent some areas more than they do others, membership in geographical groupings is fluid, and areal preferences can change over time. Mobility, interpersonal frictions, post-marital residence changes, and attempts to make the maximum use of scattered resources, underlie the kind of "mutability" referred to by Osgood. Each family at Colville Lake, for example, tends to alternate among a number of preferred camping spots, and this type of fluctuation may occur from year to year or over a number of years. Families also use different campsites for different seasonal activities, and so population distribution is constantly being altered from month to month. As each of these moves may bring a household into contact with other, named groups, multiple camp memberships can yield a corresponding complex of identities. In addition, a geographical grouping may cease to exist if people stop using the area, or if the regional population declines. According to Osgood (1932) and Sue (1964), for example, this has been the case with Petitot's *Bâtards-Loucheux* or *Nne-la-gottine* ("End of the Earth People") band of the Hare, which had disappeared by the 1920's as a result of population depletion and shifts by survivors to other areas.

Finally, specific post-contact conditions, especially disease, starvation, and the concentration of people around forts, have continually affected the nature of Hare geographical groupings throughout the nineteenth and twentieth centuries. Starvation has occasionally occurred up into modern times, and small-pox, measles, and other epidemic diseases introduced by Europeans, have periodically decimated the Hare and their neighbors since the eighteenth century. The combined effect of these factors is illustrated by the history of the various nineteenth century bands which once inhabited the northern part of the Hare's territory, and which have since declined, coalesced, and collected at Good Hope and Colville. Families from the former Anderson River and Mountain bands, for instance, were eventually absorbed into the Colville grouping in the early 1960's (Hurlbert, 1962, p.25). The bush community is thus an amalgamation of the members and descendants from several such local groups, who have focused their activities in this region in recent decades. The over-all picture, therefore, is one of fluctuation in band composition and terminology over time, and a generalized fluidity in the people's social structure and spatial clustering. [9]

3   KINSHIP AND THE CONTINUITY
OF THE BAND

The composite origins of the people of Colville Lake are consequently submerged now under their current status as a single community. The various names by which the people are known, however, and the designations which they themselves acknowledge, indicate their affiliations with several earlier groupings. They continue to be called the *dalagot'ine*, which emphasizes their identity and affinity with the major band which hunted in their region in the late nineteenth and early twentieth century (Sue, 1964, p.55). Some of the people similarly recognize the terms *khachogot'ine, nelagot'ine*, and *dutagot'ine* as applied to themselves, all of which are earlier band names for north, east, and northeasterly groups (Petitot, 1875, 1876, 1889, 1891; Osgood, 1932). The residents of Good Hope also call them the *k'apamituegot'ine* ("The Ptarmigan-net-lake People") and "the Lodge people," the latter term being derived from the fact that some of the band's ancestors were the most isolated and northerly of the Hare, which led the early priests and traders to refer to them as the "Gens du Large" (cf. Petitot, 1891, p.362).[10] "Lodge" is thus an English corruption of this early French term.

The various band terms represent the geographic rather than the tribal nature of Hare groupings, and the contemporary history of the Colville Lake community graphically illustrates the role that kinship and fluidity have played in the survival and adaptability of the people. Prior to the 1960's, the groups in the Colville area had undergone a fifty year period of gradual attrition, which reduced their total population from a size of about 200 in the first decade of the twentieth century to a core of only twenty-eight people in the mid-1950's.[11] Several factors contributed to the decline of the community, primary among which were influenza and cholera epidemics, and a high incidence of tuberculosis which had persisted over a period of many years (Hurlbert, 1962, pp.13-14). The Colville band also lost many of its members through migration to Fort Good Hope as the expanding population and facilities of the town attracted more and more native people to it. High fur prices during the 1930's induced and enabled many people to build houses around the fort, and it was also during this time that the first permanent trapping cabins were erected on Colville Lake's south shore. When a sharp decline in fur prices occurred after the Second World War, however, and the tuberculosis rate increased, bush life suddenly became less economically and physically viable, and the movement of people to the fort was

augmented. This was spurred on by the opening of a government
nursing station and school there, an increase in government financial
assistance for Indians, and the availability of more wage employment
in the Mackenzie valley region in conjunction with DEW line (radar
station) construction and the federal government's Northern
Development policy. As a consequence of these factors, by the winter
of 1956-1957 there were only seven households that were still spending
most of their year in the Colville area, and the bilateral composition of
the reduced band at that time is illustrated in Figure 4.

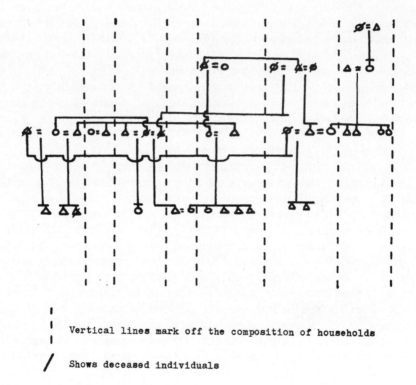

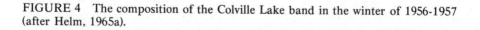

Vertical lines mark off the composition of households

Shows deceased individuals

FIGURE 4   The composition of the Colville Lake band in the winter of 1956-1957
(after Helm, 1965a).

For the handful of people who continued to live and hunt in the
Colville region during this era, there will always be a clear distinction

between the continuity of their own life style in the bush and the new patterns which lured the other families to the fort town. They see themselves as the people who "resisted the gradual abandonment of their traditional lands by the majority of the Gens du Large" (Helm, 1965a, p.374). To these elderly villagers, possessed of a sense of pride and history, there is a deep feeling of affinity with the outlook and ways of the "old timers" who coped with the northern forests — as they themselves have always done — in an earlier period. This sense of nostalgia and kinship, so real and immediate for many of them, was expressed by old Joseph when he recalled the years of his own youth in the late nineteenth century.

When I was a young boy, we never knew about a stove. We used to wear caribou clothes. We always made open fire. Sometimes we had fire inside a caribou hide tent. It's real funny. It's bad. The smoke goes in your eyes and it's real sore, real bad. We used to laugh at each other. If the smoke goes in your eyes you want to get it out. It's almost like snowblindness. We used to wear just caribou hide clothes. It was real warm in them. A guy will wear warm clothes if he's smart. If he's not smart he'll be cold in the winter, just shivering. If a person's smart, most of the people will stick with him during the winter.

We went to the Barren Grounds four or five weeks before Assumption Day. We passed the Horton River and there's no trees; just willows real low, like blankets thrown on the ground. Those willows, that's what we used for wood, to make tea or cook food. Once the water boils we keep throwing meat inside. We have no tent that time. The people bring poles along with them and put caribou hides over them and sleep under that.

A guy who really traps hard, who gets lots of marten, that's the guy who gets a seven-by-seven foot tent. All the rest of the guys use caribou hide only.

If we go to the Barrens we kill the first caribou and use the hides for a tent. Sometimes we go for five weeks with no wood. Just use willows. We go down there just for clothes and tents.

When I was a little bigger than Antoine (i.e., around eleven or twelve years of age), my parents wanted to go to Good Hope. The people out here used to go there. It was my first time and when we hit the high hill near Good Hope, we could see big houses just like this. It was my first time seeing buildings. And I just stand there and look at them. In the store was tobacco; sometimes no tea, no matches that time.

There were no matches and we used flint, that's what we used for lighting fire and lighting pipe. That time we really suffered. I was raised up when white men came to this country. The people before me really suffered hard. The people long before me, they're the ones who used to live on arrows only. The people in my time were raised up with guns so it was a little bit okay. The first gun wasn't like these kinds of guns — it was a muzzle-loading gun. At that time I used to be real strong. If I run I'll never stop for a long ways.

Now there are not enough people. When I was little there were lots of them, some of them real old. When I was as big as Antoine, some of them were even older than I am now. There was an old man Eh-ga, and Da-šey, Bele-ahn-šu, Ši-geh-ho, Luzon. There were more old men; their hair was real white. They can't even walk good. They were the people who lived on arrows. Some of these men had strong power, "hay aay yaay

aay," and that's how they sing when they do magic. That time even the young boys get strong magic power, and now these boys don't get them.

When there was no food, no meat to eat, some of them used to sing. Now people are just like white men, they have no magic. Even me I don't have any left.

While the true past of which old Joseph speaks can only be recaptured in words and memories now, recent events have wrought certain changes which, to an extent, have re-established a modern version of this earlier reality. In essence, the fate of the Colville band has undergone a dramatic reversal since the community's low point in 1957. This has been primarily due to the fact that by the late 1950's, the rapid expansion of Fort Good Hope was beginning to manifest itself in the form of some pervasive social and economic problems. The town's population was outstripping the natural resources of its environment, and wage labor opportunities were not increasing sufficiently to keep pace with the demand for them. People who had received some education, and those who had become used to wage employment as a new way of life, were reluctant to return to living off the land, and these and related acculturative factors combined to produce a situation in which welfare payments and drinking were taking on the dimensions of a new life style for a large segment of the fort's population.

In reaction to these developments, the Canadian government personnel who were responsible for the Good Hope region undertook a program to encourage the people to make greater use of the abundant fish, game, and fur resources of the Colville area.

In the fall of 1959, a winter road was cut through the woods between Fort Good Hope and Colville Lake at the cost of $5,000 to facilitate easier and faster travelling for trappers. In 1960, a private trader opened an outpost at the southern shore of Colville Lake which saved . . . long trips to town for supplies (Sue, 1964, p.82).

The establishment of the trading post marked the beginning of the revival of the community at Colville Lake. The immediate effect of the store was to encourage more of the original band members to spend a greater part of their year in the Colville area. With supplies available locally, shortages of goods and mid-winter trips to Good Hope for re-stocking were no longer necessary hardships for the people. Many of the natives took advantage of this opportunity to shift their residence back to Colville Lake. The chance to return to their original territory on a more permanent basis, coupled with the better subsistence and fur resources of the region, and the absence of the drinking and welfare problems of the fort, were strong inducements.

In the next few years, some of the people began to construct new homes at the village site, and the government assisted and encouraged them by supplying building materials. Within a few years, the community had achieved a high degree of economic self-sufficiency from Fort Good Hope, and trips between the two settlements became more a social matter than one of survival.

In the summer of 1962, a Catholic priest was assigned to Colville Lake and a mission was built there. The missionary's presence in the village enhanced its appearance of permanency and made it that much more attractive to people. It also obviated the need to go to Good Hope for major Church holidays. More of the band's original families moved back to Colville, and summer trips to the fort declined. The last family to make this seasonal journey by dogpack did so in the summer of 1964. Some families and individuals who had never lived at Colville also moved there, although several of the latter, plus a few of the old families who had considered returning to the village, eventually decided against it. At present, consequently, twelve of the settlement's fourteen native households consist of persons from what the people call "original Colville Lake families." [12]

The blood and marital ties which interrelate these households provided the kinship network upon which the reformation of the community was based. New members of the settlement also joined it via similar sets of relationships, their close kinsmen in the village serving as their sponsors for community membership. Ties to brothers, sisters, parents, and spouses' families in the band, were all utilized in drawing people into the community, or in re-affiliating them with it. In moving to the settlement, the people's decisions reveal a trend towards the reunion and solidarity of groups of siblings, and a combination of families who have variously opted to affiliate with either the husband's or the wife's kinsmen at different points in time. Since individuals and households in the community alternately camp with matrilineal, patrilineal and marital kin in different years and at different seasons, there is really no consistent or dominant pattern in the people's residence choices, and, in the long run, flexibility and bilaterality emerge as the over-riding features of the social system. [13]

It thus becomes evident, in immediate historical perspective, that kinship not only played a central role in maintaining the band during its period of decline, but that it was also an instrumental medium for reviving the community when new conditions made such a revival both opportune and desirable.

The flexibility and fluidity of the kinship system in this regard becomes manifest when one examines the lines along which people were recruited to the re-formed settlement. The recruitment procedure can be analyzed visually by taking the social structure of the band at its nadir in the mid-1950's (Figure 4) and contrasting it with the social structure of the community ten years later (Figure 5) when the band's revival had been fully accomplished. The darkened individuals in Figure 5 show the new members of the community who joined, were born into, or rejoined the band after the establishment of the trading post and mission. Each of these individuals shows one or more ties to members of the core population, and several people show numerous links with this group. It is important to note that this figure provides only a partial presentation of the kinship links within the community, and a more detailed picture, i.e., one which was extended vertically and horizontally to show ties through deceased ascending generations and additional kinship links, would be so complex that only a three-dimensional model could adequately portray it. This figure does serve, however, to indicate the magnitude and complexity of band interrelatedness, and to convey the more visible features of the system.

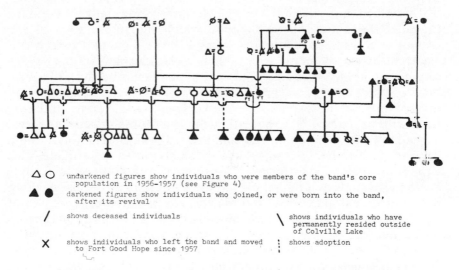

△ ○ undarkened figures show individuals who were members of the band's core population in 1956-1957 (see Figure 4)

▲ ● darkened figures show individuals who joined, or were born into the band, after its revival

/ shows deceased individuals

\ shows individuals who have permanently resided outside of Colville Lake

X shows individuals who left the band and moved to Fort Good Hope since 1957

⋮ shows adoption

FIGURE 5   The composition of the Colville Lake band in 1967.

It is important to emphasize here that this figure provides only a partial presentation of the kinship links within the community, and a more detailed picture, i.e., one which was extended vertically and laterally to show ties through deceased ascending generations and additional intermediary collateral links, would be so complex that only a three-dimensional model could adequately portray it. This figure merely attempts to indicate the magnitude and complexity of band interrelatedness.

The way in which people joined the community can be illustrated by the families of Peter and Lena Dehdele, and Fred and Thérèse Yawileh (cf. Figure 5). Fred left his parents' family in the late 1950's and moved to Good Hope, where he began living with his future wife Therese. They camped with their various kinsmen from the fort over the next few years, and raised a number of children. When they finally married, Fred's family — including Andrē, Berona, and old Joseph — came to town from˙Colville for the wedding, and soon after, Fred, Thérèse, and their children moved back to the bush community with them. The new couple eventually built a cabin for themselves, and they have been living in the village now for over ten years.

Lena and Peter Dehdele, on the other hand, are originally from the Good Hope area, but in the early 1960's Lena's sister's family took up residence at Colville Lake, and soon after Lena's parents did the same. At around that time, Lena and Peter — who had been married at a young age and had always had a stormy relationship — separated from one another, and Lena then moved to Colville to join her sister and parents. She and Peter also had a young daughter at the village who had been adopted by another band family several years previously. A year or two after Lena's move, she and Peter reconciled their differences, and he joined her at Colville. Peter had some other relatives in the village as well, including a male cousin, and Thérèse Yawileh, who was actually the daughter of one of his older brothers.

As these two cases illustrate, a married couple has considerable flexibility in choosing their residence because of the options which a bilateral system presents to them. Personal sentiments, likes, dislikes, and other non-kinship factors can thus be incorporated into decisions without violating a kin-based system of affiliation (Helm, 1965a, pp.371-372). The over-all structure of the rejuvenated Colville Lake community, which is summarized in Figure 6, shows some of the primary kinship ties that currently connect the adult men and women who head the village's native families.[14]

A social feature consistent with the bilateral structure of the settlement is that ties through one parent are not especially emphasized by the people over those through the other parent. Individuals associate and affiliate as much with their mother's kinsmen as they do with those of their father. Philip Ratehne, for example, variously fishes with his father's brother and drinks with his mother's brother, just as his parents, Wilfred and Bertha, alternate camping alliances between their respective siblings. Furthermore, and despite the prevalence of bonds between brothers in the community, the fraternally-linked families of the settlement do not regularly join

The Trail of the Hare

and cooperate on a permanent basis. Rather, they each maintain separate households, and though they sometimes camp together and hunt with one another, the degree to which this is done is highly variable. Only the two sets of parent-son related households, Yen's and Yašeh's, and Andrē's and Fred's, are relatively cohesive, and even they go their separate ways for at least part of every year. Underlining the flexibility of the entire system, therefore, is the persistently autonomous cultural role of the nuclear family as the people's major socio-economic unit. The history of any family, when it is considered as an affiliating group, reveals multiple ties with different kinsmen at different seasons during each annual cycle. Beyond the nuclear family, therefore, the more extended, bilateral ties which each person traces in the community constitute loose kindreds rather than

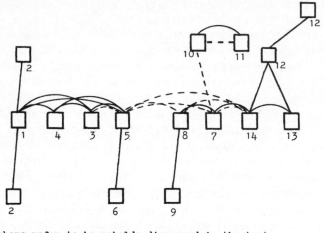

Numbers refer to households discussed in the text

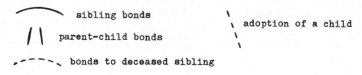

sibling bonds

parent-child bonds

bonds to deceased sibling

adoption of a child

FIGURE 6   Primary kinship links among village households.

The term "primary" refers to parent-child and sibling bonds between households. Some households have more than one primary tie between their respective members: e.g., in numbers 3 and 5, two brothers married two sisters; between numbers 7 and 14, there was a sister-exchange marriage. A child from household number 10 has been adopted into household 7, and a second child from household number 10 has been adopted into household number 11.

formalized and defined groups (cf. Freeman, 1961). Thus, the natives extend the value-laden term *sagot'ine* ("my people") to include all of their kinsmen, and they make no sharp distinctions between their patrilineal and matrilineal relatives. *"Sagot'ine"* consequently describes a social universe in which all people are potential allies and from which each individual creates a personal world.

Flexibility is also evident in the way the kinship terminology itself is used: kin terms are sometimes extended (jokingly or seriously) to non-kin to indicate the way the people perceive the closeness of their interpersonal relations, regardless of actual genealogical ties. Adult male friends who are not actually related by marriage nevertheless address one another as *sala*, "my brother-in-law," to verbally demonstrate their sense of affinity.[15] When Wilfred Ratehne's family "adopted" me as a fictional "brother," the understanding was that I had acquired all the rights and obligations that went with that status. Thus, although the people associate certain behavioral norms — such as intimacy, aloofness, reserve, joking, respect, and deference — with particular kinship relations, actual patterns turn out to be very loosely defined beyond the range of the nuclear family and lineal kinsmen.[16] This supports Helm's argument that

. . . one trend of the "internal readjustment to the altered conditions of life" (Murdock, 1949, p.199) by the Northern Dene has been toward the loss of significant behavioral distinctions between certain categories of relatives, (and) toward less correspondence between terminology and behavioral patterns . . . (MacNeish, 1960, p.287).

In many of its structural and interactional features, therefore, the community conforms to the fluid patterns of social organization that have been found to characterize other contemporary Athabascan groups in the Arctic drainage region.

If we digress for a moment and expand our historical perspective beyond the twentieth century, we find that a dual emphasis on the nuclear family and on some sort of fluid bilateral system was evidently operative in the aboriginal and post-contact period as well as the modern era. Helm (1965a; Helm and Leacock, 1971) has argued persuasively for their adaptive significance under the environmental conditions prevailing during those times. During these centuries, the Hare and other Northern Athabascan bands were subject to periodic and widespread starvation, as well as population decimation from epidemic diseases and the raids of neighboring groups, including Eskimos, Kutchin, Chipewyans, and Cree. Starvation was due to the people's dependence upon migratory and cyclically flunctuating animal populations, such as caribou, hare, moose, fish, and waterfowl, and the literature of the nineteenth century is replete with descriptions of cannibalism, hunger, and death among the Hare and other Mackenzie area peoples.[17] In late April of 1811, for example, the fur trader W. F. Wentzel wrote the following account from the site of Fort Simpson on the Mackenzie River:

> This last winter has been the most melancholy and most disastrous that could ever have befallen to any one single man to support without becoming torpidly stupid or totally senseless. Our distresses and sufferings have been so great, that, of four Christians who were left at this establishment last Fall, I am the only survivor . . . all my men are dead of starvation . . .
>
> I am unable to describe my own position; all my Indians have starved more or less; from one small band only, I received news yesterday-evening that five were dead of hunger; but of the majority of the Natives, I have not heard of since the month of November, they were already at that period gnawing the clothing they had upon themselves.
>
> Hares have totally failed throughout all parts of the country and large cattle (i.e., large game) have been uncommonly scarce at this place in particular, and the cold has been, this winter, the severest I have ever yet known. The ice on the Grand River (the Mackenzie) is no less than four and a half to five feet thick, and at this late date none of the snow has yet disappeared in the woods (1889, pp.106-107).

According to another nineteenth century observer, John McLean, conditions of starvation and cannibalism were more prevalent among the Slaves and Hares "than any other of the kindred tribes" (1932, p.343). William Hooper (1853, p.305), writing of the 1840's, reported that the Indians around Fort Good Hope were "dying in crowds." In 1844, the explorer Henry Lefroy recounted the following incidents among the Hare at Forts Simpson and Good Hope:

> As it was, there had been great scarcity for three or four years, and a frightful famine only the previous winter, accompanied by numerous acts of cannibalism. The Hare Indian woman who washed for me, known as the *"Femme du Diable,"* was protected from her husband at the Fort, because he had killed and eaten one or two other wives. Some starving women, who had already eaten their husbands, fell upon the Scotchmen who were carrying a mail, killed them as they lay asleep, and devoured them. They told me at Fort Good Hope that the scenes enacted just outside their palisades were harrowing. The cause of it all was the failure of rabbits from some epidemic, and of reindeer (caribou) . . . (1938, p.88).

These conditions continued not only into the post-contact period, but up through the first decades of the twentieth century as well. One woman at Colville Lake is the sole surviving member of a family whose other members starved to death in the area north of Aubry Lake in

1905. Yen Behdzi, who was born in 1898, described one incident of starvation in the early years of this century in the following words:

When I was young, four men and two women and seven children starved to death. At that time they were getting no rations. Now old people get rations. They're lucky. When I was small these guys starved to death because there was no food. When we were going after them, two men were already dead and two women buried them. They were wrapped in blankets and had spruce piled on top of them and had a ribbon tied up on a tree to show that these two guys were dead. There was one guy at the north end of the lake and one guy at this end. They both starved. That's what I know.

Other elderly people in the village recount similar stories of starvation from around the same period, and Sue reports that in 1904, "20 people who were hunting in the Mountain area died from hunger" (1964, p.55).

The people's traditional belief in personal guardian spirits, and their former reliance upon medicine men (*ehts'ehgont'ene*), divination, animistic procedures, and shamanistic curing as means of communicating with natural and supernatural forces, may have eased the stress of their hardships and shortages in earlier times; but even with a modern technology at their disposal, death by starvation occurred within the Colville band as recently as 1921 (Sue, 1964, p.231). Martin Yawileh, whose grandfather old Joseph is supposed to have been a very powerful medicine man in his youth, explained that:

The medicine men knew about animals, ground, trees, anything on the earth. Anything that is on the earth could sing to the medicine man and then he would have it for his helper. That's how he got his power and how he made people well. A man who knows about plants, or other things, for instance, could grab a person, sing over him, and make him well.

Martin's father André said that

a man would sometimes just know that he had the power to sing to certain animals. He may have been out hunting or travelling and then wolf or caribou or some other animal would speak to him and then he had it for life. A man would also know sometimes because these things happened in a dream.

The Hare continue to place a strong emphasis on the predictive efficacy of dreams, and they stress this as an important source of the old medicine men's power (Sue, 1964, pp.361-366).

In times of extreme hardship, it was these powerful medicine men who would go into a trance and sing to their guardian spirits to help the people secure food. "If a man knows about caribou," André continued, "he can sing to the caribou and a big herd will come if he is really strong and has strong medicine." The *ehts'ehgoⁿt'ene* of the Hare

also permitted themselves to be suspended in the air to facilitate communion with their guardian spirits (Jenness, 1967, p.395),

and they had a powerful reputation among their own and other people which only began to decline in the mid-nineteenth century as a result of white contact (Franklin, 1824, p.261; McLean, 1932, p.324; Richardson, 1851ii, p.22; Sue, 1964, p.366).[18]

Another facet of the people's earlier dependence upon medicine men is reflected in one of the tales in the Asoneh cycle. It shows that even when surplus food was cached for times of need, raids by enemy bands, or the depredations of wild animals, were occurrences which intensified the severest threats to the people's existence. In Paul Behdzi's version, this story involves the neighboring Kutchin or Loucheux, but Paul and the other people emphasize the tale's similarity to their own ancestors' plight.

Asoneh was northeast from here in the mountains. The Loucheux buried some drymeat (*iⁿyegoⁿ*) for the winter under the ground. There was a grizzly bear (*sašo*) near there, just near the ice house. The grizzly was killing lots of people.

The Loucheux were coming back to the place where the meat was buried without anything. They were starving. Two boys went to that place. But they were killed; and two older boys went and they were also killed.

So these two boys also never came back. Then they sent two older men to get the meat. They didn't know what had been happening there. So the two men were coming to the place. They saw a big mound near the place and it was the grizzly. The grizzly ran after them and took one of them away. So the other one came running back home and said: "There's a grizzly here who took my friend." Everyone said: "We are going to starve because the grizzly is right on the food we buried." The Loucheux said it was too bad that Asoneh wasn't there.

The year before Asoneh had been staying with an old man, and the old man was now staying with these people. The old man thought of Asoneh. Just when they were thinking about him it was getting dark and they heard someone coming. It was Asoneh who came to that old man. And the old man said: "Is that really you Asoneh?"

Everybody said to him: "We're just starving because the grizzly's on the buried meat." They told him that nearly everyone had been killed by the grizzly. After a while Asoneh went out and he met a little boy. He asked the boy which way the people went for the grizzly bear. The little boy pointed and said: "This way. There are two roads. They go on one and after a while they cry and come back. The grizzly took one or two guys each time."

It was getting dark. There was moonlight. The old man went to sleep. So Asoneh went out and went on the road. He saw a big thing on the hill where the Loucheux buried the meat. The grizzly came running after Asoneh. He was coming right near Asoneh, and so Asoneh jumped right over the grizzly bear with his snowshoes. He jumped back and forth over the bear and each time he hit him over the head with a stick. He wanted to tire the bear out. He kept jumping over him and hitting him between the eyes. Both of the grizzly's eyes came out.

Asoneh was sitting, resting beside the grizzly bear. Asoneh was wondering: "I can't leave the grizzly like this." So he broke up a lot of wood. He propped up the grizzly with the pieces and he also propped his mouth open with a stick. He faced the bear, on the road, to where the people would come from. Then Asoneh went back home. When he got back he went to sleep. The old man knew nothing of what Asoneh did.

The old man said to Asoneh: "Please go with those men when they go to the grizzly." And Asoneh said: "When they go, I'll go with them." So the old man said to the men: "Asoneh will go with you, so you had better hurry up." Everyone said "Yes" and they went.

Asoneh was walking behind and those men were walking ahead of him. They yelled: "The grizzly is coming already!" Those guys then ran back. The old man ran back too. Asoneh was still walking towards the grizzly and the old man saw him. He said to the other men: "You don't have to run because Asoneh is still walking toward the grizzly. What's the matter with you?"

The men saw Asoneh walking right up close to the grizzly. So Asoneh took his stick out and the grizzly fell down. He was frozen up. Asoneh asked these men: "Why do you run away? This grizzly is frozen."

Then they went to the place where they buried the drymeat. They threw away the meat with the blood on it from the men that the grizzly killed and they took only the good meat. Some of them had already died from starving. They gave the meat out to the people.

The old man said to give Asoneh two girls and he can camp with us three times. Everybody said yes. They were looking for two good, cute girls.

Asoneh was camping with the old man. Those girls came into the house and sat down waiting for him. But Asoneh was a really good guy. Asoneh told them: "Go out. Me and the old man are going to sleep. We don't need you here." He chased them out.

The next morning Asoneh was gone when the old man woke up.

Another story, told by Joseph Tehgu, shows the special relationship between a man with strong medicine and his guardian spirit, and it also recalls the stresses of warfare and raiding by the Chipewyans in early historic times.

The people were staying at *Lugewatue* (Whitefish Lake), and everyone was visiting nets. They said visitors are coming from *Denedigo^{n}tue* (Those-men-were-killed-there Lake). Everyone was just excited because visitors were coming. They were survivors from the Chipewyans who had been killing people at *Denedigo^{n}tue*. The people at *Lugewatue* saw the smoke from there.

Everyone was killed at *Denedigo^{n}tue*. The Chipewyans took off for *Sašoyetue* (Great Slave Lake) and the *Lugewatuet'ine* (the Whitefish Lake people) went out after them. They got to Great Slave Lake. The Chipewyans ran on the lake and these guys were crying because their parents had been killed by the Chipewyans. The people asked each other: "Someone of you has to do magic (*ehts'ehneh*)." Some of them said no. But one of them knew about crow and so crow came to him. The man took a little piece of ice and put it in the crow's mouth. Then the crow took off on Slave Lake.

The Chipewyans were in the middle of the lake and a big cold wind started blowing. They all froze to death. There was one guy named Tsurayule who made it across Slave Lake. And one other Chipewyan made it across after Tsurayule. So there were two Chipewyans. They made fire. The second one was a young boy: when he got warmed up, he just fell down dead. Tsurayule almost froze to death too. His eyes were getting blurry. He saw things. He said: "There are too many mice around here." Tsurayule was sitting down and then he fell backwards dead.

One other man was saved of the Chipewyans. He was the only one who did not freeze to death. He had no food. He cut off his parka and he was wearing caribou hide. He took his belt off and made a hole in the ice and tried to fish with his belt and some caribou hide at the end of it. He pulled a loon up out of the lake. He knew something this man: he was a magician. Old-timers magic is strong. He ate the loon up and then he took off. Then he met some of his Chipewyan people leaving to come after the people from around here. He said: "Don't go because all your people were killed by a big wind on the lake." So everyone quit. All the Chipewyans gave up the idea.

In those days, the people weren't afraid of killing each other.

The assistance that the Hare received from "people with strong medicine" may have mitigated their plight in former times, but more drastic measures were often necessary to cope with serious and ubiquitous privations. Aboriginal and more recent recourse to such population control devices as infanticide, especially female infanticide, and the abandonment of the aged and the infirm, testify to the severity of environmental pressures in the area (Petitot, 1889, pp.154-157; Keith, 1890, p.119; Hooper, 1853, p.319). The people's ability to resort to these measures added flexibility to their kinship system by giving families options in the matter of how to deal with economically marginal individuals who also inhibited their mobility. These ecological stresses, and the people's cultural response to control the size and composition of their groups, gave to them and the other Indians of the sub-Arctic the lowest population density of any people in the New World: one scholar has placed the aboriginal Hare population at 750 (Mooney, 1928, p.26), and another has estimated a density for all the boreal forest groups of only 1.35 persons per 100 square kilometers (Kroeber, 1939, p.143; cited by Helm and Leacock, 1971, pp.370-371). [19]

Given the inevitability of starvation and recurrent disasters for northern natives, it is most likely that it was the basic fluidity of the kinship system itself which allowed people to initially respond to and ultimately recover from these decimations by shifting residences, requesting hospitality, affiliating with other kinsmen, and then reconstituting communities of the survivors and the unafflicted. As one anthropologist has summed up the social implications of the northern Indians' ecology:

We know from reports in the last century that the Mackenzie River Dene, although in possession of iron ice chisels and firearms, nevertheless periodically suffered from drastic depopulation through starvation . . . The concurrence of the low point in the rabbit cycle, of severe ice conditions not permitting net setting, and/or fish failure, and of regional failure of moose or of caribou migration would impose absolute starvation for several or many weeks. Severe famine and population loss under exactly such circumstances were described by Wentzel . . . in 1811. Could conditions in truly aboriginal times have been better? What I am stressing is not merely that aboriginal Dene populations were small in size and low in density, but that population was unstable, with decimation through famine occurring at what may have been rather cyclical intervals. When such disasters struck, "multiple kinship avenues" to new affiliations as old ones collapsed may well have been crucial in permitting quick regrouping of survivors . . . (Helm, 1965a, pp.381-382).

The decline of the Colville Lake band through economic and epidemic factors in the twentieth century was a crisis whose nature and magnitude were similar to those described for earlier periods, and initially, bilateral networks allowed most of the group's population to be successfully re-integrated into Fort Good Hope. Later on, when the opportunity to revive the community arose, "multiple kinship avenues" [20] were again utilized to re-form the band in accordance with this underlying pattern. The fluidity of population movements, and the flexibility of the kinship system in allowing people to move around and reconstitute their groups in this fashion, thus stand out as basic social features which have both historical depth and contemporary importance for the members of the Colville Lake community.

4   KINSHIP, GENEROSITY AND EMOTIONAL RESTRAINT

Another feature of the flexibility displayed by Colville Lake's kinship system is the variable way in which people treat kinsmen of different degrees of relatedness. Pronounced disparities can be found in the extent to which attitudes and behavior are standardized for close and distant blood kin, and for people related by marriage; and the degrees of latitude exhibited in this regard reflect the cultural themes of generosity and emotional restraint. This can be seen through an analysis of kinship patterns and the kinds of expectations and obligations that the people associate with them.

For the members of the Colville Lake community, although extended bonds of kinship are utilized in the formation of the camping and hunting alliances which grow out of their semi-nomadic economy, the nuclear family remains the basic social division in the people's lives. It is the residential unit, the main locus of economic cooperation and the division of labor, and a source of material and social support. It contains each person's closest kinsmen, and so it is also the locus of the strongest affective ties in each individual's social sphere. It involves the people among whom the bonds of generosity, interdependence, and mutual aid are the strongest, and social relations exhibit a combination of warmth, respect, and restraint. The respect that children show for their parents, and the bonds that siblings establish with one another, ideally continue into the children's own adulthood, thus perpetuating the family's cohesiveness over time. Relations between grandparents and grandchildren, and parents and their young offspring, are especially warm, and the display of affection by and towards children is one of the few culturally permissible emotional expressions in the community. Adult siblings of the opposite sex, as well as husbands and wives, although possessing great affection for one another in most cases, often repress the demonstration of their sentiments. Therefore, although all the natives of the community can trace bilateral and marital ties with other village residents, social bonds remain the closest within the nuclear family, even though their low-keyed warmth is often hidden from the observer by a demeanor of restraint and a particulate sense of mutual respect.

It is significant to note that the latter day economic emphasis upon the nuclear family is probably a point of continuity with earlier forms of social structure. Historically, it has been shown that the introduction of a trapping economy among native peoples has led to an increased focus on the family at the expense of wider band ties (cf. Murphy and Steward, 1956; Leacock, 1954; Jenness, 1967, p.257; Helm and Leacock, 1971, p.365). This is because trapping necessitates the fragmentation and dispersal of bands into small groups of family units for the effective exploitation of widely dispersed fur resources during most of each year. Larger social groupings during the winter and spring, therefore, become economically inefficient, and dispersal becomes more pronounced and more prolonged than under previous conditions.

It can be suggested that the crucial economic role of the family, combined with the premium that survival in the bush places upon a smooth-working, cooperative social unit, are factors which would be conducive to an emphasis upon emotional restraint as a behavioral norm. Strong affective outbursts of either a positive or negative nature could seriously disrupt the harmony which is necessary to family and camp life. The pervasiveness of emotional restraint at all social levels in the band lends strong support to such an interpretation. This argument is strengthened by the fact that almost all cultural means of coping with stress and tension, such as the use of mobility and withdrawal as techniques for escaping unpleasant encounters, the frequent participation in gossip, and the redirection of aggression towards dogs and inanimate objects, are essentially patterns which allow the people to avoid direct emotional confrontations. [21]

Beyond the nuclear family, a wide range of kinsmen is recognized by all community residents, and extended kin ties continue to play a very important part in their lives. The ingatherings of the annual cycle, and the relationships involved in the continually changing bush partnerships that the people form, serve to maintain their social networks on a number of different levels. The natives continue to stress their interdependence with their kinsmen and fellow band members, and, as is the case with their own families, they look to one another for mutual assistance, generosity, and companionship. Beyond a certain range of kinship, however, interpersonal ties tend to be loose and diffuse, and outside of a married adult's immediate in-laws, who usually warrant deference and respect, a person's blood and marital kin do not elicit uniform attitudes and behavior within the band as a whole. While obligations are strongly felt among family members and some more distant relatives, the fact that large kinship networks are rarely organized in nature permits them to be utilized with the kind of flexibility that we have demonstrated in other regards.

The diffuseness of expectations and obligations beyond a person's immediate family and parents-in-law allows for a high degree of fluidity in establishing camping alliances and other social ties. Affiliations can and do fluctuate according to both season and activity, and the make-up of bush camps during the winter and spring can sometimes show a turn-over of better than fifty percent of the personnel within a period of two months. Patterns nevertheless emerge which permit the observer and the people themselves to speak and think in terms of partnerships, friendships, and networks. The flexible use of kinship as a social feature is reinforced by the fact that kinship is only one of several factors involved in the formation and maintenance of close ties. Other variables, including age, sex, personality, degree of acculturation, allegiances in local disputes, participation in drinking, and the size of economically viable seasonal groupings, all influence the various sets of relationships found within the community.

In many cases, these non-kinship factors supercede kin ties in the development of close bonds. Heavy drinkers camp and trap together more frequently than they do with non-drinkers, even if the latter are close relatives, and kinship considerations may also become secondary if similar acculturative experiences — such as schooling or outside wage employment — have bound non-kinsmen together in a long-standing friendship. Furthermore, the village has a predominance of people under thirty years of age, and because of the cultural emphasis upon avoidance and restraint among adult persons of the opposite sex, especially if they are kin, young men and women often establish their closest ties with non-related age mates of the same sex. The friendships of teen-agers Philip Ratehne and Gabyel Behdzi, of conservative Monique Yawileh and tradition-minded Yerimen Behdzi, and of Lena Dehdele and Paula Limertu, both bilingual, educated, and relatively Westernized, illustrate the formation of just such bonds.

Ties are also affected by the type of relationship that a linking kinsman or kinswoman has with a particular relative of a given person. In relationships between a father's brother and a brother's son, to cite one such instance, each of the cases in the village is strongly influenced by the kinds of ties maintained by the connecting brothers, as well as by the relative cohesiveness of their households. Leon Behdzi and his brother Yen, for example, are both tradition-oriented, non-drinking, and monolingual individuals, who are drawn together by their quiet, conservative philosophy, as well as by their bond as siblings. They are much closer with one another than either of them is with Pierre, their heavy drinking, more acculturated brother. When Leon, who has no adult sons in the village, needs help or assistance, he and his daughter Yerimen usually call upon Yen's son Yašeh rather than Pierre's boy Gabyel, for it is with Yašeh — and with Yašeh's father — that they share a common outlook and strong sense of mutual respect. Not surprisingly, Leon and his daughter camp much more frequently with Yen's and Yašeh's households during the winter than with any of their other — and equally closely related — village kinsmen.

The *ad hoc*, fluid nature of each individual's social network leads to a certain amount of tension among the people as a result of the wide-ranging and pervasive expectations for generosity among kinsmen and *sagot'ine*. This situation affects patterns of emotional expression within the community because in cases where non-kin stand closer to a person than some of his own relations, there is room for ambiguity and ambivalence whenever the issue of that person's responsibility to kinsmen and friends is raised. The villagers are very conscious of their own and other people's behavior in the areas of hospitality and reciprocity, and they are anxious both to receive their share of others' largesse, and also to maintain their own status and reputation for magnanimity. When the actions of individuals do not coincide with what others expect of them, strong sentiments are raised which must be dealt with in some way. Stinginess, and the failure to cooperate and provide hospitality, thus put the themes of interdependence, generosity, and emotional containment to an acid test, for these values are among the primary cohesive forces uniting the community. The way in which these values are elaborated and reconciled with one another, then, is crucial to an understanding of the nature of social and ecological adaptations within the band, and we shall therefore examine how the people cope with these ambiguities.

One of the primary functions of a cultural emphasis upon sharing is that it serves to relieve aspects of environmental stress by insuring the distribution of scarce resources among kinsmen and fellow villagers. The corollary of reciprocity means that each person has a claim upon the game killed by the people to whom he is obligated to distribute his own kill. Ideally, things should balance out in the long run, while in the short run the chances for the well-being and survival of group members are increased.

The value of such an ethic under aboriginal conditions is manifest, and currently the successful hunter or fisherman is still expected to share and distribute part of his food catch among kinsmen and band members. This is particularly so in the case of large game (i.e., moose and caribou), and fish. Moose are rare in the Colville area and they are hunted mainly in the summer and fall, viz., seasons during which fresh meat is at a premium since there are no caribou herds in the area. The successful hunter usually gives the moose away to another person (such as his father or a close friend), and the latter is then expected to supervise the butchering of the animal and the distribution of its meat among the people. Upon receiving news of a moose kill, all the men of the village, along with some of the adult females, go to the site of the kill by boat, on foot, or with dogsled if the season permits, and the meat is then distributed among them. The man who shot the moose receives his share as well, and he and the person to whom the animal was given usually retain a good portion of the meat, in addition to keeping most of the much-valued hide.

Gross inequalities in hunting luck can be a source of stress and envy within the community, but the fate of a slain moose illustrates the subtle way in which these potentially disruptive emotions are handled. At a material level, disparities in luck are redressed by redistribution mechanisms, although envy may more often be repressed or rechanneled rather than annihilated by these means. At a social level, however, the meat and hide received by the successful hunter ultimately come to him as a gift from the distributor rather than as a direct windfall, and envy of him is thus less concentrated. The distributor, who also retains a sizable percentage of the animal, similarly comes off in a good light as a man who is generous with other people's largesse. This variation on redistribution, by deflecting envy, dilutes it. The egalitarian outcome of the situation maximizes band survival by guaranteeing people a minimum level of access to food. One can thus argue, as others have done for such negatively experienced psychological phenomena as stress and anxiety, that the fear of envy, when its manifestations are culturally institutionalized, can be made to serve some important and unexpected, positive social functions.[22]

Generosity involving fish operates differently among the people. Each household has nets set the year round to get food for human and dog consumption, and no one is expected to distribute his daily catch on a regular basis. If a particularly "meaty" fish (e.g., a large trout), or several especially favored fish (e.g., loche) are caught by a person, some of this fish may be given to his parents, or a married son, daughter or sibling. The distribution occurs on a small scale, however, and it does not involve the obligatoriness, the amount of food, or the number of people that are concerned in distributing a moose-kill. Methods of preserving and storing fish allow surpluses to be kept for future use, and this is important in view of the people's continuous and daily need for dogfeed. More intensive generosity with fish occurs when a close or distant kinsman, or a friend, has run out of fish for dogfeed on some particular occasion.

This latter condition can come about in a number of ways. Some people, for example, are much less assiduous than others in laying up a large surplus of fish. This can leave them without dogfeed at those times of the year when fish become hard to get: this occurs most often during freeze-up and break-up, as well as during the coldest months of the winter (January and February). At such times, the people in question may have to turn to kinsmen and friends to fill their need, and people are expected to respond positively to such requests for generosity. People who return to the village or switch campsites are often without dogfeed for a few days until they can reset their nets and get their own fish. During this interval, they rely upon the generosity of others to feed their families and their dogs. A man who has had bad luck in his fishing, e.g., in cases where the fish have moved from the part of the lake where his nets were set, can also count on the generosity of kin and friends to help him out in his time of need. Similarly, people are expected to help feed the dogs of any traveller who visits their bush camp, as well as offer hospitable treatment to the traveller himself.

Generosity involving caribou meat presents yet a third pattern of distribution. At the present time, caribou are generally plentiful in most parts of the Colville region during the winter and spring. Most households, therefore, have an equally good chance of acquiring sufficient meat for themselves, and there is no binding obligation or expectation that people should distribute most of their meat among the other families on a regular basis. Persons sometimes present one another with caribou heads, tongues, and fetuses — all of which are considered delicacies by the people — but this is only an occasional and unformalized type of prestation. However, there are also some serious circumstances in which entire families may be without meat for a considerable period of time. Some households contain better (or more) hunters than others, and some families may find themselves camped in an area where the caribou did not come through that particular winter. In such cases, the people without meat generally do ask for some from those who were more fortunate. Their request is stated in an oblique and stylized manner, however, the needy person simply noting his lack of meat to the other party, who is then expected to understand this as a plea for caribou. [23] The people without meat may actually offer to buy some from the others, but this is rare; rather, there is a tacit expectation among the villagers that the families that have had greater luck at the hunt should offer some of their kill to those with little or no meat. This is especially the case if the men of one household have killed a very large number of caribou at one particular time.

The concept of generosity is not extended to cover the distribution of small game (e.g., hares, ptarmigan, and waterfowl) or fur animals, but it does include liquor, homebrew, and invitations to brew parties. Non-edible items which are considered to be personal or family property by the people, such as dogs, sleds, household supplies, sewing materials, rifles, traps, and a wide range of other commodities, are similarly the subject of claims by one's fellow band members. Such goods are loaned out rather than given away, however, and reciprocity may ultimately take the form of a loan of a different piece of property or perhaps a direct gift of food.

In addition to generosity in terms of food and materials, the people's concepts of interdependence and reciprocity also extend to matters of hospitality, cooperation, and mutual aid. People adopt and care for one another's children, they help each other in moving to and from bush camps, they get one another firewood in cases of immediate need, they do sewing for each other, they camp with one another for varying periods in the bush, and they also offer each other assistance by lending and operating boats, motors, and other equipment. Generosity therefore covers both goods and services, and these two aspects are often interchangeable in terms of the reciprocity involved in the people's behavior. When Wilfred Ratehne's son Philip, for example, had camped with some relatives for an extended period of time one spring, he brought these people several quarters of caribou meat the following winter. After Leon's daughter Yerimen had done a great deal of sewing for Maurice Bayjere's son Luke, Luke cut several cords of wood for her family when Leon was taken ill a few months later. I found that my own attempts to reciprocate rather than simply repay the services that people provided me with were warmly received and appreciated by them — much more so than the money with which the trader and missionary usually paid the people for food and labor.

Adoption is a process which also crystallizes some crucial values for community members. The motives for giving or taking a child in adoption are diverse, and in their variety they exhibit some of the basic social, psychological, and survival considerations which concern the people. A family, for example, may offer a child to some kinsmen if their own household already has more members than can be successfully maintained. Berona and André Yawileh have raised a grandson of theirs from Good Hope because the boy's parents could not manage with the large number of offspring that they had already produced. If a man or woman dies or is taken seriously ill, young children may also be given in adoption to ease the other spouse's burden. Wilfred and Bertha Ratehne provide a case in point, for they have brought up Suzanne Dehdele, one of Lena Dehdele's daughters, because the child's mother was stricken with tuberculosis soon after Suzanne's birth. In addition, in some cases, a child whose paternity is in doubt, or who was conceived outside of marriage, may be given to another family to raise in order to relieve the tensions that are developing between a husband and wife. A son whom Albert Limertu had fathered in a common-law union prior to his marriage was eventually returned to the boy's natural mother because the child's presence was creating intense friction between Albert and his new wife Paula.

People accept or ask for children for a variety of reasons as well. Infants and youngsters are loved and valued by the people, and kinsmen and close friends are anxious to help a child, and his or her parents, in times of distress. Adopted children are raised with great warmth and affection, and Western notions of legitimacy and illegitimacy are irrelevant in influencing the position and treatment that a child ultimately receives in his adopted home. No person is permanently stigmatized because of the conditions surrounding his conception or upbringing. Adopting a child is also an excellent opportunity to publicly display one's generosity and good-heartedness, and it simultaneously demonstrates to everyone the competence and self-sufficiency of a couple in their being able to provide for an extra person. Adoption is thus not an entirely altruistic endeavor some of the time, and childless couples are especially anxious to adopt, not only for the companionship, but also so that, in their old age, there will be someone to take care of and support them.

Adoption is thus a social feature which embodies the themes of kinship, flexibility, and generosity. It is a process which distributes children among the people who most need and can best care for them, and it solidifies and extends kinship networks while enhancing specific reputations. Children, as a source of interest, also become a medium of exchange and expressiveness, and they are not only adopted with great ease, but are also sent, from time to time, to live temporarily with relatives in different communities and encampments. They thus experience, during their early years, various periods of residence with aunts, uncles, and grandparents, and they consequently are exposed to — and participate in — a substantial network of people. They come to define their social world, and its associated expectations and obligations, in a broad manner, and this prepares them for coping with a diversity of people and values in their adult lives.

This brief summary of kinship, generosity, and sharing among the people, while it omits some features of the complex, does serve to indicate its central place in their lives. The various expectations and obligations we have noted are most strongly felt among close kinsmen, particularly nuclear family members and lineal kin. Ideally, however, and depending upon the particular situation and needs at hand, these themes can be extended to encompass all of one's *sagot'ine*, viz., in the case of Colville Lake, all the natives of the village, including blood kin, in-laws, and unrelated friends. Yet, it is among these very people that tensions over generosity may threaten to erupt into disruptive outbreaks — and so it is at these times that the ethic of emotional restraint, and the social mechanisms for re-channeling emotionality, such as gossip and mobility, may now come into play most importantly as behavioral devices for maintaining a minimal degree of peace and order within the band.

If one compares the way in which the generosity ethic operates in regard to moose, caribou, and fish, to take just three examples, it is evident that the system is flexible enough to allow different kinds of expectations to be in force according to the degree of scarcity of the various commodities. The system is flexible, however, not only in terms of the scarcity of goods and services involved, but also in regard to the varying needs that people have at different points in time. An individual's friends, close kinsmen, and distant relatives may each experience shortages or the need for assistance during different parts of the year, and the ethic permits the individual in question to act generously in accord with current necessities and his own circumstances. Conversely, a family that is in need of help can usually call upon, or choose from, a wide range of kin and non-kin to assist them, basing their choice upon the current economic position of their various *sagot'ine*, and their past history of mutual cooperation. The motives and dimensions of adoption display a similar array of options.

Since a person's possession of surplus food, time, or equipment is partly a function of his luck in a somewhat unpredictable environment, a rigid set of rules that bound him to dispensing his goods and services through a rigid network of kinsmen might not benefit those who were. most in need at any particular moment. Conversely, again, a family that could only rely upon specific relations in order to obtain assistance might find themselves, at certain times, without access to those persons in the band who could help them most in their current distress. Given the persistence of a bush way of life and its attendant ecological stresses for the people, therefore, one can suggest that a flexible implementation of generosity as a cultural value allows for the redistribution of scarce goods and services in a way that maximizes the well-being of all concerned.

What makes the flexible elaboration of this theme possible is the people's consciousness of their interdependence with one another and the inherent fluidity of the social networks through which these realizations are made to operate. Kinship and other social modalities allow different kinds of relationships to be utilized and activated under different circumstances, including those occasions when stress and jealousy are either overtly expressed in conflict or only covertly experienced as restrained sentiments. When tense and anxious conditions weaken some of the bonds in an individual's kindred or social set, flexibility again permits him to reconstruct his personal network along new lines and thus continue to survive and participate in the life of the community.

The cultural emphasis upon emotional repression and restraint is similarly tied to the interrelatedness and interdependence of band members. As was argued previously, cooperation and mutual reliance among interrelated people in a harsh environment places a premium on peaceful interpersonal relations. At the same time, the social and ecological sources of stress which these conditions engender are such that tensions and conflicts are a potential cause of serious social disorder. Hence, adherence to a cultural theme of restraint in emotional expression is one possible way of securing a minimum level (albeit a superficial one at times) of peaceful and cooperative group existence.

An emphasis upon emotional restraint does not, of course, actually relieve the stresses and tensions that it represses. One would expect to find, in such a situation, that there are other culturally sanctioned means of emotional expression which would permit the release of these tensions while allowing the community and its constituent groups to continue to function at an effective level. This is true among the people of the band, and modes of relief and sanctioned emotional expression occur in a number of ways: these include drinking behavior, humor, rough treatment of dogs, shifts of residence, gossip, and a high level of mobility. The fact that these expressive acts usually occur in a predictable manner generally allows people to explain, adjust, and react to them in socially acceptable ways which do not provoke immediate retaliation or disruptive responses. Consistent with the ethic of restraint, mild or excessive provocations rarely evoke an extreme reaction.

While the following chapters explore these behavioral modes in greater detail, a few dimensions of stress response may be cited here to illustrate the nature of the coping process. Shifts in residence, for example, are usually explained by people as being due to ecological rather than interpersonal factors. Drunken comportment is similarly excused by them on the basis of the cultural notion that drunken individuals cannot be held responsible for their private or public actions. Explanations of stressful encounters thus minimize the roles of the persons involved, and instead seek their origin in non-human factors. Furthermore, expressions of jealousy and anger which stem from the frequent tensions of the generosity ethic are almost never directly made to the person whose behavior brought these feelings about. Rather, vindictiveness is rechanneled in gossip and mimicry, and it is manifested in more indirect retaliation, such as in the covert distribution of the offended person's own foodstuffs. Similarly, sexual jealousies between husbands and wives are rarely expressed when the people are sober. Interpersonal stresses generated by prolonged periods of small-group isolation in the bush are channeled and dissipated in a number of ways, including strenuous chopping of wood, travelling, beating of dogs, and occasionally violent outbreaks when drinking occurs. With the exception of the latter, therefore, direct emotional confrontations among adults are rarely experienced.

The pervasiveness of kinship ties in the community is one of the primary social conditions that makes a generalized pattern of emotional restraint possible for the inhabitants. With kinship serving as a key medium of interaction, interrelatedness acts as a major check on aggression in accord with the belief that kinsmen should ideally be treated in a kind and open-handed manner. The flexibility of the whole system is again manifest in the fluid way in which it allows redressive measures, pressures for peace and reconciliation, and stress-reducing steps, all to be implemented in an *ad hoc*, yet effective manner. Social control is largely normative and behavioral, and sanctions are basically informal ones The band recognizes no real political authority among its members, and such devices as gossip, embarrassment, humor, temporary ostracism, and the withholding of generosity and hospitality, are among the most efficacious ways to bring a person back into line.

These non-political modes of social control are made possible by a cultural ethic of flexibility, interdependence, generosity, and restraint, whose themes thus exhibit a high degree of consistency and accommodation with one another: each contributes to the maintenance of the social system while it reinforces the validity of the other values. When the pressures for restraint break down from time to time, as also happens periodically with those for reciprocity, the flexible way in which social networks can be dissolved and reformed again gives the people the opportunity to revitalize some of their social ties while temporarily relaxing other ones. Interdependence is thus never really denied as an existential reality, but rather it is channeled by the people in different directions at different times. Bonds with close kinsmen continue as the core of each person's social set, while other relationships are utilized or deactivated as circumstances warrant and as possibilities permit.

5 IMPLICATIONS

The values that have been focused upon here, along with some of the specific ways in which they are expressed and implemented, can be found in many other northern peoples and in other hunting-and-gathering groups in the world. In a recent symposium on hunting societies, fluid modes of social organization, and a flexible approach to residence and group composition, were found to be characteristic of many of the populations that were considered (Lee and DeVore, eds., 1968). Bilaterality, as Murdock (1968) noted, was especially prevalent among North American hunting groups, a point re-emphasized by the discussion of social structure among the Dogribs, Northern Athabascans, and Eskimos (Helm, 1968a; Damas, 1968; Balikci, 1968). A cultural stress upon sharing, generosity, and hospitality was similarly found to have a wide distribution, and the frequent recourse to group fission as a means of resolving conflict also emerged from the comparisons (Lee and DeVore, 1968; Turnbull, 1968a; cf. also Netting, 1971; Service, 1966).

Elsewhere, in a volume summarizing the culture of the Canadian Eskimo, Valentine and Vallee (1968) have brought together a number of essays which stress the inherent flexibility of Eskimo life styles and orientations, including kinship, social organization, and responses to modernization. Works by Chance (1966), Damas (1963), the Honigmanns (1965), and Willmott (1960) point out similar features in specific Eskimo communities. Other studies, dealing with Northern Indians, have brought out some of the same emphases we have noted among the people of Colville Lake. Athabascan groups demonstrating some or all of these themes include the Kutchin (Slobodin, 1960a), Kaska (Honigmann, 1949), and such Arctic drainage peoples as the Slave (Honigmann, 1946; Helm, 1961), Dogrib (Helm n.d., 1965b; Helm and Lurie, 1961), Bear Lakers (Osgood, 1932), and Chipewyans (VanStone, 1965). Northern Algonkian peoples, including the Cree (Chance, 1968; Sindell, 1968), the Montagnais-Naskapi (Lips, 1937; Leacock, 1969), and the Ojibwa (Hallowell, 1946; Landes, 1937a, 1937b; Rogers, 1969a, 1969b) have been shown to have many of the same cultural emphases.

The general features noted above can be found to occur not only among the more nomadic and marginal hunters of the Arctic and sub-Arctic regions, but also among hunting societies from very different ecological and cultural situations. Helm (1968a) and Woodburn (1968), for example, point out that the nature of Dogrib socio-territorial groupings — which is quite similar to that found among the Hare — is duplicated by !Kung Bushmen, Mbuti, Ik, and various Australian bands, as well as by Eskimo and other Northern Athabascan peoples. These and other studies, such as those by Turnbull (1961, 1968a) on the Mbuti and Ik, and Hiatt (1968) on the Anbara, have also noted the existence of the thematic features we have stressed in several African and Australian societies. The point being made here, of course, is not that these cultural patterns are universal traits for hunting groups, for the latter can be found to differ on a great number of parameters, including the nature of band composition and social organization, the types of authority, decision-making and social control that are operative, and the modes of — and motives for — cooperation, hospitality, and food distribution. The wide incidence of the features discussed, however, does indicate their adaptive significance for hunting groups in general, particularly those found in the rigorous northern latitudes where their occurrence is especially prevalent.

It must be emphasized that the existence of these themes may not always be directly expressed in a culture, although their indirect and subtle manifestations can often be detected in many areas of life (cf. Opler, 1945, pp.198-200). The people of the Colville band, for example have no word which corresponds to "flexibility" *per se*, nor do they state this concept, in a straightforward manner, as a cultural theme. However, the people do value and hold in high esteem an individual whom they feel to be malleable, adjustable, and capable of adapting to diverse ecological and social situations. When they praise a person like Leon or Peter Dehdele for being "a good bush man," they mean not only that he possesses all the skills necessary for living off the land, but also that he is alert and innovative enough to meet the challenges of any unusual circumstances that may arise. The successful person is thus a flexible one, an individual who can alter materials and rely on inventive procedures when his situation calls for such adaptations. In social contexts, flexibility is often given expression in the way that people boast of and enumerate the various friends and kinsmen that they have, or could have, lived with in the past, and with whom they may yet live or camp with in the future. This is not merely a way of describing the extensiveness of one's *sagot'ine*; it is also an affirmation of how many social possibilities a person has at his disposal, as well as the fluid way in which he can actualize them.

Flexibility, restraint, and generosity are values which also find expression in the affirmation of other cultural themes, some of which can be considered as corollaries of those delineated above (cf. Opler, 1946). One of the most clearly stated values among the Hare is freedom, viz., the freedom to live as one chooses, to move when and where one pleases, and to schedule, order, and arrange one's life as one wishes. The people of the band are continually contrasting the type of existence that they lead with that found in Fort Good Hope, and one of the great advantages with which they characterize the bush and the village is the freedom of life style that it permits them. As they express it, this involves the absence of many of the unpleasant features of the more urbanized town, including freedom from overbearing Western time schedules, authoritative whites, discrimination, high rates of drinking, violence, gossip, and overcrowding. Freedom is also defined positively by them in terms of the relatively more independent decisions they can make concerning their associations, residence arrangements, physical movements, drinking habits, and the timing of their work and leisure.

Freedom, in this sense, is cognate not only with flexibility, but also with the people's stress upon individualism, anti-authoritarianism, and independence. Their dislike of "bossy" or pushy persons, and their positive evaluation of self-reliance and individual competence, are consistent — though not synonymous — with their emphasis on freedom and flexibility. Furthermore, their focus on individuality, autonomy, and independence also expresses the theme of emotional restraint because the people insist that proper behavior includes the norm of non-interference in the lives of others. Taken together, these attitudes and orientations comprise an independent outlook which resembles the variously individualistic or "atomistic" ethos that Honigmann (1946, 1949, 1968), Hallowell (1946), Landes (1937a), and others have found to be characteristic of both Northern Athabascan and Northern Algonkian groups.

While the people of Colville Lake can be both flexible and restrained, as well as free and independent, it is evident from the history and current life style of the band, that its members are also highly interdependent with one another. They are bound together by ties of kinship, intermarriage, friendship, generosity and mutual reliance, a set of conditions and emphases which constitute counter-themes (Opler, 1945, p.198) to the autonomous values described above. Given the nature of the people's existence, both *in*dependent and *inter*-dependent orientations are of prime adaptive significance for them, and a one-sided emphasis on one set of values without the other would probably be socially and ecologically unfeasible. These existential attitudes are also reflected in the mythology and lore of the people. Thematic studies that have been done on folktales from Fort Good Hope, and from the people's regional neighbors the Chipewyans, have revealed a complementary emphasis upon dependency and self-sufficiency in the folklore of both these groups; a balance between these value-orientations was especially evident in the traditional materials collected during earlier times (Cohen and VanStone, 1963; Cohen and Osterreich, 1967). At Colville Lake, where a corresponding balance among traditional needs and motivations is still in force, the people's themes — and their corollaries — help to bridge the inconsistencies that exist between these two sets of values. Nevertheless, many cultural stresses within the band derive from the ultimately irreconcilable nature of the "independent" and "interdependent" ethics. People trying to maintain their autonomy continually experience their reliance upon others, just as they are periodically confronted with the dependence of others upon themselves. The restrained way in which such stresses are usually coped with by the people helps to minimize their destructive impact, just as flexible approaches to life and social relations permits the band members to simultaneously elaborate and participate in each of these contrasting themes without directly denying either of them.

   In recent years, a number of ethnographic studies in the North have documented the persistence of the themes we have discussed among Athabascan, Algonkian and Eskimo peoples who live in more urbanized settings. [24] The cognitive and behavioral problems which confront these groups are immediate and pervasive, and they hinge upon not only the inherent complexity of larger and more heterogeneous situations, but also upon the ambiguity in role and personal expectations which such conditions generate. The folklore analyses cited above, for example, which compare traditional and contemporary native persons, have shown that more Westernized Indians reveal — in their projective fantasy material — a level of dependency which significantly exceeds that found among their ancestors, and analysts have argued that this is in part the outcome of the people's increased involvement in Federal welfare programs. [25] Although the social and historical material from Colville Lake concerns a people who have not really experienced the full dimensions of this kind of Westernization, the band's contemporary involvement in a traditional life style does provide a necessary picture of the cultural patterns which precede these more urbanized dilemmas. While a detailed analysis of these latter situations is beyond the scope of this study, certain of their dimensions can be delineated here in order to indicate some of the directions in which contemporary social change is proceeding.

To begin with, it is imperative to note that generosity develops as an increasing source of tension in an economy and way of life that are becoming more and more oriented towards aspects of the "Protestant" rather than the Indian ethic. When people are taught that they will be esteemed for accumulating and hoarding rather than for distributing their wealth, they will encounter difficulties if others in their society still have strong, traditional expectations of sharing. The stress between the two ethics is especially felt by the most acculturated northern natives, who are torn between their old obligations and their new goals. The confusions and frustrations of people in this cultural limbo can be particularly difficult to bear if they live in a social context that gives them few emotional outlets. As long as these tensions persist alongside an emphasis for emotional restraint, one can expect that the few affective releases that the people permit themselves, especially drinking, will continue to be used extensively.

A new dimension has also been added to the traditional theme of interdependence. At Colville Lake, for example, in addition to bonds within the band *per se*, the presence of permanent white residents in the community has led the people to develop new styles of relationships with these men. In some cases, these have taken the form of patron-client roles, a phenomenon of increasing native dependency which Vallee (1967) and others have noted occurring in many other northern settlements. While the outsiders and the natives both derive certain benefits from such a system, interdependence is cast in a new form because of the unequal power, prestige, and wealth that the white patrons and their native clients command. Not only do native people have to adapt to the new and largely dependent roles that they play vis-à-vis the whites, but interdependent roles within the native population are also affected when people start looking to the whites, rather than to their own kinsmen, as the main focus of their obligations and expectations. Under such circumstances, kinship relations become more tenuous and difficult to maintain, especially in cases where extended kinship networks were not organized to begin with.

With attitudes towards generosity and responsibility undergoing a simultaneous redefinition, the nature of social relations within these increasingly urban communities is being radically transformed. As changes continue in this direction, people who were once band members and villagers gradually come to think and act more like "townsmen" (cf. Honigmann and Honigmann, 1965; Ervin, 1968, 1969). If we are to understand the problems that confront these new, native urban dwellers in the North, we must seek to realize the depth and significance of the attitudes that they bring into their new environment, as well as the way in which these values have traditionally been integrated with one another in the past. This is one of the most basic lessons that the people of Colville Lake can teach us.

PART 3

Stress and Mobility

1 INTRODUCTION

There are many circumstances in a life which compel people to live together. In his *Notes From A Dead House*, Dostoyevsky wrote of prison life in Siberia as "forced coexistence," and explored, with wit and compassion, how the men of czarist Russia dealt with the fate of their sentences. Coexistence is not always compulsory, however, not even in the North, for outside of prisons people can choose and create, or at least modulate, the content of their company. There is thus freedom within the conditions of survival, even if existence is only possible within the context of kinship.

Although they may be lightly experienced or left unconsidered much of the time, the motives which draw people together are deeply textured, and so are the forces which drive them apart. For the Hare, whether it is habit, kinship, and obligation, or necessity, desire, and a reluctance to confront life alone, existence apart from one's *sagot'ine* is seen by people as unsatisfying and impossible. In the modern era, it was social as well as economic motives which contributed to the persistence of the Colville Lake band, reaffirming both a network of affiliations and a style of life. Yet, as the dimensions of kinship reveal, there is tension among the very people who make one's life both possible and meaningful. Many of the sharpest personal anxieties with which individuals must contend stem directly from the environment, and these material dimensions of survival, in their turn, invest social life with some of its intensest ambiguities. Ecological sources of stress, particularly scarce fur and food resources, the need for adequate shelter, and the physical hardships involved in obtaining these necessities, clearly persist as features of life for everyone, threatening people's well-being in different ways at all seasons. In concert with these dilemmas, however, people must experience their companions and families as well, and they must relate simultaneously to a social and a physical reality that is demanding in its intimacy, and often frightening in its immediacy.

The social, psychological, and cultural stresses which affect the

85

people are of equal if not greater impact than their ecological situation, and they derive, in large measure, from the group dynamics of a semi-nomadic existence. The band's yearly and necessary alternation between social dispersal in the bush and community ingathering at the village creates extremes of isolation and concentration for the individual, and modes of behavior must be malleable enough to preserve the nature, efficiency, and satisfactions of each of these polar situations. The people's social dilemmas encompass more than densities and durations, however, for stresses are also experienced in connection with acculturative differences, drinking patterns, socialization processes, marital problems, allegiances in local disputes, and, as we have seen, expectations for generosity and reciprocity.

Given the people's interrelatedness, and the strong emphasis upon emotional restraint which characterizes most Northern Athabascan groups, interpersonal aggression as a means of relieving tensions among adults is rarely exhibited, being almost entirely restricted to periods of heavy drinking. Most responses to stress therefore tend to be either repressed or otherwise channeled. An important consequence of this is that both social and ecological tensions enhance the people's level of movement as a stress-reducing mechanism: situations which threaten the equilibrium of groups are more often dissolved than directly confronted, and individuals thereby reduce stress by redefining circumstances. Mobility among band members thus tends to be maintained at a high level during all periods of the year, with movement operating as an important device for dealing with a variety of social and ecological contexts. This section examines the interrelationship of these stress and mobility patterns, and relates them to a range of other coping techniques which are also employed by the people.

2 DISPERSAL, STRESS AND IDENTITY

The dispersal of the Colville band which occurs with the freeze-up of the lakes and streams each October, inaugurates a period of the year during which the people face some of their most severe stresses. Environmentally, they now have to contend with the harshest weather, the greatest discomforts, the hardest work, and the most threatening dangers of the annual cycle. Accidents may include axe and knife cuts, gunshot wounds, pulled muscles, smashed fingers, and potentially fatal falls through the lake ice. The possibilities of suffering frost-bite, freezing to death, getting lost in storms, and experiencing extreme hunger are all increased. As we have seen, deaths from freezing and starvation have occurred within the lifetime of many of Colville's adults: consequently these hazards are regarded by the people as very real threats, and are not looked upon by them as just vague memories from the "old days," or as events occurring only in myths and folktales.

Since aboriginal times, the food resources of the people have been relatively unstable, and while contact with Euro-Canadians has introduced a technology which alleviates some of the resulting environmental hardships, this has not changed the nature of the principal food sources themselves. Thus, trapping, hunting, and fishing activities each continue to present their particular frustrations and hazards. The distribution of caribou within the band's game area varies seasonally and annually, and locales that are rich in animals one winter may provide relatively poor hunting in the next. The supply of fish in certain lakes or at specific campsites can also vary over time. Traps and traplines are disturbed by wolves and wolverines throughout the winter, resulting in the loss of valued furs and the need to reset or redeploy one's traps. Heavy snowfalls cover up both traps and trails, making travelling arduous and trapping tedious.

Despite the difficulty and frustrations of winter life in the bush, the people actually look forward to this dispersal, and they feel minimal hostility towards an environment which strikes the outsider as intensely inhospitable. Instead, winter is eagerly anticipated by them, and its challenges welcomed for their variety. After being gathered together at the village for nearly three months, the people are weary and often tense with one another's company, even somewhat bored with the repetitiveness of summer existence. The hurried preparations of the autumn — the sewing of clothes, the repairing of sleds, the training of dogs — these are the more visible signs of an underlying feverishness and rush of activity. People are continually in and out of one another's houses, and travelling between the settlement and the outlying fish camps, in order to trade, borrow, exchange and sometimes purchase the equipment that they need to complete their winter outfits.

In the weeks before the people actually pull out for their trapping areas, the community is partially dispersed at the fish camps which dot the shores of Colville and Aubry Lakes. There, where they are close to, but not in continuous contact with one another, clusters of families are scattered among the better fishing spots, laying up supplies of dog food, and experiencing a foretaste of the greater isolation yet to come. At this point in the yearly rhythm, however, the prospect of isolation does not carry the stigma that it will later bear, for separation now presents itself as a release from already over-strained social bonds. Similarly, what will soon become the physical burdens of the bush now appear as renewed challenges, a true change of pace and style, the novelty of which is itself a source of excitement and anticipation.

When the people finally scatter and move to their base camps, then, pushing their boats up narrow streams, and driving their dogs over naked, snow-patched ground, they go to confront a stressful environment with the full *élan* of stress-seekers. A world which, in its dangers and life-supporting possibilities, is ambiguous at best, is met with a duality of attitude possessed of its own ambiguities. The bush is simultaneously threatening and inviting, and the people perceive of it and accept it on both these terms. Stress is thus a two-edged sword, cutting out a realm of danger and dis-stress on the one hand, and opening up an area of challenge or eu-stress on the other.

If the bush is a heterogeneous source of stress for the band, it is also an intrinsic part of the people's identity, and it is this latter source of motivation which most fully comprehends the community's perception of the forest. The bush is the people's most visible and immediate link with their past, and involvement in it becomes an act of tradition, a bond with the generations which preceded them. "To be *dene*, an Indian," as Yen once declared, "is to live in the forest"; to give this up is to lose one's ethnicity, "it is to become like a white man." While some people in the band feel this much more strongly than others, everyone experiences a clear sense of distinctiveness from the Indians who live at the fort, for, as André says,

they are the people who have given up the old ways. They forget what it is like to be *dene*. It is only us who remember.

For all the people then, regardless of their personal degree of involvement in the bush, returning to the forest each year, and seeking one's livelihood from it, is an act of reaffirmation, a participation in a native identity which is a very deep part of the people's individual and collective self-image. It was in this spirit, in September, that Philip Ratehne spoke with enthusiasm of the winter, and of our forthcoming departure for the bush:

That's the real Indian time of the year. None of this sitting around like this all summer and just taking out fish. In the bush that's when we really know how to live, and then you'll see how tough we are. Sure it's hard, but when you learn how to take care of yourself then you really learn to love it. That's when you think "this is the real good Indian life. It's hard but it's our own good way." Maybe some white men don't understand it, but that's because they never lived like us.

3   LIFE IN A BUSH CAMP

Philip's vision is a true one, and the contrast with white perceptions is apt. But the problems of maintaining both life and identity in the bush requires tolerance and competence as well as enthusiasm, and as I later discovered, not all of the people are as equal to the task as they believe themselves to be. Once the villagers have achieved the privacy of dispersion, they must then confront its loneliness, and having anticipated the challenges of survival, they must now face its hazards and frustrations. The first few months of the winter, which I spent with Philip's family, showed me how some of the most capable of the people dealt with these stresses while trying to maintain both themselves and their unity.

The freeze-up of 1967 occurred on the night of October 13th, and within a week of that date the shoreline areas of ice around the lake were thick enough to allow us to travel. I went out on the ice for the first time with some of the Behdzis a few days later, helping them to set and then check their fish nets. In the meantime, the Ratehnes and I were getting the final items of our outfit together, and we were ready to leave the village about a week before the trapping season officially began. We divided our supplies up among the family's three sleds — Philip's, his father Wilfred's, and his brother Adam's — and we first journied to the fish camp of Wilfred's brother George, located about fifteen miles north along the east coast of Colville. Wilfred and his wife Bertha decided to stay there for a few days and then relay their equipment in stages, and so leaving them and Adam behind, Philip and I pushed ahead, carefully picking our way over the still young and dangerously thin crust.

It took us several days to break a trail over the sixty-five miles of rough ground which separated our trapping camp from the village. The dogs, who were still far from their peak condition after a relatively idle summer, strained under the heavy loads of equipment in the sled. They were also difficult to handle, the younger ones reluctantly pulling in a team for the first time, and the older ones readjusting to life in harness. On alternate stretches of this northward trip, Philip and I took turns pushing the sled from behind to aid the dogs, and walking ahead with an axe, clearing the path of trees and brush.

At the campsite at *Lugetenetue*, on a high bluff overlooking a large lake, we cleared the snow from a level patch of ground, and pitched our canvas tent. Then we laid a carpet of spruce boughs on the inside floor, and moved in our sleeping bags, sheet-metal stove, cooking utensils, and other gear. While I staked out the dogs and went to cut firewood, Philip set to work building an *alahfi* or storage platform for the family's fish, caribou meat, and other supplies which could not be stored in the tent itself (cf. Figure 7).

The second day at *Lugetenetue*, Philip and I set a fish net and cut some brush for the dogs to sleep on. Late the following morning,

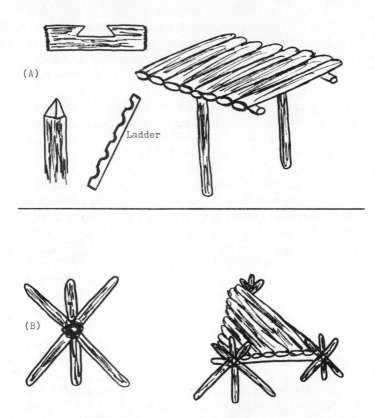

FIGURE 7   Types of *alahfi* or stages.

Adam and his parents arrived, and the dimensions of the camp expanded: saplings were cut down at half-height to one side of the tent for chaining up the new dogs, and two more fish nets were placed beneath the lake ice (Figure 8). There were, after all, five people and twenty canines to be fed now, and there might not be any caribou in the area for several weeks yet. Bertha fixed up the spruce floor and rearranged the tent's contents, pushing the canvas walls out as far as she could, and holding them in place from the inside with vertical stakes. She piled up more snow and brush around the outside base of the walls, thus sealing the inside off from the wind, and keeping in the warm air created by the stove. Space was at a premium within the tent, and Bertha tried to expand its area, not only to accommodate the five of us, but also to make room for the large amount of clothing and equipment we had brought with us (Figure 9). Sleeping bags, cooking

(C)

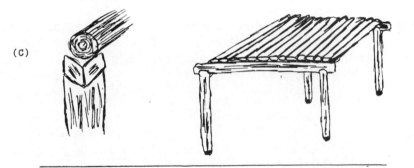

(D)

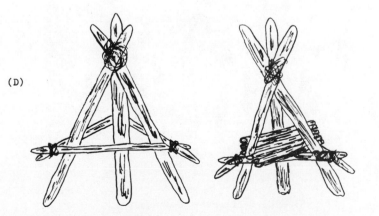

gear, sewing materials, spare mukluks, pants and mittens, a radio, candles and a gas lamp for illumination, a water bucket, a large sack of flour, cartons of food, salt, tobacco . . . all of these had to be placed at a safe distance from the stove. Dangling from the ridge pole of the tent was a rack from which we dried out our clothes at the end of the day, and rosaries and calendars hung pinned to the canvas walls. Outside the tent itself were our rifles, extra fish nets, traps, fur stretchers, a five gallon drum of gasoline, axes, and additional tents and stoves for overnight camps on our longer traplines.

The inventory was impressive, and it mirrored the people's commitment to an acquired form of Western materialism. What had taken us so long to prepare for the bush had been the collecting of such an array of items, and what had lengthened our final journey had been the necessity of transporting so much in our small sleds: hence the slowness of Philip's progress, and also the need for his parents to relay most of their supplies. Clearly, the people's mobility was limited by the burdens they imposed upon themselves, and I began to see part of the reason why band members no longer travelled as far, or as extensively, as they did in the old days. People who depended heavily upon Western materials — and the Ratehnes, as it turned out, were neither the best nor the worst in this regard — had less freedom of movement, not merely because of the quantity of goods they

FIGURE 8   Layout of bush camp.

transported, but also because they had to remain within access of the village for purposes of re-supplying themselves. Trapping has thus not only re-oriented ecological concerns by shifting the people's focus to different game resources, but it has also affected the modes and conditions of mobility by placing life within a new material context.[1]

The people's survival is persistently demanding even within this more limited geography. Bertha soon set out snares for ptarmigan and hare, bolstering the family's food supply until fishing and hunting became more productive. With the camp established and the fish nets set, the men now began their trapping activities. Adam and Wilfred

FIGURE 9   Inside of a bush tent.

decided to run a joint line to the east of the camp and then split in different directions after having set out "one day's travelling" worth of traps. It was first 'necessary to break a trail in this direction, however, and I went with the men on this arduous, initial trip. We left camp at eight in the morning, and the men shared the work of taking the lead, one man hacking out a path and the other one following behind with the dogs. We gradually moved into an area of high ground where Wilfred said "the marten signs were good," and then he and Adam began to alternate setting their traps just off the trail (Figures 10 and 11). We eventually made a fire to boil tea and have some lunch in the afternoon, and then continued to set traps for another two hours before turning back towards camp.

The next day we returned to extend the trail, putting out more traps, and pitching a tent about twenty miles from our base camp.

FIGURE 10   Trap set: enclosure or "pen" set for marten.

Wilfred and Adam then set a net in a nearby lake so that they would have dog food whenever they visited this new camp in the future. They laid out some traps within the vicinity of the tent itself, and on the following morning they went off in separate directions — each of them on snowshoes — to set their own lines. When we travelled back to our main camp the next day, having set out over 170 traps altogether, we found two marten in the previously arranged traps, plus three rabbits who had gotten caught while trying to reach the bait at some other sets. Whiskeyjacks, a species of small jay who abound in the woods, had also touched off four other traps in attempting to steal the bait. As Adam noted, with a touch of frustration in his voice, a man is helpless against these small animals, for every trap that they disturb remains inactive until the trapper comes that way again and re-sets it. In this way, a man can lose his chance at a considerable amount of fur

FIGURE 11   Trap set: leaning set of "hung bait" for marten.

during a winter, since marten, foxes, and weasels who are attracted by the bait will never be caught in already triggered traps. While a good trapper tries to visit his sets every five or six days, it is difficult to keep to a strict schedule because of weather conditions and subsistence needs. As I witnessed many times during the winter, men experience a keen sense of frustration and anger when they see a trail of marten tracks leading up to a trap that already has a worthless whiskeyjack in it.

While Adam and Wilfred had been busy for several days to the east, Philip had travelled on his own to the north, setting out a line of 100 traps. Energetic and resourceful, Philip prided himself on his toughness and trapping ability, and the previous winter, at the age of sixteen, he had taken more fur than most of the older men in the band. Now, back at the main camp, Philip checked the family's nets, and found only eighteen fish. With food supplies low and dog food almost gone, he went hunting to the northeast the next day, indicating that he had seen some caribou tracks in that direction while he had been laying out his trapline.

By late that evening, however, he had returned empty-handed, even though he had seen a number of small caribou herds from a distance. Philip tried again the next day with the same result, and Wilfred came up with only a dozen fish from our nets. Only Bertha's snares seemed to be reliable, and so — within the first few weeks — we were already "back to choking rabbits" for our supper. There was some difference of opinion within the family that night over whether or not we should broach our supply of "store" food (*molep'ere*, "white man's food") so early in the winter, and Wilfred and Adam — who took opposite sides on the issue — shot some quick and angry glances towards the floor as they avoided one another's eyes. Philip, somewhat put out by what he felt was his unfair burden of responsibility in the family, took an oblique swipe at Adam by suggesting to his father that they would not have been faced with this dilemma if Adam had spent as much time searching for food as he had done for fur. Before anyone could respond, however, the debate was frozen: Adam reached out for the bucket near his sleeping bag and announced, in restrained, neutral tones, that he was going to get water from the lake so that they could boil some tea. Wilfred silently fingered some spruce needles which lay by his feet, and without any further words, the matter was ended.

The issue was a small but indicative one in the life of the camp: enthusiasm was being tempered by routine, and routine was yielding up its tensions. The deprivations of the winter were making themselves felt a bit earlier than expected, and the family was responding with some muted strains. While the tenseness of the evening had dissipated itself in silence and activity by the time of Adam's return, it was clear that the tenor of existence had changed — however subtly — and that the stresses of the season were upon us. The immediate quarrel had quickly passed beyond mention, but it had left in its wake raw nerves and heightened sensitivities.

In the following weeks, the family began to feel the full brunt of winter. Adam and Philip each got a few caribou within the next few days, but fishing remained poor, and so some of the meat had to be fed to the dogs. Wilfred and Adam gave up a day of trapping to re-set their nets in a different part of the lake, and Philip deferred a visit to his lines in order to cut a large supply of firewood for his mother. Bertha, who usually had her adopted daughter Suzanne to help her with camp chores, was alone these first few weeks because Suzanne was off at another camp, helping her natural mother Lena Dehdele care for a new-born baby. With Bertha's arthritic knee paining her, more of the camp work fell to her sons, limiting the time that they could devote to hunting and trapping.

Philip's traps had yielded him a good number of marten in the first three visits that he had made on his line, but on his fourth trip out he discovered that a wolverine had gotten on one of his trails. The animal had religiously followed the path on most of its fifteen mile route, and in stopping at each set, it had carefully avoided the trap itself and removed the bait. As Philip travelled along the trail, he saw — from the leg stumps and bits of fur left in some of the traps — that he had actually caught three marten and one red fox, but that each of these animals had been found first by the wolverine, and that nothing of any value now remained. On his return trip to camp, therefore, Philip made two special sets with very large traps, hoping to catch the wolverine in the event that it continued to raid his line — a pattern which, he explained, the wolverines often followed.

In early December, the cold and snow combined to increase the family's difficulties. A two-day storm deposited enough snow to cover up most of the men's trails, and so the next time we each went out, it was necessary for us to walk ahead of the dogs for most of the route in order to beat down a new path with our snowshoes. Adam had failed to mark many of the places where he had made his sets, and without the tell-tale blazes and cuttings on the trees, he was unable to find a number of his traps. The wind-blown snow had also buried many of the men's other sets, and so the fur yield was disappointingly low. Having exploited their areas for over a month now, each of the men began to pick up some of his traps and branch off into new regions.

Fresh trails were broken in different directions, and Philip, deciding to strike off to the west, removed his overnight tent and fish net from his northern line, and established an entirely new outpost camp on a different lake.

Soon after these new lines had been laid out, however, an intense cold spell put a sudden end to all activity. Wilfred and Adam, trying to reach the main encampment before nightfall, both suffered frost-bitten cheeks on the final leg of their long journey. The next morning, with strong gusts blowing at air already cooled to -25° F, the wind-chill prevented us from leaving camp. The first day in the tent was a welcome rest, but by the third morning our immobility was becoming its own burden, and people were turning irritable. Furthermore, Wilfred was worried about his lead dog, who had become lame on his last trip out, and Adam, who had shot several caribou a few days previously, was anxious to retrieve the carcasses that he had been unable to haul back before the storm set in. When the weather finally broke on the fourth morning, then, everyone was up early, and with noticeable relief and anticipation, the dogs were quickly harnessed. The men were soon dispersed for the day, and for the family as a whole, the dangers of the environment now seemed a welcome alternative to the confined conditions of the camp.

4   STRESS AND RESPONSE PATTERNS

This tension between togetherness and separation, and the people's shifting exposure to social stresses on the one hand and ecological pressures on the other, was as characteristic of individuals within the band's larger encampments as it was for small groups like the Ratehnes. Later in the winter, when I stayed with three of the Behdzi families, and another time, when I camped first with the Yawileh households and then with the Dehdeles and Godantos, the rhythm of life continued to fluctuate — in each of these groupings — between emotional and social extremes. The parameters remained the same regardless of the size of the encampment: the bush provided a challenging escape from the stresses of what was invariably a closed society, and the camp, in its turn, became a haven of company and comfort from the solitary strains of the forest.

Even in mid-December, when Yen Behdzi's family came to join Wilfred's group, bringing Suzanne along with them from the Dehdele's, the style of life at our camp was not appreciably altered, and Yen's move, in itself, illustrated the nature of mobility and discontent in a multi-family encampment. The Behdzis had been staying with the Yawilehs, but the younger men from these two families had found it difficult to trap with one another. The good fur areas in the vicinity of their main camp had been limited, and so the men were restricted in their trapping range. Each group came to feel that they were being hampered by the other's presence, and — according to Yen's son Yǎseh — the Yawilehs kept asking for so much fish that he and his brothers felt they were caring for the dogs of both households. Before matters could deteriorate, however, Yen decided to move his family, and so he, his wife and his sons, gathered up their tents and traps, and journeyed — by way of the Dehdele's — to Lugetenetue.

Socially and psychologically, as the incidents conerning the Ratehnes and Behdzis reveal, the winter dispersal makes the greatest demands on interpersonal relations and individual stress tolerance. This is in large measure a consequence of the fact that, as compared to aboriginal patterns, trapping fragments native communities into even smaller and more dispersed groups than a strict subsistence economy would necessitate. The resulting tensions among small group members who must work, live, and cooperate with one another at close quarters are heightened by their ultimate sense of isolation and boredom. Social milieus are severely limited for extended periods of time, and people are deprived of the amenities and pleasures of more gregarious situations. While there is a degree of excitement and stress-seeking in confronting the challenges of the bush, relations within the small, isolated camps eventually become strained because of the abrasive nature of interaction under these confined conditions. Minor events or habits overlooked during periods of communal ingathering may now become highly visible and irritating. The fact that dispersal phases usually coincide with the environmentally harshest periods of the year further increases the potential for intra-group stress and friction.

As the winter progressed, I had the opportunity to live with many different families, and to compare their distinctive responses to the challenges of the bush. After staying with about two-thirds of the band's households for extended periods during the winter and spring, some stylistic differences emerged from their stress patterns. I found that it was the most acculturated people in the band, i.e., those who had had the most experience in living, working, and going to school in Fort Good Hope and other large Mackenzie settlements, who demonstrated the most pronounced ambivalence about bush life. When the people were ranked according to such criteria as their amount of outside living experience, their ownership and use of Western commodities and equiment, their participation in such Western-derived forms of leisure as radios and magazines, and their degree of bilingualism and literacy, the villagers formed an acculturative continuum with large clusters of individuals at both ther "conservative" and the "highly Westernized" poles. As is the case with other Canadian Indians and Eskimos in similar situations, many of the people near the "Westernized" extreme exhibited varying amounts of cultural disorientation. This was seen in problems of self-identity, feelings of inferiority, aspects of cognitive dissonance, involvement in violence and drinking, and ambiguous attitudes towards "bush" versus "fort" styles of living (Chance, 1968, pp.572-573).

It was these acculturated individuals and families who found the winter months of trapping particularly stressful, especially because of their heightened sense of isolation. Whereas they and the other people of the band were equally cut off from one another and the settlement, it was not the people's physical isolation, but rather their *perception* of their isolation, that most affected their behavior and mental state. The persons who were socially and physically separated from other households, but who — as most of the Behdzis and Ratehenes — nevertheless sensed a proximity or relationship to them, were clearly less distressed than the acculturated persons who needed a larger and more immediate social presence.

The acculturated and more traditional members of the community, then, were differentially affected by the various social and ecological tensions of life, and this was reflected in their respective mobility patterns. For example, the people of the band responded to the hardships and dangers of the bush by trying to keep their trapping and hunting camps within a sixty mile radius of the settlement. Besides making travel to and from the village less difficult, this also gave them easier access to the medical aid that the missionary offered and to the supplies that could be bought at the trading post. Traditional families, however, placed less reliance upon Western goods than did more acculturated households, and so it was the men from the latter families who made the most frequent trips from the bush to the settlement during the course of the winter. Albert Limertu, for example, made six journeys to Colville from his bush camp during the period between freeze-up and Christmas. His family's shortage of even minor supplies was a sufficient excuse for most of these trips, and between the "shopping" and the drinking that he did at the village, he was away from his traplines for about a third

TABLE 3
Sexual division of labor among adults

Men	Women
Hunt large game: caribou and moose; haul game back to village and camp Hunt smaller game: waterfowl, hares, etc.	Do some hunting of small game Snare ptarmigan and hares Assist in the butchering of small and large game Treat (i.e., clean, scrape and tan) caribou and moose hides Manufacture dried and smoked meat and babiche
Set and check fish nets in the summer and winter Prepare and fix nets Construct and repair canoes, scows, and outboard motors Manufacture ice picks and ice scoops	Check nets in the winter Help to prepare and fix nets Clean fish Manufacture dried and smoked fish; collect firewood for smoking and cooking fish during the summer Sew canvas covers for canoes
Do most of travelling, transporting, trail-breaking, and dog driving Care for and train dogs; shoot dogs when necessary Construct and repair sled and braker Make trips from bush camp to village for re-supplying	Some women drive dogs during the winter All help in the care and feeding of dogs Make and repair sled wrapper
Cut and haul firewood throughout the year Construct saw-horses	Help in hauling and cutting firewood throughout the year
Train sons and help care for children	Do most of caring for children, and train daughters
Construct village houses Set up bush camps with women Construct stages, caches, and dog compounds Do some cooking and sewing Make frames for snowshoes Do shopping in village; sell family furs	Set up bush camps with men Care for tent and house, including cleaning, and cutting of spruce boughs Cook, sew, make and repair clothes Help put webbing in snowshoes Do shopping in the village Pick berries in the fall
Do most of fur trapping Skin and stretch hides Do most of wage labor	Do a small amount of trapping Help to skin and stretch hides Do a small amount of wage labor
Manufacture homebrew	Manufacture homebrew

of this time. Acculturated individuals like Albert consequently spent
less time living off the land than did more conservative band
members, and this frequency of movement was as much a reflection of
psychological stress as it was of ecological necessity.

Patterns of travelling not only reflected these subcultural
differences, but they also indicated distinctive mobility styles for
males and females within the band. In all the families, the men

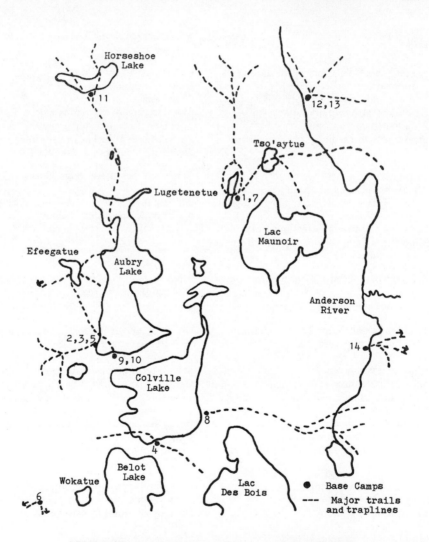

MAP 4   Trapping camps: early winter dispersal, 1967.

engaged in activities which made them considerably more mobile than the women (Table 3). Women's tasks usually kept them in and around the family residence both when in the bush and in the village, whereas the men were frequently gone for several hours to several days in connection with their responsibilities for hunting, fishing, trapping, and transportation. One index of the different levels of mobility characterizing the two sexes was that only three of the community's

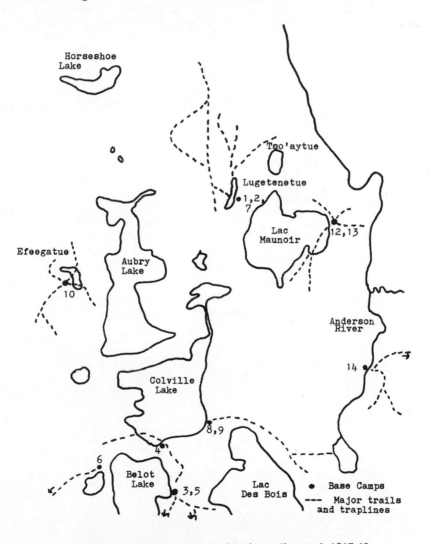

MAP 5   Trapping camps: mid-winter dispersal, 1967-68.

thirty-six dogteams were regularly used by women in conjunction with their household tasks and labors. Bertha Ratehne never went further from our camp than her hare snares, and even Albert's wife Paula, who had her own dogteam, rarely travelled further than her family's fish nets, visiting the village and other camps for only a fraction of the time that her husband did.

By keeping a detailed account of daily movements in all the camps that I stayed in, I also came to realize that young men did considerably more travelling than older males, the former making the

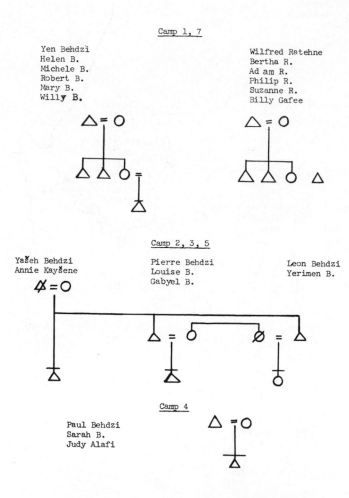

FIGURE 12 Composition of early winter camps.

most frequent hunting and trapping trips, as well as the most numerous visits to Colville Lake, neighboring camps, and Fort Good Hope. The division of labor in some families, in which younger men actually specialized in hunting and trapping while older men did most of the more sedentary fishing, was another factor in the differentiation of mobility by both age and sex. On a more limited spatial scale, similar patterns of work and movement distinguished the activities of younger women from those of older females within households. Some of the younger adult women, such as Sarah Behdzi's daughter Judy,

Camp 6

Charlie Behdzi
Adele B.

Albert Tahso
Angele T.   } from Fort
Clara T.   Good Hope

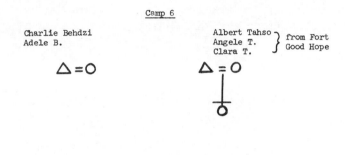

Camp 8

George Ratehne
Christine R.
Mark R.
Jack Eddee
Elizabeth Nota

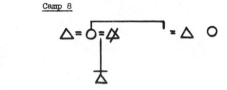

Camp 9, 10

Albert Limertu
Paula L.
Cecile L.
Rose L.
Bella L.
Jonas Tahso

Peter Dehdele
Lena D.
Cathy D.
Jean-Marie D.

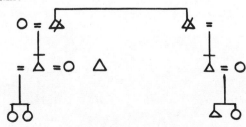

and Berona's daughter Monique — both in their twenties — actually
set short traplines of their own, giving them a greater range of activity
and movement than their mothers.

Whole families in the community were also more or less mobile
than other residential units — differing from one another in how far
they went from the settlement to trap, how long they stayed out in the
bush, and how much territory they covered during their stay there.
Albert's repeated trips to Colville, for example, contrasted with the
more persistent trapping efforts of Wilfred's sons, who did
considerably more travelling in their subsistence pursuits than did
Albert in his attempts to escape from them. This spatial dimension of
mobility is illustrated by Maps 4 and 5, which show the distribution of
band members among hunting and trapping camps during two parts

Camp 11

Thomas Godanto   Batiste Sašo

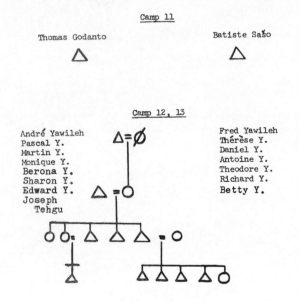

Camp 12, 13

André Yawileh
Pascal Y.
Martin Y.
Monique Y.
Berona Y.
Sharon Y.
Edward Y.
Joseph
  Tehgu

Fred Yawileh
Thérèse Y.
Daniel Y.
Antoine Y.
Theodore Y.
Richard Y.
Betty Y.

Camp 14

Maurice Bayjere
Dora B.
Luke B.
Alfred B.

of the winter of 1967-1968. Figures 12 and 13 (which accompany these maps) show the composition of these various camps, and reflect the kinship and non-kinship bonds influencing these winter alliances.[2] It can be seen that only one household in the community (#4) actually trapped in the area of the village itself, all the other people placing their base camps from fifteen to seventy miles away. Certain individuals and families were thus five times as distant from the settlement as others, and the traplines and hunting trips of the men in these far-flung groups often carried them well beyond a 100 mile radius from Colville. The men in these latter families scarcely ever

Camp 1, 2, 7

Yen Behdzi
Helen B.
Michele B.
Robert B.
Mary B.
Willy B.

Yašeh Behdzi
Annie Kayšene

Wilfred Ratehne
Bertha R.
Adam R.
Philip R.
Ousanne R.

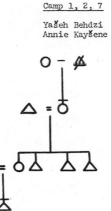

Camp 3, 5

Leon Behdzi
Yerimen B.

Pierre Behdzi
Louise B.
Gabyel B.

Camp 4

Paul Behdzi
Sarah B.
Judy Alafi

FIGURE 13   Composition of mid-winter camps.

returned to the village between holidays, and with their greater tolerance for the strains and demands of the bush, they supported their families well, and collected a considerable amount of fur.

5   SPACE, TIME AND TENSION

Beyond variations in styles of movement and dependency, the families of the band also followed some common strategies in locating themselves in time and space. In choosing their winter trapping camps each year, the people attempted to enhance their security and

Camp 6

Charlie Behdzi
Adele B.

Camp 8, 9

George Ratehne   Albert Limertu
Christine R.   Paula L.
Mark R.   Cecile L.
Jack Eddee   Rose L.
Elizabeth Nota   Bella L.
                        Jonas Tahso

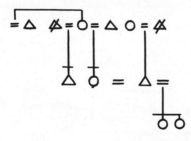

Camp 10

Peter Dehdele
Lena D.
Cathy D.
Jean-Marie D.

Camp 11

Left the Colville Area

minimize environmental stress by staying in areas well known to them. Most families tended to alternate among a series of favorite camping spots, using them over a cycle of several years, or, in some cases, occasionally returning to one site for two years in succession. Familiarity with the region's topography and its fuel, fish, meat, and fur resources provided some insurance against the threat of serious deprivation and hardship. Nevertheless, the occasional unpredictability of fish, game and fur from season to season and year to year, and the eventual depletion of fuel and fur in repeatedly used areas, necessitated that several families switch their camping grounds once or more during the winter and spring. Furthermore, with the seasonal transfer from the winter trapping of marten and fox to the spring hunting of beaver and muskrat, it was also necessary for the people to move into areas better suited for these particular fur animals. Living off the land thus required constant mobility in terms of day-to-day subsistence and trapping activities, as well as the periodic movement

Camp 12, 13

André Yawileh
Berona Y.
Martin Y.
Sharon Y.
Monique Y.
Edward Y.
Pascal Y.
Joseph Tehgu

Fred Yawileh
Thérèse Y.
Betty Y.
Daniel Y.
Antoine Y.
Theodore Y.
Richard Y.

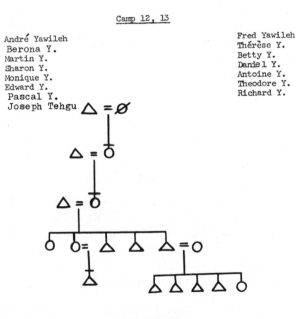

Camp 14

Maurice Bayjere
Dora B.
Luke B.
Alfred B.

of entire camps because of the availability of resources and the seasonal changes in primary economic concerns.

For the people of the Colville Lake band, as well as for the members of other hunting groups in the world, each of the major annual phases may involve several shifts or subsidiary moves by which the trend toward population dispersal or concentration is gradually increased; that is, extreme conditions of dispersal or concentration may be reached in a series of stages rather than in an abrupt manner. Such a pattern is approximated in the way that the people of Colville disperse for winter trapping activities each year. That the people of the band do not like to go too far too fast is due both to the burdens of travelling and to the seasonal readjustment to conditions of bush living. The people therefore move away from the village in a series of steps. Several families may leave in a group and then set up a fish camp for a period of one to several weeks; only after such an interval of partial separation from the area of the settlement do households which have arranged to trap together finally split off from the larger group. Households may also travel out together and, over a period of several days or more, camp with one another at increasingly greater distances from the settlement. After such a succession of moves they eventually separate off as each family or group of families approaches the region in which it is going to trap.

Furthermore, the villagers do not like to move out en masse: only one or a few families may leave at a time, and the dispersing of the whole population is spread out over a period of several weeks to a month. The dispersals in January and at the start of the spring hunt in late April are relatively more abrupt because they involve the movement of a smaller amount of equipment to camps which, in many cases, are already established. They also come after much briefer periods of residence in the settlement. The general pattern of movement during these seasons nevertheless remains consistent with that of the early winter dispersal because people continue to travel to their camps in a series of phased moves. The gradualness of all three of these dispersals points up the fact that conditions of band concentration and band fragmentation are relative, the spatial distribution of community members displaying many different degrees of population density during the course of each annual phase. While extreme conditions of dispersal and concentration are reached during certain parts of each year, the transitoriness of these polar situations indicates that there are stresses implicit in them which impel the people to periodically either dilute or concentrate their social milieus. Density controls and spacing devices thus appear to be operative during all seasons of the annual cycle, and to reflect both the social and the ecological dimensions of population mobility (cf. Birdsell, 1968; Deevey, 1968; Turnbull, 1968b).

The people's need for, and love of movement as a simultaneously ecological, social, and psychological process has been one of the prime reasons that they have consistently opposed all governmental attempts to create fixed and registered traplines in their region. They recognize that what may be an administrative convenience for whites often bears little relationship to Indian reality. While administrators have in fact created large "hunting areas" for most official "bands" in the North. they have not forced the issue by imposing smaller family trapping areas within these zones. As the people themselves emphasize, the fixity of a trapline contradicts the fluidity of the environment, as well as the flexibility of native life styles — features whose relevance game officers and other personnel often fail to take into account.[3] As I learned from experience during the winter and spring dispersals, the social motives for mobility are especially immediate for the people, often outweighing strictly ecological considerations in the spacing and structuring of their groups.

These factors can be seen at work in the interpersonal and psychological sources of stress which affect band members during phases of residence in the bush. The trapping partnerships, and the co-camping and travelling arrangements which underlie the people's groupings are made, as we have seen, on the basis of kinship ties, friendships, and similarities in the ages and acculturative levels of the adults involved. Within the population limits set by the fur and food resources of a particular region — and given the environmental and social conditions of winter life — people feel more secure staying in relatively large, multi-family encampments, especially those which contain at least two or three able-bodied, adult males. In camps of this type, the work and travel loads can be divided up, and companionship is enhanced while isolation is diminished.

The rare individual who actively or directly seeks isolation as an end in itself may become a source of worry and concern for the people, and the abnormality of such behavior invites comparison with the fate and dehumanization of *lariyin* or "bush men." Even young children are sensitized to these consequences of prolonged separation, and they learn to evaluate people's actions with a view to such a possible outcome. George Ratehne, for example, frequently found the company of his demanding wife Christine quite intolerable, so after bringing her to the village at the beginning of Christmas, he returned to his bush camp and stayed on his own there for the next three weeks.

This was not the first time that he had voluntarily separated himself from spouse, family, and society, and nine-year-old Cathy Dehdele, reflecting the tenor of community gossip, once said:

Him, that silly George, he just like to stay alone in the bush all the time. He don't have no one with him. Why soon he's just like a "bush man."

To the people, then, co-camping arrangements ease the physical and social hardships of life, and they are viewed as being consistent with both the nature of man and the nature of his environment. Like many other devices resorted to in order to cope with and reduce stress, however, these alliances and arrangements are also productive of stress. The time and space dimensions of each camp often combine to promote the very incompatability they are designed to mitigate. People must not only endure one another for long periods, but they must do so within the area of close, canvas tents. It is paradoxical that the very people in North America who, in a gross ecological sense, have the lowest population density, end up in a social architecture of such confined spaces. Despite the interrelatedness and friendliness of the individuals who compose the various camps, then, tensions do arise over such concerns as generosity and work loads, dominance patterns and bossiness, and jealousy and mistrust. Trapping partners sometimes become jealous of one another's good fortune, and hence occasionally suspect that traplines have been tampered with and robbed of furs. Thomas Godanto confided the following thoughts to me about the behavior of Batiste Sašo, his partner from Good Hope:

He was always making up stories. One time I ask him how many traps he set and he say one hundred fifty. The next time Batiste he say only one hundred. You see? That first time we go visit our lines he say he got sixteen marten but the next chance I ask him he says maybe nine or ten. There's something wrong there with that guy. You can't trust what he says. I got my feelings . . . That short line I set near our overnight camp was full of good marten signs. So why I never caught anything there? But Batiste he pass that way when he go to Colville. I'm not saying anything sure, but it looks funny. Those could be my furs sitting at the store right now.

Although feelings such as these rarely result in public accusation, they may generate an atmosphere of mistrust which ultimately threatens the harmony of camp life. The particular trapping partnership referred to above was abruptly dissolved after two months because of the suspicions and antagonisms that had developed between Thomas and Batiste, and this was not the only such incident that occurred during the winter.

Similar tensions may be produced by the presence, in a camp, of an especially "bossy" or overbearing person whose actions conflict with the people's emphasis upon independence. This ethic of non-involvement is a positive one to the people, stressing, in their view, a basic respect for other people's individuality and self-esteem. In concert with these attitudes, leadership among the Hare has traditionally been exercised in an informal manner, rather than with direct and abrupt shows of power and force. Persons who violate these unwritten norms by acting in authoritative or presumptive ways provoke either ridicule or rejection, and they create the kinds of stresses which ultimately destroy relationships. Lena Dehdele once summarized the consequences of this kind of behavior by referring to the actions of Thomas Godanto, her sister's son:

Oh that Thomas just like to tell everybody his own business. He like to be boss and give orders. That's why no one go with him. Last winter that happened when he trapped with my brother Jean from Good Hope. He says Thomas always telling him what to do. So they argue lots and then Jean pick up his traps and pull out.

Generosity, another dimension of proper conduct, can also be a source of stress and provocation if a person's behavior is not congruent with the expectations of others. The real or apparent failure of an individual or family to contribute or reciprocate in proportion to the largesse and efforts of others in an encampment often leads to strain within the group. To an extent, stresses over generosity within the community stem from two conflicting sets of social and economic orientations held by the people. On the one hand there is the traditional band ideology of interrelatedness and sharing, cooperation and hospitality. On the other hand, however, there is the more individualized and familistic economy which develops with a trapping way of life. It places families more on their own than in the past, and while it increases their dependence upon the fur trader, it decreases their interdependence with other households and *sagot'ine*. Families own more material and capital goods than previously, and fur and money are not shared within the village the way meat and fish are supposed to be. The fur trade, by emphasizing the socio-economic importance of the family at the expense of the band community and its ties, thus injects a degree of stress and ambiguity into the entire generosity ethic, straining its operation on many fronts.

Peter Dehdele, for example, had put up a large supply of fish during the fall and early winter at his base camp on Aubry Lake (Map 4, Camp 9, 10). Although a highly acculturated individual in many regards, Peter was one of the best trappers in the band, and he had established this cache of dog food so that he would be relatively free to trap during most of November and December. In these warmer winter months, he explained, marten continue to move around freely, thus making them easier to trap than in the later and colder months when they tend to stay underground.

When Peter and his family were joined at Aubry Lake by Albert Limertu and his household, however, Peter's fish supply started to disappear very quickly. Albert needed dog food while he set his own nets, and he often left some of his dogs with Peter when he went on his periodic trips to the village. Without any surplus fish of his own, Albert also turned to Peter's cache whenever his day's fish catch was poor. Peter, who prided himself on his even-temperedness, and who sees himself, above all else, as a generous person — a man "with a good heart," as he expresses it — finally lost patience with Albert, and several arguments ensued. When visiting neighboring camps, the two men complained about one another's behavior to other people, and they eventually went to trap in different areas following the Christmas ingathering.

Albert, in his turn, experienced some of Peter's frustration later that same winter from one of his own trapping partners, Jonas Tahso. According to Albert:

He (Jonas) didn't bring much to our camp. Just a box or two of stuff from the store. Then he never shot much caribou either, or cut any wood for us. Me, I'm doing most of the work for everybody. He come and stay with us a long time and that's the way he act. He should know better (than) to treat people that way.

As Albert added, when later recounting this episode, he finally felt that he "had had enough of that," and let Jonas know that he could either work or get out. Things eventually became so strained in the camp that Jonas — just as Albert himself had done earlier that winter — did indeed pack his gear in his sled, and move away to stay with some of his other kin in a different region.

6   RESIDENCE CHANGES AND DAILY MOBILITY

When personality conflicts, sharing, and other sources of stress become manifest within an encampment, mobility in the form of a change in residence by one of the individuals or families involved is

PLATE 1   The village of Colville Lake, as seen from the southwest curve of the bay.

PLATE 2   A dogteam entering a winter encampment.

PLATE 3   Children at their family's mid-winter trapping camp.

PLATE 4   Cleaning and scraping
a caribou hide from which the hair
has been removed.

PLATE 5   Unloading caribou after a successful hunt.

PLATE 6 Beaver pelts being
stretched at a spring hunting
camp.

PLATE 7   A trapper with part of his winter catch of marten at the trading post.

PLATE 8   Old Joseph at the age of ninety.

occasionally the outcome. Many of the residential shifts which occur during periods of bush living can be traced to social causes of this nature rather than to ecological pressures. People nevertheless often give an ecological rationale for their moves, explaining a residence change in terms of their need for better fishing or trapping conditions, rather than citing the more pressing social circumstances which really motivated them.[4] It is only later that the true reasons are brought out. When Albert and Peter first split up at Aubry Lake, they euphemistically explained to people that they were not getting enough fish there to support themselves. The separation of the Behdzi and Yawileh households cited earlier, however, was indeed partly due to a scarcity of fish and fur near their camp, a paucity which became so aggravated later that the Yawilehs themselves abandoned the site for a new area.

When families moved their trapping camps to a different region, they often took up residence with households which they had not previously been associated with that winter. A comparison of Figures 12 and 13, for example, reveals that the make-up of trapping camps changed considerably from one part of the winter to the next. Fishing and hunting encampments near the settlement, which were formed by families between trapping seasons, also involved residence changes and varying alliances over time. The composition of these latter groups, in fact, often changed from week to week during some periods, and people frequently shifted their residence between these nearby bush camps and the village itself. The same pattern of fluctuation characterized the composition of certain task groups, including the families collected at the sites of major wage labor projects, such as the logging and construction operations contracted for by the trader. The personnel of each of these seasonal encampments was continually being modified as people sought to alter their immediate social environments. Within the space of five weeks during one spring, there was a turnover of forty percent of the people who made up the band's five major camps during that period: most of these moves were later found to be occasioned by drinking disputes between members of co-resident families at logging sites. As Table 4 makes abundantly clear, when I compared camping alliances at different time horizons in 1967-1968, I found that not one family in the entire band had maintained a consistent camping arrangement with any other household during that entire year.

Existentially, there was another form of mobility that was even more pervasive than residence changes as a stress-reducing device. Hunting, fishing, trapping, snaring and wood-cutting activities each took family members away from the camp for at least brief periods of time on almost every day, allowing them to separate and escape from the other people. This other dimension, then, involved the daily movements and temporary separations of the people which stemmed from the nature of economic activities and the division of labor within each camp. The short-term dispersals of the people in subsistence and trapping pursuits thus provided "cooling off" periods of several hours

TABLE 4
Camping affiliations of Colville Lake families, 1967-68 †

House-holds	1	2	3	4	5	6	7	8	9	10	11	12	13	14
1	—	B,C	C				A,B							
2	B,C	—	A,C		A		B							
3	C	A,C	—		A,B									
4				—										
5		A	A,B		—	C		C						
6					C	—		C						
7	A,B						—			C			C	
8					C	C		—	B					
9								B	—	A				C
10							C	A		—			C	
11											—			
12												—	A,B	
13							C			C		A,B	—	
14								C						—

A... Camping affiliations during early winter dispersal (1967)
B... Camping affiliations during mid-winter dispersal (1967-68)
C... Camping affiliations during spring dispersal (1968)

† The table omits individuals and families from Fort Good Hope who spent part of the winter and spring with various Colville families. Numbers refer to families discussed in Part II, and in earlier sections of Part III.

to several days during which tempers were restrained and emotions repressed. When people were reunited after such an interval, relations in the camp were usually resumed without reference to the previous tense situation: group members could thus continue to live with one another under at least surface equanimity. Emotional repression of this sort is a key feature of the Hare behavior and value system, and the recourse to mobility as a means of avoiding disruptive encounters was one of the major techniques employed in the process of restraint. Movement, a basic feature of the Hare's ecology, therefore also served as a stress-reducing and conflict-avoiding mechanism.

The anxiety and stress that people experience over the possibilities of emotional display serve the important social function of reinforcing the whole pattern of restrained behavioral expectations. When the limits on appropriate behavior are overstepped from time to time, temporary or long-term residential shifts are a resort which explicitly avoids and implicitly denies the social clashes which have developed. As far as public sentiments are concerned, the physical dissolution of an unpleasant situation is tantamount to social amnesia — the mention of such incidents becoming as socially taboo as the kinds of behavior which originally prompted them.

These and similar conditions also characterized the tensions which arose within family units in the bush. The environmental hardships, isolation, and boredom that men and women experienced contributed to the amount of stress and friction which developed among them. The periodic absence of men in the course of their trapping and hunting activities, however, allowed hostilities to be dissipated or repressed by them and their wives, and it gave all family members a respite from the abrasive interaction which often occurred within the cramped quarters of the family tent. Trips were therefore looked forward to by both the mobile and the sedentary members of an encampment. Mobility of this sort, in fact, was one of the few ways in which band members could actually obtain a certain degree of individual privacy from one another. A much calmer atmosphere prevailed in the camps following the separations based upon such routine economic pursuits.

When I analyzed the various contexts in which emotional displays took place while the people were living off the land, I found that the process of expressing and displacing hostility often occurred along the lines of a pecking order. Men, when they were angry, picked on their wives, their children, and their dogs. When their husbands were gone, the women often yelled at their children. The latter in their turn focused their hostility on one another and on their pups. Among the dogs there was also a hierarchy of aggression based on dominance patterns. Every living thing in the camp was thus involved in an established order of emotional expression and release.

Without mobility and the chances for separation, displacement, and restraint that it provided, it is problematical whether bush life could have been maintained within the emotional limits that the people permitted themselves. The social and psychological value of movement seemed to be as significant for them as was its ecological utility. Their great emphasis upon freedom and self-sufficiency placed particular stress upon mobility as a means to the independence which they so highly prized. Travel, then, became something of an end in itself, taking on the dimensions of an expressive activity, besides being an instrumental aspect of survival and subsistence. The flexibility of the people's relationship to their social and physical reality thus drew much of its strength from the fluidity which mobility allowed.

If lack of privacy and territoriality were aggravated by the smallness of a tent, movement allowed for the unambiguously free use of space by individuals. People on the move were confined only by the narrowness of their trails, but they could break and follow a trail in whatever direction they chose. The people's love of mobility, and their respect for the "tough traveller,"[5] suggest the trail itself as a metaphor for life: behavior and trails are both bounded, one culturally, the other physically, but the person who can move within these limits enjoys the freedom and openness which existence provides. People participate in a sense of liberation when they journey, and this is as rewarding for them as the incidental measure of privacy that they thereby also achieve.

7　REUNION, PRIVACY AND PUBLICITY

Ultimately, the stresses of the bush affect everyone to some degree, and the eventual resolution of hardship and isolation comes with the periodic reunion of the entire band. Just as mobility invests the life of the bush with variety, the whole rhythm of the people's existence is punctuated by the major ingatherings of each year. The Christmas, Easter, and summer reunions vary in their length and hence in their intensity, but they share in the qualities of release, and in the ultimate re-creation of both community and its particular problems. Counterpointing the stresses of dispersal, then, are the alternate styles of communal life, possessed of their own attractions and tensions.

People anticipate their seasonal returns to the settlement with the same spirit of *élan* that they approach their moves to the forest. Now, however, it is an encounter with society rather than with environment which excites them, and the days of arrival pulse with the comings and greetings of each family. Although the people of Colville do not think of their lives strictly in terms of ingathering and dispersal, they do conceptualize the year in a manner which is congruent with these major phases of movement. They talk of "hard" and "easy" times and "bush" and "holiday" periods, and in conversation they often divide the annual cycle into the harshness of the winter and the ease of the summer. Each of the seasonal ingatherings constitutes, as Bertha explained:

. . . the really good times of the year for us. All the peoples are together and then we really happy to see each other. No more being cold and hungry and not so much hard work. Everybody just visits lots, have parties and drinks, and have a good time.

Having a large number of persons gathered in one place is seen by the people as requisite to a "good time" or holiday. At the beginning of the summer reunion, Adam Ratehne once said:

We can't have much of a party with just a few guys here. We should wait till more people come in from the bush. They maybe we'll put up a brew pot or drum dance and really start. It's best when the village is full up and there are lots of people for visiting.

The relative size of groups at different times of the year thus has its psychological as well as its ecological significance (cf. Mauss, 1904-1905). Densities reflect, resolve, and contribute to both the enjoyable and the stressful conditions which affect the people. One dimension of this is the variation in seasonal preference and mood that occurs from person to person according to time of year. Whereas acculturated people find bush conditions more stressful than traditional natives, the latter, in their turn, experience greater anxiety over the drinking behavior which now occurs during village ingatherings. Though all the people are subjected to stresses in both environments, then, and although they all enjoy the ease and security of community life, the relative significance of the tensions they feel in these two settings varies with personality and orientation.

The sense of ease, comfort and community with which ingatherings begin for the people constitutes a dramatic change from the frequently uncertain and fragmented nature of their lives in the bush. Yet, just as the experience of the forest perceptibly shifts from an attitude of stress-seeking to one of stress-avoidance over time, village existence also modulates its tone as the novelty of communal life gives way to its own tensions and banalities. The slow-paced tenor of the long summer may proceed for several weeks before conflicts develop, but the shorter, more intense reunions of the winter holidays, condensed as they are in time and mood, compress these same rhythms into a briefer span.

Stress and mobility during each of these village concentrations stem more from social than environmental causes, although tensions derived from the latter are not entirely lacking. Each family's possession of fish, caribou meat, and hides varies with effort and luck, and the perceived balance of generosity can be as much a cause of stress within the community as it is in the context of the bush camp. The same applies to the sharing of valued and important pieces of equipment — such as boats, outboard motors, gas-powered chain-saws, tools, dogs, and sleds. The heightened social life of village reunions increases the rate at which interactions, exchanges, requests, gifts, and loans take place; and it also ensures that people's actions in these areas of life occur in a highly observable and public manner.

The publicity of life in the village makes the lack of privacy a prime source of stress and irritation. The ability of people to conform — or to appear to conform — to social norms rests, in part, on their capacity for impression management, and this, in turn, is a function of their control over the information that others have about them.[6] Privacy and secrecy thus affect one's public as well as one's self-image, with personal reputation and self-regard hanging in the balance.

The openness of the village area itself (cf. Map 3), and, until recently, the unpartitioned nature of most of the people's own dwellings, are spatial features which limit their access to family and individual privacy. The diagram of the Dehdele's household (Figure 14), a representative village dwelling, illustrates certain aspects of these information and interaction processes. Because most of the people's houses are single-room structures like the Dehdele's, there is little privacy from observability within each building. People are hidden from one another's view only when it is dark or when they are in their sleeping bags. Except in the case of children at play, no attempts are made to obtain privacy by erecting temporary barriers, by turning one's back and withdrawing into a corner, or by simply ignoring or refusing to acknowledge the presence of others. Aboriginally, women were isolated during their menstrual period, but there are no longer any institutionalized forms of seclusion among the Hare. Sulking or withdrawal from interaction within a home are prompted only by serious quarrels among household members. Mary

Behdzi once withdrew from her family in this way for several days after she and her mother had argued heatedly over a marriage proposal that Mary had received. Such marked emotional expression among adults does not constitute an everyday means of access to privacy, however, and people in the settlement were struck by the singularity of Mary's reaction.

The stresses of gossip and living together were once expressed by Bella Sinta, a young woman from Fort Good Hope who came to Colville in 1971 to stay with her relatives, the Yawilehs. One night, in a confessional mood following a brew party, she took my wife and I aside, and complained that although she had been good to the Yawilehs and had worked hard for them, the women in the household nevertheless spread gossip about her sex life, and gave her a "bad time." As Bella herself explained:

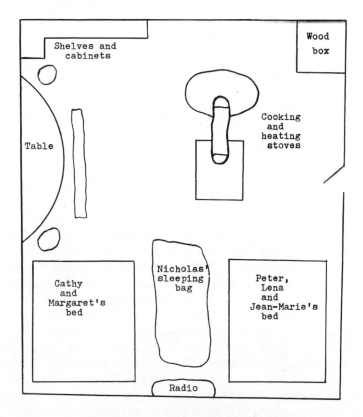

FIGURE 14   The Dehdele household.

Those Yawilehs, they're my cousins. My own cousins. So why do they talk about me like that and tell people stories? Since I came to live with them I thought I got along good with everybody. The old man André and his son Martin, we get along fine. But it's that fat old woman and those two girls who start the trouble. Once, that Martin, my cousin, I washed all his clothes for him. Him, he didn't ask me or nothing. I just went ahead and did it on my own. That's the kind of person I am. I took all his clothes and cleaned them for him. Just like that.

But my own cousin, that older one Pascal Yawileh, that Ehja (a nickname), he started a fight with me two days ago I think it was. He's bothering me all the time. Grabbing at me, you know. For no reason. So finally I went after him and hit him with a stick.

Those two girls, that Monique and Sharon, gee they're lazy. They just sleep all day, never do any work. They lie around all the time. It's okay if you're pregnant, then you can sleep two or three hours during the day. But them, they're not pregnant. They're just like that. Them they sleep all the time and don't work. But me, I'm a hard worker. Why are they like that? I haul water and everything. I'm just an Indian. A real Indian woman. I can do everything. That Monique Yawileh, she says she can't make drymeat. How is that? An Indian woman should know that. But her she just doesn't do any of it that Monique.

That fat old woman, she and her daughters just talk about me all the time. When I came here I met that Michele Behdzi, and he asks me if I want to get married. But those Yawilehs, that old woman and her girls, they start telling all kinds of stories about me. Why? For no reason. That Berona says that Monique is proud. What that mean "proud"? That Monique is "proud"? It doesn't mean anything to me. But they keep telling stories to people about me. My own cousins, those Yawilehs. Me and that Michele, we were going to get married on July 15th, but now they ruined that. Everything was nice. The people were good and everybody here at Colville was nice. But then those Yawilehs, that fat old woman, started talking and telling those stories. So now it's off. Me, I think I'll go back to Good Hope. I can't live here like that when my own cousins treat me that way and just ruin everything for me.

Bella's story illustrates how co-residents and kinsmen can increase the exposure of individuals to communal awareness.

Although the people's cabins would seem to provide families with at least one private domain within the public sector, even here there is a high degree of spatial permeability. The view of villagers into other people's households is cut off by the walls of the structures, but doors are never locked during the day, and people freely enter one another's homes without knocking or asking permission. This behavior is modified only when a brew party is known to be going on inside, in which case people generally do knock first. The villagers usually lock their doors and draw their curtains when the whole family retires at night, and the lack of smoke coming from a household is also a sign that its residents are asleep. Though drunken people may continue to bother a household at very late hours, sober individuals do not disturb residences showing these outward signs of retirement. In and around each household, the only form of total individual privacy from direct observation is afforded by the use of the family outhouse.

Just as there is little visual privacy among the villagers, auditory privacy is also limited. Within a house, people speaking in the tone of voice normally used by the natives can be heard anywhere inside the small structure. Gossipers may drop their voices to achieve intimacy, but the lowered sound and the observability of their behavior serve as clues to other people as to what they are doing. The sound of voices that are raised during arguments carries easily beyond the house and attracts the attention of people outside. Where houses are close to one another, disputes and fights at drinking parties can often be heard in the neighboring residence. Drinking parties themselves usually contain several eye- (and ear-) witnesses to such incidents. These conditions enhance people's awareness of others' conflicts and jealousies, and thereby heighten their own embarrassment when they realize that their neighbors know the same things about them.

Sleeping arrangements in the village are such that married couples have their own beds, although in some cases, as the Dehdele's, it is shared by an infant. In small households of three or four persons, there is generally sufficient room on sleeping platforms for all the people, but in larger families, one or more members may have to lie on the floor in their sleeping bags. Night-time sexual activity can be overheard within houses, but it is impossible to say to what extent people intentionally listen for it, or are inhibited by the possibility of others listening. Children are exposed to and witness sexual relations from a young age, which helps to foster the people's easy acceptance of sexuality among adults and adolescents. When some of the village children were gathered in my cabin one morning, a nine-year-old girl accused her friend and age-mate of the following:

Ah, Cecile, you you're always staying up at night to listen to your father and Paula. You try to hear them talking and making love. You told me yourself you just pretend to sleep. You, you're always doing sneaky things like that.

Casual comments by some of the adults also reflect their sense of the lack of sexual privacy in their houses. Cecile's father Albert once took Paula on a summer hunting trip with him to Aubry Lake and, before departing, he jokingly said:

Well, me and my wife we gonna go and have ourselves a second honeymoon I guess. Just the two of us and the ducks. No one else to say good morning to.

Albert's neighbor Peter Dehdele once commented:

Me and Lena are going by boat to the north end (of Colville Lake) to get the rest of our stuff from there. We'll leave all these kids here with Albert's mother to watch them. It's vacation time, yes sir. Just like when we were young again. My wife will think she's twenty. No worries so long as the boat don't leak.

It is noteworthy that privacy in these cases resulted from the mobility of the persons involved, i.e., the temporary residence shifts and their departure from the village. In a somewhat similar vein, young, unmarried adults having a sexual affair often resort to liaisons in the bush near the village, or they take advantage of a house left empty by the departure of one set of parents.

Though privacy from visual and auditory surveillance is minimal within village households, there is a certain degree of what could be called "spatial privacy." This concept and the behavior it refers to concerns a type of individual territoriality which can be considered an extension of the notion of "personal space" (Sommer, 1959, 1969; Hall, 1969). By "spatial privacy" I refer to the fact that individuals become associated with certain areas within houses, and that these areas are utilized by them much more than they are used by other household residents. A certain degree of exclusiveness and "personalization" may pertain to these locales. Other family members may in turn have their own spatial domains which similarly afford them some physical privacy within this highly social situation.

The most prevalent and clear-cut instances of this type in the village relate to the space occupied by a person's bed or sleeping area. People who are in their house during the day or evening usually sit, recline, or work on their own beds. Women sew, men carve, teen-agers listen to the radio, and young children play, each on his own sleeping platform or sleeping bag. Individuals are rarely seen using other people's sleeping areas for these and other activities. This pattern may be partly due to a scarcity of other household furniture, which in most cases amounts to simply one table, a bench, and a few chairs or stools. However, if there were no such pattern of personalized territory, the people's use of household areas would be far more randomized than it is, since the areas so utilized are neither economically nor socially specialized in any other way.

The concept of spatial privacy gains further support when one considers how the people treat the areas around their sleeping platforms (Figure 15). The personalized use of the latter extends to the floor area around sleeping bags and to that under bed platforms.

People usually store individual property there, and no other members of the household would disturb this "cache" without permission. Items kept in this way include children's toys, extra clothing, hand tools, sewing materials, pieces of hide, combs, brushes, magazines, cards, letters, and tobacco. Young adults and older people often have small boxes or cardboard suitcases in which such items are kept, and the privacy accorded to these containers turns them into a form of "ego index" (Schwartz, 1968, p.748). The "private" treatment of

FIGURE 15   Sleeping area and personal space.

personal property stored in this way contrasts with the people's handling of less privatized items, such as their boats, saws, sleds, and dogs, i.e., items which are on public view and which can be sold and loaned to other people.

One can also note that spatial privacy within households extends in some cases to include wall space. People who have sleeping platforms often display and store property on the walls near their beds. One can find magazine pictures, photographs, letters, rosaries, fur auction schedules, calendars, and other items in these regions. If the wall is covered with cardboard or paper, literate adults sometimes write amusing comments or keep count of their fish catch in these spaces. Though some of these articles and items are clearly less personalized than others, the fact that they have all been placed there by one person — and can only be removed by that person — renders the space a private one. Like the containers noted above, wall areas thus serve as ego indexes and they also constitute a means of personal expression. Walls, sleeping areas, and associated floor spaces, therefore, afford the people of the band a degree and type of privacy which visual and auditory conditions would otherwise deny them.

8   DRINKING, STRESS-SEEKING AND MOVEMENT

As the stresses of privacy demonstrate, considerable tension in the village also derives from the chronic brewing and drinking which characterize major ingatherings. People set up two to five-gallon pots of *kontweh* (literally, "fire-water") to ferment soon after their return to the settlement, and a round of parties is begun which only ceases with the re-dispersal of the community. *Kontweh* is inexpensive and simple to make, requiring sugar, water, yeast, and a fruit or carbohydrate base such as raisins, beans or currants. All the ingredients are available at the local trading post, and the mixture can be drunk within twenty-four hours after brewing begins. While some adults also make *kontweh* in the bush, the difficulty of transporting large amounts of brew materials to distant campsites limits most of the people's drinking to the village environment. Heavier drinkers in the community sometimes also order more expensive, hard liquor from the government store at Norman Wells, and their bottles of rum and scotch reach the village whenever one of the trader's supply planes comes to the settlement from that town.

While at one level drinking qualifies as a leisure activity along with gambling, visiting, traditional drum dances, and the occasional movie shown by the priest, it differs from these latter pursuits because of the degree of emotional expressivity which accompanies it. While drum dances are exuberant and hypnotic in their communal and rhythmic movement, drinking is clearly the most cathartic of all the people's activities, crystallizing and fomenting so much of the latent and otherwise inexpressible hostility in their lives. Repressed feelings and jealousies from diverse sources — including stinginess, marital tensions, insults, quarrels, and the events of previous drinking sessions themselves — may all be exposed during these encounters. While the parties at the beginning of each reunion are basically friendly and euphoric, violence eventually emerges from drinking after an ingathering has been in process for a while. During the summer this may not occur for several weeks, but at Christmas and Easter times, with their intensity and high rates of interaction, parties may occasion aggression within the first few days of the reunion.

The children of the band are exposed and accustomed to these incidents from an early age, but youngsters who have spent the winter at the residential school in Inuvik find the violence and drinking of the summer the most difficult part of their readjustment to the community. Children are allowed the freedom of the village during all ingatherings, and no attempt is made to shelter them from brew parties, or from their sexual and aggressive overtones. Young people learn to adjust to drunken behavior with an accomplished air of stoicism and resignation, and people thus become socialized to drinking patterns, violence, and sexuality at a young age. The place of brew in the ethic of generosity, and the significance of drunken comportment in the people's emotional economy, make it imperative for individuals to accommodate themselves to these styles, just as the ubiquity of these patterns makes it difficult for people to avoid participating in drinking once they have reached adolescence or young adulthood. Violence involving their parents nevertheless visibly distresses and embarrasses the young children, who react as nine-year-old Cathy Dehdele did to a fight involving her father:

Gee, you know I got real scared last night when they were drinking at my house. They was all yelling and me I couldn't sleep. Then my daddy and Albert got real mad and started pushing each other, so everybody starts shouting to them. Then those other guys stopped them and so Albert he left. But after that me I still couldn't sleep the whole night. I get too scared when those things happen.

After a night of nearly continuous drinking and episodic violence at another house, Cecile Limertu (aged ten) confided to me her feelings about Albert's treatment of her step-mother Paula:

When my daddy drinks he always beats up poor Paula. Her she don't do nothin' but he pound her up anyway. Sometime I think what it's for. I sure wish he wouldn't do it. Paula she always cry and later my daddy sometime say he's sorry. It's bad for me in that house when that happen. When we're in the bush it's not so bad 'cause then there's not so much brew.

Children not only learn to cope and put up with drinking situations, but they also learn to interpret them in the same conceptual manner used by adults. Among the people, there is — at a conscious level — a basic attitude of leniency towards drinkers and their behavior: a person is not considered to be responsible for his or her actions when drunk because, as Mary Behdzi explained, "he just don't know what he's doing then." As Cathy Dehdele once observed of an incident:

Oh look at that Jonas beating his dogs. He's so drunk he can't think what he does. That guy just lose his head when he drink.

The fist fights, shoving, shouting, flirtations, acid mimicry, and hurried sex which stem from drinking sessions derive less from the lowering of inhibitions by alcohol than they do from the people's cognitive appraisal and cultural definition of brew parties as times of excess and expressiveness. Jealous spouses, spiteful neighbors, and angered kinsmen may now both create and respond to the substance of their stresses, seizing on the drinking situation rather than the drinks *per se* as their excuse. Homebrew in particular is a mild concoction, and because the people rarely let it ferment for more than a day or two, its alcoholic content is generally in the range of eight to twelve percent. At parties, however, behavior quickly becomes voluble and animated even before many of the people have finished their first drink. *Kontweh* thus serves as a social lubricant (Netting, 1964, p.381), not so much because of its physiological effect, as because of the nature of the situation it defines. Brew is believed to release inhibitions and relieve responsibility, but this is more a product of attitude than chemistry.

At a deeper level, however, what is overtly excused by the people may carry covert connotations of responsibility and blame. Just as generosity is an openly applauded but privately monitored pattern, drunken behavior creates its own reputations and records. As Luke Bayjere once reflected, in a Socratic mood, "I never try to drink so much that I can't remember or know myself." People realize the instant publicity that their behavior receives, and they later experience embarrassment — a very painful emotion for the Hare — over the actions of their close kinsmen and themselves. When a brawl breaks out in the village, people call out to one another "free show, free show!", and faces quickly appear in all the community's doorways and windows. Unless serious harm seems imminent, however, the observers rarely interrupt a quarrel, and with the full, vicarious pleasure that the role of spectator allows, they instead enjoy the display of emotions and violence.

While drinking thus serves as a standardized, sanctioned form of emotional release, it actually operates to inaugurate and perpetuate (rather than simply to dissipate) stresses within the community. Though surface relations usually remain quite amiable after a party, the events which occur at drinking incidents are remembered and often resented by the people. What is initially forgiven by the participants is not necessarily forgotten. Grudges and animosities stemming from various sources are often harboured until some future party, at which time their release and expression again raises the level of tension within or between families. People's generosity with brew is itself a crucial feature of interpersonal relations, often provoking jealousies and stresses in the same way that participation in drinking helps to overcome the usual limits on emotional displays. It is when drinking behavior surpasses these limits that culturally sanctioned hostility occurs in its most visible and often its most violent form.

Gabyel Behdzi once observed of the whole drinking pattern:

There's always trouble around here when people drink. They're always fighting, but I don't know why. Nobody knows why I guess. Just always trouble like that.

Another time, however, Gabyel himself suggested that stress-seeking was part of his own motivation for drinking:

Me, I should go over to Father and buy up some of that liquor from him. Then get drunk again and tie one on and get in trouble once more. One time is not enough. Two times in trouble, that's the way to do it. My stomach's bad, but that don't stop me.

Philip Ratehne perhaps came closer to some of the more personalized motives when he discussed the sources of anger among the people:

Indians are real bad for getting one another angry. They're not like white people, you know. They get onto one another. That's the way they are. Real Indians are "pushy". . . . they talk smart and ask for things when they see they want it, so they're always getting each other angry. They talk lots and get pushy and don't know when to stop. Then they get mad and fight and drink or just pull out.

Because of the process of repression, the observers of drinking incidents, and even some of the participants themselves, often do not fully understand the causes which underlie their acts. The motivating factors may occasionally be openly expressed by one of the people, but more often the actual sources of the specific conflict are not immediately evident. One consequence of this pattern of restraint and delayed release is that although a great deal of drinking occurs from the very beginning, for example, of the summer ingathering, it is usually several weeks before tensions build up to the point where people find it necessary to leave the settlement in order to find relief from the conditions of life there. This time lapse between the beginning of a period of drinking and its culmination in some form of mobility similarly affects the rhythm of each of the other annual periods of population concentration.

Drinking is not the only way in which tensions are produced and reduced within the village context. People seek, experience, and relieve stress in a number of ways, some of which are direct and obvious, others more muted and vicarious. Drum dancing at the village is a cathartic, communal display of ritualized energies, drawing together the efforts and sentiments of the entire band, and epitomizing the collective force of each reunion. Participation in sports and gambling provide means for seeking and dissipating stress, allowing for physical and personal competition within limits and without violence. Card games and sessions of *udzi*, a native "hand game" played to the accompaniment of fast, rhythmic singing and drumming, generate considerable excitement on the part of participants and observers alike.[7] The very heated, tactile sport of "boys against girls" — in which the opposing sexes try to retrieve a rubber ball from one another by means of shoving, grabbing, tackling, and wrestling — affords young adults a sexual and physical outlet for energy and aggression. In addition, the drama and narrative content of both native folklore and Western movies, which the people listen to and watch with great intensity and interest, furnishes them with the opportunity to participate vicariously in the stresses of fictional and mythical characters.[8]

Attending movies with the people provided me with an especially striking example of their use of vicarious affect, for the old Hollywood Westerns that the missionary sometimes showed were occasions for true audience participation. These movies displayed a range of emotions and behaviors, such as rage, jealousy, love, kissing, fighting, slapping, and caressing, which the people did not permit themselves to publicly indulge in under normal circumstances. It initially came as something of a shock to me, then, that when scenes portraying these feelings and activities appeared on the screen, my neighbors — in fact the whole audience — responded to them with enthusiastic laughter, cheering and booing. As in their witnessing of other people's quarrels and drunken disputes, individuals thus found a setting within which emotions could be vicariously displayed and enjoyed without contradicting the strictures of restraint.

Furthermore, the ubiquitous gossip and humor which punctuate the people's conversations allow many individuals to express and redirect their hostility in verbal guise. They thereby deal with personal jealousies and anxieties in a non-provoking manner by faulting their neighbors in the company of sympathetic listeners. The people are highly accomplished mimics, as attentive to the nuances of their *sagot'ine* as they are to the features of their ecosystem: subtleties of behavior become the substance of ridicule, and the pointed, detailed nature of gossip is informed by the limited privacy and openness of village life. Few marital disputes go unnoticed, and it is the rare idiosyncracy of speech which remains unechoed. Gossip and humor thus provide important devices for handling and displacing community tensions, but persons who are the objects of talk also experience themselves as the subjects of other people's comments. One man's humor then becomes another man's stress, for it is difficult, within the confines of a small community, to avoid becoming the content of other people's discourse. The Hare thus illustrate the kind of anxiety which Heidegger (1962) defines as the sense of "being at issue" (Bakan, 1968, p.81), for people do literally experience their own existence as an open question, the outcome and substance of which become a source of doubt and uncertainty.

In comparing the people's transactions at the village and in the bush, their own responses indicate that they variously experience either too much or too little of one another at certain points in the year. Brewing, drinking, interaction rates, violence, and publicity are situational stresses consequent to the intensity and density of ingatherings. Because behavior, embarrassment, and the "information overload" of gossip at such times are both products and enhancers of spatial relationships, the proxemics of band reunions become one of the key dimensions that people must contend with in order to cope with their stresses. Hence, mobility, as a density and a spacing device, becomes an important part of the people's repertoire here, just as it does in dealing with the simultaneously compact and dispersed conditions of the bush.

Specifically, daily activities during different reunions, such as checking fish nets and rabbit snares, gathering berries, hauling firewood, and going hunting, all provide a temporary change of social and physical surroundings for band members. Once again the men are relatively more mobile than the women in this regard, but the crucial point here is not *who* moves the most as the fact that movement by *any* segment of the population provides separation and relief both for those who depart and for those from whom they take leave (Schwartz, 1968, p.742). One consequence of this pattern, however, is that the rare cases of complete withdrawal from interaction within households usually involve women: whereas men can more easily leave the community when tensions and anxieties become oppressive, women — with their lower access to movement — must resort to other coping techniques, among which are immobile retreat and a turning inward.

Also indicative of differential stress response are the mobility styles of traditional families. During the late winter and summer ingatherings, it is they rather than the acculturated people who seek long-term separations from the village by moving to caribou-hunting and fishing camps in the region of the settlement. Whereas acculturated people find the isolation of the bush hard to take, the traditional families find the drinking and tension of the more concentrated village situation the more stressful of the two environments.

Some highly acculturated individuals also express dissatisfaction with the situation at Colville — not because they find the social life there too raucous, but rather because they often find it too limited. Like the traditional families they have recourse to mobility as a solution, but for the acculturated people it is the size and excitement of Fort Good Hope rather than the solitude of the bush which is sought. Some of Colville's young, unmarried men who, like Adam Ratehne, have been unable to find wives in the community, also travel to Good Hope at these times in order to visit girl friends and seek out future mates. There is an imbalance in the ratio of marriageable men and women in the band, impelling some of the "surplus" males to travel in search of spouses. Several of the young adults are too closely related to even consider marriage with one another, further limiting the possible unions within the community. Of the twenty-nine people in the band between the ages of sixteen and forty-five, only eleven individuals are married (five males and six females), and thirteen out of the eighteen unmarried adults are men. [9]

Aggravating the stresses of this situation is the fact that, in many cases, Colville mothers have blocked the marriages of their grown daughters because of their reluctance to lose the labor and services of these girls: adult daughters take on most of the responsibility for designated female tasks within households, relieving their mothers of their hardest chores. Berona has consequently objected to proposals received by both Monique and Sharon Yawileh, and Mary Behdzi, who — like the Yawileh girls — is in her late twenties, has been frustrated several times by the obstructing tactics of her mother Helen. This promotes inter-generational conflict and ambiguity within families, since young adults who are seeking to establish their autonomy are simultaneously still trying to respect the roles of their elders and parents. Clashes between mothers and daughters, and the frustrations of single men, consequently add to the stresses and problems of the community.

There are thus diverse motives for travelling to Good Hope during holidays, ranging from excitement and escape to sex and marriage. It is significant, however, that the various individuals and families who journey to the fort usually return to Colville Lake well before the particular holiday they are enjoying has concluded. After a week or two of town-living, they often find that the countervailing stresses of the fort — including a certain amount of discrimination, the presence of the Royal Canadian Mounted Police, the high cost of living, and a greatly augmented level of drinking and violence — are even more oppressive than the tensions experienced in the small bush settlement. In retrospect, it often seems that they find it more enjoyable to remember and anticipate the fort rather than to experience it. Similarly, just as people welcome a return to the village after a prolonged period in the bush, the members of the band are equally anxious to disperse once more to trapping, hunting, and fishing camps·following an extended reunion. The people can again provide ready ecological explanations for leaving the village, but as André Yawileh once remarked from the peace and solitude of the family's bush camp:

When we are out here alone you know it is hard for us. But sometime I think it is even harder for us to live like that together. We just bother each other too much. That brew does it sometime I think. People shouldn't argue and be jealous but they do. Here in the bush things can be tough, but you're not troubled so much as back in Colville. So the winter is good for something too.

9   CONCLUSIONS AND IMPLICATIONS

Social and ecological sources of stress and mobility are dimensions of life in all human societies. Each group, however, exhibits distinctive patterns in regard to the types of movement and the content of the tensions which concern its members. The life style of the Hare Indians at Colville Lake combines features of traditional sub-Arctic hunting bands with adaptations to the conditions of Western contact. The villagers are therefore involved in a series of tensions derived from two different cultural traditions. Within the framework of a highly mobile existence, the people respond to a wide variety of stresses with a number of different coping techniques. The primary aspects of their mobility are ecological, being a function of the people's dependence upon migratory and sparsely distributed faunal resources. The size and nature of the human groups created by the movements of the band are in turn productive of a series of social and psychological tensions which are partially relieved by additional mobility.

Mobility is not always the primary device resorted to for the relief of tensions; for instance, drinking and aggression towards dogs are two alternative modes of stress release. A great deal of verbal aggression is also displayed in the high level of gossip maintained by community members. Vicarious emotional participation — channeled through gambling, sports, folklore, mimicry, movies, and other people's quarrels — is also an important part of the band's psychic economy. In addition, tensions stemming from the village feud between the fur trader and the priest, which are considered in detail in the following section, are dealt with by the people through such mechanisms as patron-client relationships with these white men, rather than by movement into or out of the settlement. Nevertheless, the level of mobility maintained by band members during all periods of the year, including both ingatherings and dispersals, is much greater than that required for successful exploitation of the environment. Mobility is therefore serving more than ecological needs; the social and environmental situations which obtain in the village and bush indicate that movement is regularly resorted to by the people as a way of coping with socio-ecological stress.

In the field I was initially unaware of the relationship between stress and mobility until I myself began to experience some of the same tensions which affected the people. The boredom, insularity, and hardship of the bush often stretched my tolerance and patience to the breaking point, and I started to develop deep feelings of hostility towards both my hosts and myself. I wondered, in the moments of intensest anxiety, why I had ever gone North in the first place and subjected myself to this way of life. The repetitiveness of existence, the monotony of conversations, and the compactness and privations of the camp all came to oppress me in their turn.

At first I was too guilt and doubt-ridden to express these feelings openly, but while I consciously repressed them, I unwittingly turned to my field diary as a convenient outlet for venting my anguish and frustration. When I re-read my journal while I was still in the bush, I began to recognize the process of emotional restraint and displacement which I had been engaging in. I noted that not only was I using the diary as a confessional, but that I had come to value the trapping and hunting trips, and even the daily chore of wood-cutting, as opportunities for escaping the confinement of camp. This led me to consider what stresses the people themselves were experiencing, as well as the techniques that they were using to cope with their dilemmas. Without the aid of literacy, how did people handle their tensions?

At this point my concern shifted from a focus on the material aspects of survival to the nature of human relationships within the camp. Sensitized by my own experiences and reactions, I became a much more attentive observer of individual behavior and interaction. Fluctuations in mood, petty annoyances, the treatment of dogs, and the sources of worry and satisfaction now became increasingly evident. The people's own evaluation of mobility was openly expressed in the excitement and relief that they experienced in travelling. The most striking feature about these events was the rhythmic nature of the changes in camp life and mood, and it was in trying to understand this existence as a process that the importance of restraint, displacement, and mobility began to emerge. At the village I had also been struck by the people's frequency of movement and residence shifts, and I had begun to keep a detailed, daily record of individual and family mobility. Now, when I combined the data on moods, stress sources, and mobility rates into a chronological document, the crucial role of movement in the stress coping process became manifest. Careful observation during the remainder of the year confirmed and amplified what had initially been a very tentative hypothesis based on my own experiences.

Living with the people also revealed stress-seeking as an existential feature of their adaptations. In the context of the bush, the encounter with challenge became a fundamental part of band identity, and at the village, the actively sought stresses of gambling, sports, and drinking were intrinsic to an emotional economy of well-defined release mechanisms. Taking stress and sociability in their widest senses, one could argue that a dual balance between stress-seeking and stress-avoidance, and between inter-dependence and independence, were necessary for an optimum level of individual and group coping. As an operative mode of this system, mobility was then an implicit part of the flexibility which characterized so many of the people's adaptive procedures.

Students of sub-Arctic groups have also shown that anxiety can function both as a centrifugal and a centripetal force for social systems. Latent hostility, insecurity, and fears of witchcraft, for example, contribute to the atomism of the Ojibwa and Kaska; anxiety over isolation and "bush men" operates as a cohesive force among the Kutchin (Hallowell, 1941; Landes, 1937a; Barnouw, 1950; Honigmann, 1947, 1949; Slobodin, 1960a). An important point not emphasized by previous writers is that *both* major aspects of population mobility — ingathering *and* dispersal — can each serve as a source of stress as well as a means of resolving it. At Colville Lake each of the six periods in the band's annual cycle has its characteristic environmental and social tensions. The successive periods of population redistribution relieve many stresses which have been generated in previous phases. Each new phase in its turn creates other stresses which find release in the next part of the cycle. Mobility thus serves both to generate and relieve stress within a social and ecological framework. Within each part of the cycle, day-to-day mobility and other coping techniques offer temporary respite from pressures and anxieties. The entire year is therefore characterized by a continual and dialectical alternation between periods of high and low stress: major shifts in the rhythm coincide with large-scale population movements, while changes of a lower magnitude generate mobility among smaller numbers of people.

Individual and family participation in this rhythm is affected by such factors as age, sex, acculturation level, and the division of labor. These variables lead to differential exposure, susceptibility and responses to stress on the part of community members. Responses to stress which overcome the people's usual affective restraint are channeled and displaced so that they usually come out in predictable and socially acceptable ways. These arrangements permit the maintenance of social relationships in spite of the existence of stressful situations, and the expressive and potentially disruptive acts which sometimes accompany them. The cultural emphasis on emotional containment leads people to repress, displace, or delay their reactions to provocative situations, and the vehemence and directness of their responses is therefore not as extreme as might otherwise be the case.

Given the universality of stress and mobility in human groups, there is a possibility that the type of interrelationship that has been found among the people of Colville Lake may also characterize behavior in a variety of other social systems. In order for this functional relationship to be operative, the specific tensions and movements which occur in these groups need not be identical to those which affect the Colville band. The model presented here, which differentiates social from ecological sources of stress, and primary from secondary types of mobility, should be flexible enough to accommodate a wide range of stresses, coping techniques, and patterns of movement. In applying this scheme to other human groups, it would nevertheless be necessary to separate the general from the particular in order to see if the underlying pattern is, in fact, the same as the one that has been outlined. To this end, three hypotheses are proposed as a means of testing the wider applicability of the model.

First, the interrelationship between stress and mobility that has been found at Colville Lake suggests that when high mobility is a basic feature of a society's ecology, then movement will also be utilized by people as a way to relieve social sources of stress. Mobility in such cases will therefore be greater than is strictly necessary from an ecological point of view. Such mobility can involve individuals or small or large groups, and it can encompass temporary or long-term separations or amalgamations of group members. Movement which is basically ecological in significance may be used simultaneously as a stress-reducing device, although the people involved may consistently explain mobility as a purely ecological necessity.

A second implication is that if the particular ecological situation of a group involves prolonged conditions of extreme dispersal or concentration, then these will both constitute major sources of tension for the members of the society. The stresses resulting from these extreme conditions will be coped with, in part, by forms of mobility which allow the people either (a) to escape isolation by coming together in larger groups, or (b) to find privacy from the abrasive social interaction which such large groups generate. Interaction within small groups will also be stressful over time, and mobility will here function as a stress-reducer by allowing group members temporary separations from one another. The stress and mobility dimensions of existence will therefore constitute a dialectical process.

Finally, the situation among the Hare suggests that if the people in a group are socially differentiated on the basis of sex, age, degree of acculturation, status, or some other criterion, then this will be reflected in (a) their varied exposure, susceptibility, and responses to stress, and (b) their varied modes and levels of mobility, including variable recourse to movement as a stress-reducing technique.

Each of these features of the situation at Colville Lake could be tested as hypotheses on the stress and mobility patterns that characterize other human groups. Since the conditions of life among the people of the Colville band do not occur universally, modifications of the above model, or the proposal of new and alternate schemes, are developments which are to be expected from future work. The presence of stress often serves important social functions in human society, and the necessity of considering this positive aspect of the problem as part of any cultural analysis has been demonstrated by Hallowell (1941), Slobodin (1960a), and others. For the people of Colville Lake, a degree of stress-seeking is itself an implicit part of the social ecology. In addition, the tensions which are experienced over generosity and emotional restraint help to reinforce those basic patterns of behavior which underlie the coherency of the community's social life. Child-rearing techniques also include the induction of anxiety in youngsters (e.g., about drinking and "bush men") as a way of socializing them to the expectations and demands of other people. Among adults, the anxiety of being the subject of other people's gossip and ridicule underlie the effectiveness of discourse and humor as informal modes of social control. Furthermore, the stresses which stem from isolation in the bush promote group solidarity by enhancing the desirability of village ingatherings, as well as the maintenance of large encampments during phases of band dispersal.

Since the problems and issues which have been raised here constitute a basic dimension of the human condition, I would suggest that fieldworkers should devote more attention to them than they have in the past. The process of stress production and reduction offers a context within which a large number of social phenomena — ranging from kinship relations and religion to physical mobility and economic behavior — could all be fruitfully reconsidered. Recent studies of tension and movement among hunters-and-gatherers (e.g., Turnbull 1968a) reveal how important group fission can be as a technique for the peaceful resolution of conflict.[10] The summary presented here indicates how the people of one human group are affected by a similar process, and it is hoped that future research will broaden our knowledge in this area by developing comparable models for other societies.

PART 4

The Missionary and the Fur Trader

1 INTRODUCTION

The perception of scale and dimension is one of the most deceptive
experiences of life in the North. Size, distance, and depth in the
environment can be judged only after one has learned to appreciate
sound and texture as well as sight, for spatial relationships require
sensory awareness of great subtloty. People orient themselves by such
features as the sound of the wind and the feel of the snow, and the
crucial sensations of movement are more often kinesthetic than visual
in nature.

The deceptiveness of physical space is consonant with some parallel
problems in judging the scale of social relationships. Numbers are not
necessarily equatable with power or complexity, for different people
are perceived, grouped, and experienced in different ways. Kinsmen,
friends, strangers and whites each evoke distinct responses, and
people adjust their behavior to the qualities and statuses of their
companions. Beneath the small scale of communities like Colville,
then, there also lies a subtle fabric of bonds and divisions, woven from
the nature of Indians and whites alike.

A frequent condition of fieldwork situations which often produces
both practical and methodological problems for an anthropologist is
the presence of other "non-native" persons in the community of his
study. Among the most frequently encountered individuals are
representatives of government, religious and commercial institutions,
who, in many cases, have a longer history of involvement with the local
population than the anthropologist can himself claim. It is not
unusual for the fieldworker to find that these non-native residents are
often engaged in conflicts with one another, and that, as a researcher
and an individual, it is difficult for him to avoid being drawn into their
disputes, regardless of his personal wishes or professional poses. The
influences that these outside personnel have upon local conditions,
and the relations that they maintain with the people of the

139

community, with the ethnographer, and with one another, thus constitute both legitimate areas of inquiry for the anthropologist, as well as basic conditions which affect the nature of his work.

Feud situations of this type, developing initially as personal quarrels between these white "outsiders", are common throughout the settlements of the Canadian North, and Colville Lake provides a poignant case for study. The conflict at issue there involves the community's only permanent, non-native residents, a white missionary and a fur trader, whose increasing mutual enmity over the years has crystallized certain stress patterns and identity processes among the people of the village. Specifically, the whites' feud constitutes an important source of tension for the people, who are periodically pressured by these men to take sides and display allegiances in a conflict that is not of their own making. By becoming involved in the feud, however, the people are not only subject to manipulation by the whites, but they have also learned to capitalize on their own situation by playing the priest and trader off against one another in order to derive certain material benefits from these men. Beyond this, the people have gradually come to define the feud and its protagonists as prime sources of many of their other problems, and hence the whites have unwittingly provided the community with a means of displacing anger and responsibility from some unrelated, but equally stressful areas of life. Furthermore, rather than promoting the rise of village factionalism, the feud has actually tended to foster a sense of native unity and identity by creating, among the people, a community of interest which centers around their common dilemmas in confronting and coping with these powerful local figures.

The poignancy of the village feud stems, in large measure, from the disproportionate amount of influence and power which these two white men have over the members of the band. When the people are concentrated at the settlement, the relatively unscheduled and ecologically-oriented life of the bush gives way to a more structured existence, the primary dimensions of which are set by the community's trader and priest. At the village, where they remain during all seasons of the year, these two men control many of the religious and economic aspects of the people's lives, including the distribution of governmental assistance checks, and the provision of wage employment opportunities. Beyond their traditional commercial and spiritual roles, these two men also serve as the settlement's primary link with the outside. They handle the local disbursement of mail, medicine, and money, in addition to controlling much of the flow of information and supplies into and out of the community via their access to chartered airplanes and a short-wave radio. Therefore, although the local people continue to live off the land, their lives and welfare are inextricably bound up with the goods and services, as well as the attitudes and aspirations, of the priest and trader, white men who have come to dominate their small, circumscribed world in an effective though not always conscious manner.

2   THE FEUD

The quality of life at Colville Lake is a function of many factors, including not only how man interacts with nature, and how whites and Indians relate to one another, but also with how the whites themselves have adapted to each other's presence. Given the influence of the community's white residents upon the entire village, it is therefore necessary to relate, however briefly, the short but dramatic saga of the relationship between the local fur trader and priest. Without such a summary, the bitter feud that these men have developed with one another, and the repercussions of this conflict, could not be fully appreciated.

As detailed in Part II, the village of Colville Lake is a relatively new settlement in the Canadian Northwest, and, in large part, it owes its existence as a permanent community to the two white men who now dominate so much of its life. In the winter of 1959-1960, after several decades of disease, starvation, and migration had severely reduced the size of the Colville band, an independent fur trader from Fort Good Hope opened up an outpost store on the southeastern shore of the lake. This store was first run by the Godanto family, which worked in the employ of the trader, and in the years after its inauguration, a substantial community began to develop around the trading post as families from the original band were attracted to resettle there. Then, in 1962, a Catholic missionary order which had been active in this area of the North for over a century, sent a priest to Colville for the purpose of establishing a church and mission in the village. The settlement continued to grow, and approximately a year and a half after the mission was built, the fur trader from Good Hope closed down his business at the fort and moved to Colville Lake with his family in order to run the store there himself.

Initially, the trader and the missionary got along well with one another, both feeling that their common interest lay in working towards building up the community and making it more attractive to people. This would have personally benefited both of them: one man would have a successful business, the other a flourishing parish. And so, while living in separate houses, the missionary and trader began a congenial joint residence in the village by sharing one another's company, facilities, equipment, supplies, and hospitality.

Being both strong-willed, independent, and authoritarian individuals, however, the incompatibility of their personalities, which was intensified by their focal roles in the small village, eventually led to a rupture in their relationship. The attitudes which underlay this split are evident in the tone of an informal "gentleman's agreement" that the two men made with one another shortly after they found themselves sharing the spotlight in the community. The priest, for his part in the arrangement, promised to encourage the people to sell all their furs at the trading post rather than ship them out or take them to the Hudson's Bay Company store in Fort Good Hope. The trader, in turn, being a prominent figure in the village, was to set an example for the people by regularly attending Church services, and by holding down the supply of liquor and materials for making homebrew.[1]

This *modus vivendi* was effective and operative for a period of about one year. There are numerous reasons given by each white man to explain his eventual disillusionment with the way things were working out. Each man accuses the other of a number of unfair or abusive tactics to gain advantages and pre-eminence on the local scene. Currying favor with visiting government officials and the local people, broken promises, vindictive actions, behind-the-scenes moves, and abuses of privileges, good-will, and generosity, as well as more personal and narrow accusations which need not be chronicled here, are all cited as leading up to their open conflict. Understandably, each man interprets the course of events quite differently. At the same time, however, there is a curious agreement in their respective accounts of the one event that finally touched off the feud. According to both men, it happened one Sunday afternoon when a pilot was visiting the village. He was at the mission with the priest when the trader, who had not attended Mass that morning, stopped in to say hello. The priest asked the trader why he had not been to services that morning. According to the priest, this was a legitimate question, since he felt that the trader was reneging on their agreement. To the trader, however, the implication that he was responsible to the priest for his actions, especially with the question being presented in front of another white man, was a grave insult. The trader angrily left the mission, and he and the priest have not spoken to one another since then.

This event brought feelings which had been building up for over a year to a head. Since the split, the animosity between the two men has increased, as has the number of actions that they have employed to dislodge one another from the community. To cite some recent examples, the trader has begun to circulate a petition among the people, asking the regional bishop to remove the priest from the community for his purportedly irreligious behavior. The missionary, in turn, has opened up a small store of his own in the settlement, as well as made plans for the start of a fur-marketing cooperative, in order to divert fur pelts and profits from the trader, and ultimately to drive him out of business. Both men agree that at one point a reconciliation may have been possible between them, but now they feel that things have gone too far to warrant this. What was originally a clash of personalities has since been transformed into an ideological series of moral and economic arguments: the trader accuses the missionary of unchristian and unpriestly conduct, and the missionary, in turn, argues that the trader is exploitative and abusive in his pursuit of power and profit. Nevertheless, the initial agreement that these men made between themselves, i.e., to support one another in their institutionalized roles, indicates that neither economic nor religious motives were really at the root of their differences.

The native people of the village have subsequently become involved in the actions and strategems of the feud, and they are exposed to continual pressure from both the trader and the priest to support their respective sides in the conflict. The members of the band have thus been placed in the undesired roles of pawns in a power struggle, a set of circumstances over whose genesis they had little influence. They have found that their business, their furs, their assistance checks, their credit and debt, their fish and meat, their signatures, their liquor and homebrew, their friendships and associations, and their symbolic acts of support, are all coveted prizes for which the whites constantly compete.

The missionary and trader, in their turn, each feel that, as a result of the feud, the other white man is seriously holding back the growth of the village. Each claims that the other benefited most from their original agreement, and that he therefore lost the most by breaking it. Furthermore, the trader and the priest each maintain that he himself was mainly responsible for the revival and development of the settlement. Each man also claims that if he left, the village would ultimately collapse, and that the people would move back to Fort Good Hope. They both give as reasons for this that: (a) no one would come to replace him, and (b) the people would not be able "to put up with that other man." To a considerable degree, therefore, each man's participation in the feud is bound up with his sense of mission or profit, as well as with a commitment to power, autonomy, and the maintenance of a distinct self-image.

3   INITIATION

When I arrived at the village in 1967, five years after the missionary had come, three and a half years after the trader's arrival, and two and a half years after the feud's inauguration, I was only dimly aware of what the local situation was like. I was quickly baptized into local politics by the pilot on whose plane I flew into the community. As we hovered over the village and the bay on whose shores it is located, he asked me whose dock I wanted to land at: the missionary's or the trader's. Showing a reluctance to make any kind of decision, I said that I really did not care. Besides, I offered, what difference would it make? Shocked at my naiveté, the pilot just stared at me silently for a moment. And then, in about two minutes of torpid flying and torrid prose, he quickly filled me in on the entire history of the feud — a feud whose story was apparently well known throughout the North.

Moments later, sitting in the cockpit a sadder, more apprehensive, but wiser person, I realized that some sort of decision was necessary, and so I asked the pilot to circle the village one more time. Acting on an impulse whose rationale still escapes me, I felt that I had better determine who had the bigger landing dock, the trader or the priest. And, satisfying myself that it was the latter, I asked the pilot to land there.

Almost the entire community turned out to greet the plane, the trader and his family being notable exceptions, and in a short period of time I had made a nodding and superficial acquaintance with the village's population (Figure 16). I soon found myself alone inside the mission, however, and, while talking to the priest, I became aware of how distant and deferential most of the people were towards him, as well as how hesitant they were to intrude into his company. Meanwhile, the missionary explained that the small cabin that had been set aside for me in the native part of the settlement was not quite ready yet, and that I could stay with him for the next few days while it was being fixed up. Before long, his conversation got around to the trader and the feud, and I found myself in the midst of my first indoctrination session, one that was to be followed by many others during my year's stay in the community.

Staying at the mission those first few days was an educational experience in several regards. Besides learning the priest's side of the story, I soon realized how difficult it would be for me to establish rapport with the people if I became too closely identified with either white man. From observing village patterns of interaction and avoidance, I came to appreciate the caste-like nature of social relations between Indians and whites, and its reflection in the physical

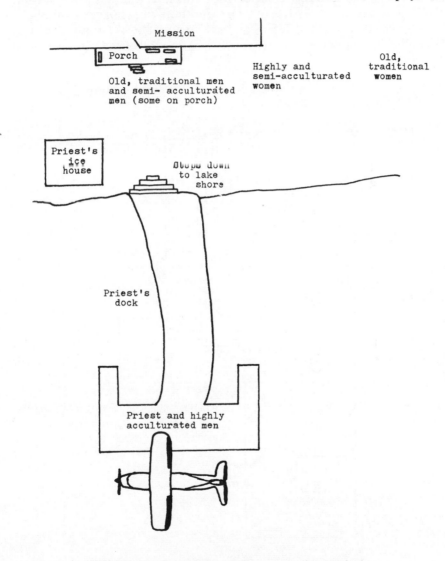

FIGURE 16   Positioning of villagers at plane arrival.

and social distances that these people maintained between one another[2] Not only did the missionary and trader segregate themselves from the people spatially (Map 3), but they carefully regulated just which parts of their homes the people could enter: certain rooms and areas of the mission and store were clearly out-of-bounds to all but a select few of the Indians, whereas the whites, as a prerogative of their status and power, could freely penetrate the living quarters of all the people if they so wished (cf. Figures 17 and 18).[3] As soon as it was feasible for me to do so, therefore, I left the mission to pay an initial

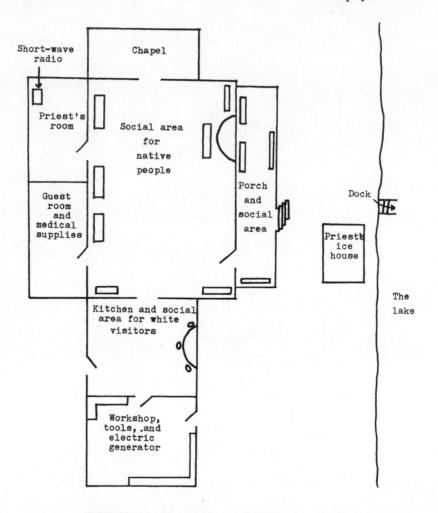

FIGURE 17   The mission at Colville Lake.

social call upon the trader, and then, at the earliest convenience, I moved into my own cabin, and began mixing with the people on a much more informal basis. My first priority was to avoid being type-cast into the same "white man's" role that the priest and trader had assumed, and in order to do that, I needed the freedom of movement and interaction that would allow me to establish a unique identity.

Within a day of changing my residence from the mission to my cabin, I began receiving a constant stream of young and adult visitors who were curious about my presence and my person. It took a bit of explanation to make clear my motives for coming to Colville, and

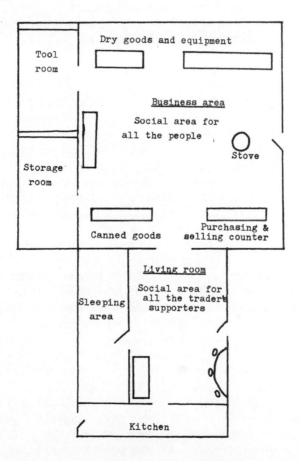

FIGURE 18   The trading post at Colville Lake.

primarily to settle the matter of why I had chosen to live in the Indian
part of the settlement rather than isolate myself from the people as the
missionary and trader had done. After a few days had passed, and I
began to cut my own wood, draw my own water, hunt for my own
supper, and "go native" in many other small ways, the people began
to appreciate the fact that I did not intend to live in the "colonial"
style of the other white men they had had contact with, and that I was
indeed serious about learning and emulating their life style. Unlike
the priest and trader, that is, I did not set my residence apart from
theirs, nor did I expect the villagers to perform essential services for
me on a voluntary or cash basis. Furthermore, given the way in which
I was conducting myself, including my physical separation from the
whites and my propinquity to themselves, the people came to accept
my publicized position of neutrality in the local feud. They thus began
to feel comfortable in my presence, and soon lost the reluctance to
speak with me that they had exhibited while I was still living in the
mission.

The feud between the missionary and the fur trader thus worked to
my advantage during my initial weeks in the settlement, because the
people came to look upon me as a sympathetic, neutral outsider with
whom they could register their complaints, sentiments, hopes, and
grudges without any fear of reprisal or recrimination. Within a
surprisingly brief period of residence among them, their conservations
with me covered a great variety of topics, ranging from the psychology
and economics of the local conflict to sex and marital problems. I thus
found myself the recipient of a great deal of personal information and
gossip within a few weeks of my arrival — and much of the
information that I received was of such an intimate nature, that it
provided me with the kinds of insights that one feels fortunate and
privileged to discover after years of careful and patient fieldwork.

It took longer to establish my position of neutrality in the eyes of the
priest and trader, and, in a very real sense, this was a struggle that I
had to keep up throughout my stay in the community. Visits or favors
to one man always had to be balanced by a comparable gesture
towards the other one, and I found myself spending an inordinate
amount of time placating, pleasing, and patronizing each of them so
as not to jeopardize my position in the village. As a result of the layout
of the community, I soon discovered, as had the people long ago, that
it was almost impossible to hide from either man the fact that one had
visited the other individual. The trader and the priest, from their
respective front windows, could each see who was paying a call upon
the other man: both the winter and summer trails to the mission and

store, whether the people walked on the land or took a short-cut across the bay by boat or snowshoe, were within the purview of each of the whites. And if bad weather or heavy winter clothing obscured a person's identity, both the priest and trader kept a pair of binoculars close at hand to aid in the process of identification. Furthermore, because the mission was raised up off the ground on wooden supports, it was even possible for the priest to see down into the shopping bags of people who passed below his window on their way back from the trader's store. He thus knew who was selling furs and buying commodities, as well as which people had been given large amounts of credit or were planning to make homebrew.

Similar to what had happened to many of the people, I also found that my earnest statements to the whites that I did not wish to become involved in their struggle was accepted by both of these men, but that, nevertheless, neither of them ever really ceased to court my favor or to try to use me as a source of information and leverage. This put me in a position to enjoy from them some of the same confidences that I received from the people, but in my dealings with both whites and natives, I was placed in a status where my trustworthiness as a confidant was continually being tested by all the interested parties. And at Colville Lake, *everyone* was an interested party.

The natives' role and interest in the feud was closely bound up with the control that the whites exercised over important goods and services in the community. Wage labor, assistance checks, medicine, loans of money and equipment, credit, Western forms of entertainment (such as movies), the provision of liquor and brew materials, and access to the primary means of communication with the outside, were all in the hands of the whites. The natives, in their turn, had the souls and the furs, and the support and the public opinion, that the whites needed to bolster their egos, their pocketbooks, and their power plays. Thus, the feud was central to existence and survival in the village, and one could not hope to ignore it and still grasp the essence of community life.

Though it was a hard lesson to learn and follow through with, I soon realized that the distinctive features of the local situation made naiveté a pose rather than a real possibility. All the villagers, natives and whites, myself included, needed to receive and give information on a regular basis lest they lose touch with the realities of life and thereby impair their ability to adapt to them. People not only needed information to survive, but the participation in gossip was also a pursuit which had its own intrinsic rewards. In the small world of Colville Lake, just as Gluckman (1963) and others have found it to be true in various settings, information and gossip were among the basic fuels of life, providing a kind of social energy which had no direct counterpart in the more material realms of food and nutrients. And to the extent that social relations were instrumental means to survival as well as expressive outlets, the useful information conveyed in gossip was a *sine qua non* of life itself.

I eventually realized that, at one and the same time, I had become many things to many people: communication channel, information filter, high-status friend,[4] local resource, experimental subject, object of trust, source of suspicion, a link in the network, an outlet for stress. Perhaps the most difficult part of the entire Arctic experience, therefore, was not adjusting to the physical conditions of life, but rather learning to juggle and play all of these roles simultaneously.[5] I was never really offstage, and I continually had to confront one or another personage in the local drama and perform in accordance with his or her expectations. This was, however, the kind of position that everyone in the village occupied to some degree, for we were all in this together. And, perhaps unwittingly taking my clue from Hamlet, I realized that the drama was an opportunity rather than an inconvenience, being a performance which could reveal much of the inner workings of the people who were caught up in it. Without expecting it to be so, then, the village play became the thing wherein I hoped to catch the conscience of the community.

4   ALLEGIANCE, ALLIANCE AND ATTITUDE

A key aspect of community conscience in the feud was the depth and variety of individual commitments to the main protagonists. The natives' leanings in the feud tended to be heavily influenced by their perception of the roles of missionary and trader, perceptions which were colored by their previous experiences with other incumbents of these positions. Historically, the native concepts of the roles of fur trader and missionary are rooted in the accumulated experiences of band members since the early and mid-nineteenth century. Nowadays, for example, the people do not differentiate between the roles of "missionary" and "priest," referring to all clergymen, in fact, as "priests" or "Fathers." This is because the conversion of all the Hare Indians in the area to Catholicism was begun in the 1860's, and so the real missionizing phase of activity has long since past. Similarly, fur trading activities in the region began in the early nineteenth century and have continued with varying degrees of intensity up to the present day. Involvement with the fur trade as a key aspect of life is thus also an established part of native existence. Based upon their past and their more recently intensified exposure to such institutionalized figures, therefore, the people are well aware of the type of behavior that these roles entail. Without, of course, using the word "role," the people have — and express — definite ideas on what they expect a fur trader and priest to be like. Consequently, it is only the role *incumbents*, and not the roles *per se*, which are new to the people of the settlement.

A contributing factor to the local feud, and to its perpetuation and intensification, has been the discrepancy that most of the natives feel exists between the ideal and actual behavior of the two white men who live in the village. "He doesn't act like a *real* priest," complain some of the people, while others protest that "the trader doesn't treat us the way he *should*." It must be emphasized that the concepts that the people hold of these Western roles, and disparities that most of them see in the behavior of Colville's two white men, vary with the backgrounds of different village residents. That is, people with different degrees of outside experience and white contact show different attitudes towards Colville's missionary and trader. The relatively more acculturated people generally sided with the trader, while the more traditional members of the band tended to be among the most consistent supporters of the priest. To express the matter somewhat differently, a small number of the most traditional natives did not find the priest's behavior incongruent with his role, and the most acculturated natives felt largely the same way — though not quite as consistently — about the trader. More pronounced and open support of the trader was connected with drinking and the wage labor situation in the community since the trader's provision of brew materials, liquor, and employment, were prime sources of his power and influence in the feud. Furthermore, the trader spoke only English, and his close contacts with the people were therefore limited to the bilingual individuals.

The most conservative members of the community, who the more acculturated people referred to as "the *real* Indians" or "those old bush Indians," were primarily monolingual, bush-oriented non-drinkers, who had relatively little experience outside the community. The more pronounced and open support of the priest by some of them related again, in part, to the provision of wage labor within the community: the priest (like the trader) offered more work to his supporters than he did to other individuals. The priest also had a good command of the native language, and so the more traditional individuals of the community had more frequent interaction with him than they did with the trader.

Although the priest and trader each had a small core of supporters, the majority of the villagers had no clear set of allegiances in the feud, and, correspondingly, only a small number of them could be characterized as being highly acculturated or highly traditional. The band's population actually formed a continuum in the areas of acculturation and allegiance, with most individuals falling somewhere in-between the two extremes on each of these issues. My status in the community put me in a position to participate in and analyze the dynamics of the feud, and, being an intimate of band members and whites alike, I could follow their respective motives, strategies, and responses on a day-to-day and issue-to-issue basis. I saw that from time to time people changed their leanings in the conflict in accordance with their perception of what actions and alliances would do them the most good. For the most part, however, the bulk of the people tried to maintain a conscientious neutrality in the conflict, desiring to enjoy the good will, the services, and the goods of both white men.

The corollary of this strategem in the realm of attitudes was the fact that most of the people felt that both white men had their faults as well as their virtues, and so in most cases, native opinions about these individuals tended to be more balanced than one-sided. In Lena Dehdele's estimation:

Father's okay and he does a lot for the people, but he shouldn't go around getting mixed up in everybody else's business.

Lena's husband Peter once complained that

Dave (the trader), he been good to us the last few years, but now he's trying to cut our fur prices too much. How're we going to pay up our debts with him? If he and Father stopped fighting, things would be better for the people.

To the limited extent that feud alliances consistently followed acculturative levels in the band, this presented an incipient, divisive factor in the settlement. There were few cases of permanent feud leanings, however, and these allegiances took the form of patron-client relationships, i.e., in return for support, information, furs, gifts, meat, fish, and other considerations, the trader and the priest each reserved for particular families most of their wage labor positions, the use of their equipment and supplies, and access to liquor, credit, and other resources and services. But such a strategy of commitment in the feud was followed by only a small number of families, and most of the people tried to play the game both ways.

All of the natives, regardless of their leanings in the feud, felt that it was in their own best interests to maintain good relations with both white protagonists because, in their view, neither of these men — by himself — could have insured the continuance of current services and the level of living in the community. That is, the goods, services, and benefits that they offered were complementary. The trader provided liquor, the missionary showed movies; the trader chartered most of the airplanes, the missionary sent messages on his short-wave radio; both men offered wage labor, but not enough — individually — to employ all the men of the village. The people, therefore, for these and other reasons, recognized the need to court the good will of both men.

Even the trader or missionary's most open supporters generally attempted to remain on good terms with the feud's other protagonist, hoping to realize some of the benefits of the "neutralist" position. Consequently, the people rarely criticized either the priest or the trader to his face, and instead used various material and expressive means to please the whites. In several cases, some of these actions were motivated by genuine friendship for these men. In most instances, however, acknowledged supporters of both whites, as well as relatively "neutral" individuals, were observed to participate in these activities in order to placate either one or both men.

The missionary and fur trader realized that most of the natives leaned both ways when it was beneficial for them to do so, and both men accepted this as one of the features of the conflict. They realized, in fact, that this type of behavior was often necessary for the people's own well-being. "I know," said the priest,

that everyone had to sign the trader's petition (against me) or else they would have lost their credit. I guess I really can't blame them for doing it.

The trader, for his part, once commented

I know that lots of them are giving caribou meat to the priest. They'd sure be in dutch with the Father if they didn't make some presents like that during the winter.

While it may appear to an outside observer that it was the whites who controlled the local drama, to the participants it was equally evident that the local people themselves were often in a position to manipulate and exploit the whites. That is, natives also used their role in the feud to their own advantage, and there were several ways in which the dynamics of the conflict accorded benefits and stress-releasing mechanisms for the people (cf. Dunning, 1959, p.118). In return for their good will and support, for example, they could secure from the whites such things as larger amounts of credit, liquor, more wage work, or the loan of some piece of equipment. They were also allowed to use the mission and store facilities for informal social gatherings, and such events were a major part of the people's leisure life.

The trader and priest accepted these and similar facets of their relations with the people as part of the dynamics of the feud. The whites were thus as much concerned with accommodating themselves to local conditions as were the people. At the same time, nevertheless, these two men continued to exert pressures for allegiance upon the people, resulting in the need for this type of dualistic behavior. In indirect and sometimes less subtle ways, the trader and priest each interrogated many of the people who visited them about the activities of the other man, a form of questioning to which I was also subjected. Everyone at Colville was an interested party to the dispute, and knowledge was a precious commodity. Whites and natives avidly sought and used information on a number of issues, including current policies at the village's two stores, the status of the petition and the cooperative, the fur and food prices being offered locally, the level of wages, and the amount of employment being made available. Many pressures and tensions consequently stemmed from the whites' behavior in these regards, and these stresses were the source of the people's most commonly expressed complaints about the feud. In the view of Wilfred Ratehne:

These guys are always after us to do this or do that. They both want our fur, they want us to sign things, they're always asking us questions. They can't leave each other in peace and so the same thing happens to us.

Most of the people of the community had mixed feelings about the trader and the priest, which could vary from season to season and even week to week. Poor fur prices, for example, brought criticism of the trader from Pierre Behdzi, but two weeks later he praised the trader's generosity when the latter gave him a contract for cutting logs. Albert Limertu, who usually thought of himself as an ally of the trader, had kind words for the priest one winter because the latter had lent him the tools he needed to fix his sled and harness. At different points in time, therefore, contradictory statements could be (and were) elicited from the people, depending upon how the course of the feud and the behavior of the two white men had most recently affected them. When people hàd complaints to express about the whites, they did it to one another, to the man whom they supported at the moment (i.e., if they had strong leanings in the conflict), and to uninvolved outsiders such as myself, but never to the missionary or trader if that particular man was not a patron of theirs. Such a move would have been seen by the people as a provocation or an invitation to trouble. As Philip Ratehne, a relatively "neutral" young man expressed it:

It is bad to get mixed up with this whole thing. You try to please everyone but it's not easy. These white guys are always fighting and getting us into it even if we don't want to. It always means trouble for us Indians.

5 "TRUTH" AND CONSEQUENCES

To the missionary and fur trader, the feud was primarily a personal concern. They each viewed it as a series of attempts by the other man to have his antagonist removed from the community. Each man saw his own actions as countermeasures to insure his self-preservation, as well as to preserve what he regarded as his unique and essential contribution to the life of the village.

Given the considerable degree to which the feud affected the lives of the people, the villagers also viewed their own actions in terms of their personal welfare. Hence, feud involvements constituted a series of pressures and stresses for them which touched upon almost every area of their lives. After a hard winter spent trapping in the bush, the people returned to the settlement to find the whites competing for their pelts by raising and lowering fur prices (Table 5), by extending or withholding credit, and by offering or denying services, jobs, homebrew materials, and liquor. When government assistance checks arrived at the settlement, the people similarly found each white man pressuring them to sign their checks over to him in order to deny the other man access to their purchasing power and business. Furthermore, during economically slack periods between trapping seasons, people discovered that wage labor positions were variously given or withheld from them as a reward or punishment for past gestures of support and friendship. Such gestures were themselves the result of other pressures and stratagems, such as "volunteering" to

The Trail of the Hare

sign a petition, join a cooperative, or offer "gifts" of meat, fish, firewood, or hides to the whites.

With two stores operating in the village as a result of the whites' competition with one another, the people found that they could get more credit by utilizing both of these outlets. The trader and the priest were each reluctant to deny a man credit lest they lose his business and his furs. Another consequence of this situation, however, was that the people found themselves going into deeper and deeper debt over the years, much more debt than they had been able to handle in the past. This provoked resentment on their part because they felt it was the whites' responsibility to control the amount of their debts so that they would never lose all their credit, or owe more than they could expect to pay back (cf. Adams, 1963, p.191). Caught between the demands and blandishments of the two white men, many people felt that they were being unjustifiably victimized. The decline in fur prices over the years, coupled with some occasional sharp profit-taking by the trader, the feeling that the missionary cheated in the handling of

TABLE 5
Fur income by household, winter of 1967-8

Household	Number of active trappers	Value of fur catch *
1	2	447.20
2	1	341.00
3	1	151.20
4	1	538.80
5	2	651.40
6	1	91.00
7	3	1,705.40
8	2	1,079.00
9	2	499.00
10	1	853.00
11	1	127.00
12	3	497.30
13	1	412.25
14	3	1,655.20

Men from Good Hope who camped for
part of the winter with Colville familes
and traded some furs at the village   <u>1,422.50</u>
    10,471.25

* Includes the value of furs that were directly shipped out by Colville trappers to fur auctions.

payments for shipped-out furs, and the people's lack of understanding about the "outside" fur market system, all added to the level of tension and rancor. In an articulate and angry mood, André's son Fred once said:

To hell with both of them. Those guys are cheating me and everybody. You work hard in the bush and then they fight for your fur. The trader's marten prices go down and you're left with nothing. If you ship them out then the priest won't show you your fur slips. What's a guy supposed to do?

The people emphasized that it was difficult for them to pay up their debts with the low fur prices that they were paid. Although most villagers were concerned with keeping the size of their debts down, one consequence of the feud over the years had been that, as debts had gone up, people came to look upon wage labor and assistance checks, rather than trapping, as the surest means of achieving the payment of what they owed (cf. Balikci and Cohen, 1963, p.40; VanStone, 1963). Hence, trapping activities, and the incentive to trap, were slowly declining as people looked more and more to other sources of income for their livelihood.

In such a situation, the individuals who controlled these other sources of income eventually came to play an increasingly decisive role in orienting community life styles. Since wage employment was such a valued reward on the local scene, the whites, especially the priest, had come to use it more and more over the years to cement patron-client relationships and to win people's support.[6] The amount of wage work offered in the community therefore increased over time, and some local construction projects, such as the priest's store, were inaugurated as a direct result of feud strategies. Consequently, periods of wage employment were eventually extended into seasons which had been previously devoted exclusively to trapping, and, occasionally, the trader and priest even "invented" jobs so as to be able to give one of their favorites a special reward.

Similarly, liquor and brew materials were made available to the people on a selective basis in order to reinforce particular allegiances. The trader recognized that increased drinking over the years was connected with the fact that the people had been catching less fur each winter, and that they gradually had been going deeper into debt. He nevertheless derived a good deal of control over the people from the fact that he was the only one who sold brew materials in his store, and that it was he, and not the priest, who allowed liquor to be brought into the village from the outside on his chartered supply planes. The fact that the people's drinking also upset the missionary reinforced the trader in his stand on this issue. Since the people's participation in drinking and wage labor cut down on the amount of time and energy that they devoted to trapping, fishing, and hunting, the feud therefore had some indirect, but very significant effects, upon the ecological patterns exhibited by band members.[7]

The increase in the people's ambivalence towards trapping and bush living as a way of life was particularly evident among the more acculturated people, especially the younger adult males. Adam Ratehne's opinion was that:

We work all winter and don't get anything out of it. I've been trying to get out of debt since last fall but I still can't do it. Both the trader and Father are out to make so much money they won't leave us anything. Maybe I should give it up and try to get work in town like I did a few years ago. At least I wouldn't have to worry that way.

It should be emphasized that the feud was really only one of several factors underlying the ambivalence of these young adults. Their acculturative experiences, along with the difficulties that many of them had encountered in finding spouses and achieving an enhanced social life, were also at the root of their attitudes. It is more accurate to say, therefore, that the feud operated to accentuate and reinforce, rather than initiate, their feelings of dissatisfaction with village and bush life. The conflict and its protagonists thus served as an excuse for gossiping and expressing their complaints about the community. Even older, less acculturated adults were frequently found to verbally redirect a good deal of their personal tensions and hostilities by displacing them towards the feud's main figurres and the situation of stress and conflict that they had created.

The phenomenon of whites feuding with one another is a common feature in isolated northern settlements, and the ubiquitousness of such conflicts outside of Colville Lake has been discussed by Dunning (1959), Vallee (1967), and others. According to Dunning, whereas in the period before World War II these settlements characteristically had a single, dominant white person, the post-war growth of the North has brought with it an influx of white personnel. Subsequent conflicts have been the result of attempts by these traditionally high status outsiders to dominate their local scenes. That is, the previous monopoly of high status by one resident white has been lost, and there is no defined order of rank among the outsiders (Dunning, 1959, pp.117-119).

Although, as we have seen, Colville Lake's history has been

different in several regards from the model outlined by Dunning, the developments in the community in its first decade of existence have yielded strikingly similar results. The genesis of the feud has had similar roots, particularly in the authoritarian personalities of its main figures. The various ways in which it has been fought out are also largely the same as those described for other communities.[8] Students of "contact" situations have also emphasized the fact that feuds among whites stem, in part, from the isolation, boredom, frustration, and monotony of their life styles. Their patterns of interaction with one another are often intense and emotionally laden because they have no one else to turn to for company, given their variously ethnocentric, "racist," or "colonialist" rejection of native people as proper companions (cf. Saum, 1965, pp.61-68; Dunning, 1959, pp.118-122; Honigmann, 1952, pp.520-521). These attitudes color and affect relations among the whites themselves by defining the range and content of appropriate friendships for them. These factors heighten the potential for conflict that Dunning, Vallee, and others have noted, based upon the personalities of these "marginal" white outsiders in the North, and the general lack of a commonly accepted hierarchy of status and power among them. When ambiguity is thus combined with authoritarianism under conditions of isolation, frustration, boredom, and intensified interaction, stress and conflict are a common outcome.

The people of Colville Lake were well aware of the ubiquity of feud situations in the North, and many of them consequently claimed not to be surprised by the behavior of the whites. As Peter Dehdele once observed,

In most places I been in, Indians get along and stick together and it's the whites who fight and cause trouble.

Despite their level of awareness, the people were nevertheless resentful of many of the local consequences of the feud, especially the air of tension and pressure that it had created. The stresses which resulted from this situation did not easily find release in everyday life. Expressions of hostility were strongly repressed among the people, and they considered it foolhardy to directly confront the whites. Their tensions found some release in drinking, physical activities, and mobility patterns, but the feud left a residue of discontent about life as a whole in the village.

On the other hand, the feud and its protagonists also served to channel and release some stresses. Tensions resulting from the feud, as well as discontents derived from personal problems, acculturative disorientations, and other sources, found direct or indirect expression in gossip and verbal attacks on the trader and priest The people frequently used me as an outlet or sounding-board for their negative sentiments about the whites,[9] and, after living with the people for a full year, both in the village and in the bush, I found that the gossip and complaints about these two men were so central and ubiquitous in the villagers' conversation that one could regard their discontent about these whites as a cohesive element in their lives. That is, the community, in part, was held together and defined by the gossip, the scandals, and the concerns which its members shared and exchanged (cf. Gluckman, 1963, pp.311-315). The fact that strong antagonism and hostility between Indians and whites was generally expressed in an indirect manner permitted relations between these two ethnic groups to be maintained under a peaceful facade (Honigmann, 1952, p.521). At the very least, the people's concern with the actions of the whites, and the importance of their own responses to them, lent a common and basic theme to everyone's existence.

The presence of these two white men also involved, as we have seen, a number of services which they provided for the people. The positive and negative aspects of the roles of these outsiders underlay the range of reactions to them that the people displayed. Dunning noted that in the settlements that he had studied, the people had to learn to adjust and accommodate to "the often unreasonable behavior" of the whites because of their dependency upon them (Dunning, 1959, p.122). At Colville, the whites also had to learn to accommodate to the behavior and expectations of the people as well, for the whites, in their own way, were as dependent upon the Indians as the Indians were upon them.[10]

Given several factors, including the strong pressures for taking sides in the village conflict, the selected allegiances that were consequently formed, and the varying acculturative backgrounds of the natives, the question arises as to why the feud did not lead to the creation of clear-cut factions in the settlement. Taking the whole social situation of the community into consideration, there were several countervailing forces in the village which mitigated against this potential for factionalism. To begin with, the majority of the people were basically "neutral" in the feud, and so their attitudes thus overlapped with those of the less numerous people at the two extremes in the conflict. In this way, they helped to hold the village together by the expression of sentiments to which everyone could subscribe, at least in part. Furthermore, leanings in the feud changed from time to time, and alliances were thus tenuous and loosely structured, except for the few cases of close, patron-client ties. With the exception of the latter, in fact, the people's leanings in the feud turned out to be a good deal more variable than the natives themselves admitted in their appraisals and perceptions of the conflict. When the villagers' expressions of sentiments were compared with their actual participation in the dispute, it was found that people changed their sides much more frequently than they could later recall.

One can thus contrast the people's "conscious models" of the feud with their actual patterns of involvement in it (cf. Lévi-Strauss 1963, pp.281-282). At any one point in time, individuals who felt antagonistic towards one of the white men tended to regard many other people as sharing the same feelings as themselves. When their own position changed, their "model" of the feud, including their perception of the behavior of other villagers, was correspondingly altered to harmonize with their new stance. The major difference between the people's "conscious" models of the feud and their actual participation in it, then, was that the former were much more static and consistent than the latter. Statements indicating fairly stable allegiances were often not confirmed, or were flatly contradicted, by people's actions, since their need for wage work, and their desire to placate and enjoy the services of both white men, induced them to periodically alter their behavior and revise their attitudes.

The fragile nature of affiliations among the people, and the way in which the drama of the feud was played out by them, thus reflected some of the influences working against factionalism. In addition to the people's dependence upon *both* of the whites, the village lacked any large corporate groups or institutionalized authority patterns around which factions could have been formed. The lack of corporate groups was evidenced in the loose ties that obtained among the networks of bilaterally-linked families. Formal leadership among the people was almost non-existent beyond the nuclear household, and people regarded the exercise of authority as an attribute of "white" status. The village's "chief," for example, a position created as an administrative convenience by the government, had no power or authority among the Indians. More influential, informal leaders operated mainly in the role of spokesmen for the villagers in their dealings with white outsiders, rather than actually being involved in organizing the people or exercising authority over them. As an extension of this attitude, therefore, individuals were reluctant to take any actions which would have been interpreted as authoritative by their fellow band members. These were aspects of the people's emphasis on individualism and non-interference with others, and harmonized with their stress on taking flexible approaches to life and its problems. Such themes did not conflict with the formation of *ad hoc* feud alliances and patron-client relations, but they did predispose people against the formation of more cohesive and visible groups on the basis of such leanings.

Another factor was the people's emphasis on interdependence, generosity, and reciprocity. The uncertainty of environmental conditions, and the fluctuations in each family's success in gaining a living from the land, made all the people of the band interdependent with one another for their well-being. The successful hunter or fisherman helped out his less fortunate fellow villagers because next month, or perhaps next year, their respective positions may be reversed. The expectations, obligations and ties that were built up in this way — especially in a community with such a small and closely interrelated population — would have made corporate factions difficult to form and tenuous to maintain.

Kinship bonds were particularly stressed among the people, and the complex network of cross-cutting bilateral and marital ties would have had to have been superceded, destroyed, or radically modified in content if factional groups were to emerge. The band's size was also a limiting factor: it is problematical whether an interdependent, interrelated community with only sixty to sixty-five people could have maintained itself under factional conditions. Furthermore, there was a sense of solidarity among the villagers as a whole which stemmed not only from their interrelatedness, but also from their status as Indians. There was a feeling, as Andrē Yawileh said, that

We Indians have to stick together in this white man's world because these white men are just out to steal everything from us.

In one frame of reference, therefore, the people — as Indians — categorically set themselves off from the white missionary and trader. In this context, the people viewed the feud as a set of conditions which resulted in their exploitation by whites. The conflict was thus, in the sociologist Simmel's words, "a way of achieving some kind of unity" (1964, p.13), and these feelings of exploitation and ethnicity were reflected and given expression in the anti-white gossip which bound the community together. In this regard also, therefore, the feud and its stresses had a unifying effect. In the face of their tensions and divisive pressures, the villagers responded by emphasizing their Indianness, their kinship ties, their distinct way of life, and their

common problems — including their hardships in living off the land and their difficulties in dealing with the local white men.

The Hare and the Dog

1   INTRODUCTION

Anthropologists often feel the obligation to play the role of tribal historian to the group among whom they have done their fieldwork. In the case of peoples without written records and a strict historical consciousness, the methods of archaeology and ethnohistory often yield novel and provocative results. While scholars who have been concerned with the Athabascan peoples of Canada and Alaska continue to work in the broad area of ethnographic reconstruction, it is imperative to realize that another, more current way of life is quickly passing away in the modern generation, and that the next few years might provide us with a final opportunity to study and understand it. Specifically, I am referring to the semi-nomadic "bush" style of life, with its economy of hunting, fishing, and trapping, which has been the primary mode of existence for most Athabascan peoples for at least the last century and a half. It is a life style that is rapidly disappearing from the Indian realm of experience in many areas of the North, and some day it may be as irretrievably lost as are the aboriginal patterns which anthropologists devote so much energy to recreating. While the opportunities still exist to study and comprehend what it is like to live off the land and survive in the forest, we should make the most of our possibilities. Not only the traditional economy of the Athabascans, but their social structure, their patterns of family life and socialization, and their personalities and philosophies, all stem, in part, from their long-standing involvement with the boreal forest. The more we can learn about the nature of this involvement, the richer will be our insights in all areas.

It is a relevant fact, and one which I think many anthropologists have experienced, that when Athabascan people speak of their past, they often talk in terms of "the good old days" — but by this phrase they refer not to aboriginal times, but rather to the period of the mid and late nineteenth century. When the Hare Indians at Fort Good

164

Hope and Colville Lake speak admiringly of "the real old-timers," they are talking primarily about Indian people who lived in the previous century, not individuals who existed two hundred or more years ago. The people's interest in their own history, although not exclusively defined in this way, does tend to focus on the post-contact, fur trapping, and fort-trading period, the era that they know best from the oral traditions of their own elders.

In this section, I would like to focus on an aspect of bush life which has points of continuity with both the aboriginal and the post-contact culture of the Athabascans, but which has received little attention from anthropologists and other scholars despite its continued significance in modern times. Specifically, I would like to explore the relationship between the Indians and their only domesticated animal, the dog, and try to delineate certain areas of canine culture which could provide us with some useful insights into Indian life styles. At first glance, a study of the cultural significance of the dog would seem to need little justification because of the ubiquity and economic importance of the animal. Perhaps it is the obvious nature of this situation which has led to its ethnographic neglect. Yet the issue is more complex and subtle than may be realized, and a few introductory comments are in order concerning the role and importance of dogs in Athabascan culture.

One outstanding fact that emerges from the literature, and from the recollections of informants in many areas of the North, is the scarcity of dogs in aboriginal and early post-contact times. There would seem to have been a paucity of dogs for hunting, packing, and traction purposes not only among many of the Athabascans, but among other northern Indians and Eskimos as well. Several studies provide evidence indicating that prior to the modern era, native groups had very few dogs, rarely enough for more than a few well-off families or bands to muster full dogteams of six or seven animals. The literature of the North covering the early periods of contact show us groups of native people who are usually pulling and pushing their own sleds, or dragging and carrying their own loads. In general, dog traction and dog packing seem to be of limited occurrence and limited significance because people could not afford to maintain many animals. As the early and oft-quoted descriptions of Hearne (1795), Franklin (1824), and Richardson (1851) make evident, women — rather than dogs — would appear to be the traditional beasts of burden among most northern groups (cf. also Jenness, 1967, pp.55, 104).

Evidence from several regions of the North further indicates that dogs became a major factor in transportation and traction only after native people became deeply involved in fur trapping and the use of a Western technology. Serious fur trapping requires a type of mobility which is radically different from the style of movement which characterized aboriginal life. People who are living off the land move in conjunction with seasonal animal migrations and patterns of resource depletion. There is no special premium on speed, nor is there an economic commitment to non-food producing faunal resources.

Trapping as a way of life introduces new considerations, primary among which is the need to travel quickly and repeatedly over specific routes in pursuit of animals that contribute little to immediate family subsistence. The effective harvesting of fur resources is enhanced by a person's capacity to visit his traplines frequently and speedily, setting up new lines and extending old ones when the opportunities to do so are propitious. Furthermore, trapping constitutes a commitment, albeit a temporary one, to a fixed area. Since a region may not contain all the resources needed for the maintenance of one's family, a trapper may have to transport much more equipment and materials than was true aboriginally (including tents, steel traps, stoves, rifles, and foodstuffs), and he may find it necessary to periodically undertake long trips from his base camp for purposes of hunting or replenishing supplies. The life of the trapper thus centers on his capacity for movement, and dogsled travel has become the basic means used to meet this need. The result is that not only do Indian trappers need and use many more dogs than was the case aboriginally, but that they also need the special kinds of equipment that are appropriate for rapid, dogteam travel. Thus Indian trappers eventually learn from whites and other Indian groups to use toboggan-style wooden sleds, harnesses, carioles, sled backboards, brakers, and all the other specialized items that are associated with the use of a dogsled.

The changed cultural significance of dogs is also related to other aspects of Western technology, especially rifles and nets, for it was the Indians' access to these latter items which enabled them to get enough meat and fish so that they could support a larger number of animals (cf. the data in Jenness, 1967, p.104; Birket-Smith, 1929i, p.170).[1] The economic and technological innovations accompanying trapping and dogsled travel thus have to be looked upon as an interrelated complex: trapping necessitates the use of more dogs, but it is the availability of rifles and commercial netting which enables the Indians to maintain an increased number of animals. This is particularly relevant in view of the fact that a high proportion of hunting and fishing activities in many communities is devoted to securing food for the dogs rather than people, underlining the focal role of these animals in the lives of the Indians.

Thus, while dogs are among the oldest of domesticated animals known to man, and while tame canine species undoubtedly accompanied Asiatic peoples on some of their later migrations to the New World, we must keep before us the realization that the development of different economies, including post-contact ones, has given the dog a variable cultural significance in North America. In more recent years, especially in the post-World War II era, there has once again been a series of major cultural and economic transformations among northern peoples. This has included the disappearance of most "bush" communities as native groups have been drawn more and more into towns and urban centers. Under these conditions, the introduction of snowmobiles and similar types of automated land transport has hastened the decline of dogs as important economic resources. Ecologically, the significance of trapping has been appreciably reduced in the last few decades, and there has also been a decline in the reliance upon hunting and fishing as subsistence activities. Since trapping utilizes dogs for transportation, and since hunting and fishing were carried out, in part, for the purpose of providing food for these animals, such changes indicate the diminished importance of dogs in Indian life in recent years.

This process of culture change has not, of course, occurred uniformly throughout the North, and some communities and bands continue to utilize and appreciate their dogs in terms of traditional bush activities. The people of Colville Laka have perpetuated just such a pattern. I would like to focus here upon certain social and psychological aspects of their relationship with their dogs because of the historical interest of such a situation, as well as for the enlightenment that this can provide us with about other aspects of Athabascan culture. In particular, I will describe how the people's treatment of their dogs reveals some basic features of Hare values, socialization processes, sensory modalities, patterns of emotional expression, and modes of social exchange.

It is appropriate that these features be viewed within the context of how the people use their dogs to further their own survival. Since the bulk of their subsistence and income is derived from winter activities, winter transportation becomes basic to the entire livelihood of the band. Life for the members of the community would therefore be unthinkable and impossible without dogs and dogsleds. Travel between the village and their bush camps; the process of setting, checking, and extending traplines; the hauling of wood, fish, meat,

The Trail of the Hare

and equipment; the movement to caribou areas; and the periodic trips to settlements to trade furs and replenish supplies, are all among the absolutely essential tasks that require the use of a dogteam. Furthermore, in transporting wood and supplies in the late spring, summer and fall, when the snow cover on the ground is poor or absent, people nevertheless continue to use their dogs as pack and traction animals. During the course of a single winter or spring, a conscientious hunter and trapper may cover 2,500 miles with his dogs, and spend literally hundreds of hours getting the necessary meat and fish to feed them. It is not surprising, then, that the condition, the training, and the food supply of their dogs constitute some of the most ubiquitous concerns of the people throughout the annual cycle.

One index of the people's commitment to a semi-nomadic life style, and a good reflection of their dependence upon their dogs, is the

TABLE 6

Distribution of dogs among the village's population

Household	Number of dogs	Number of teams
1	21	4
2	5	1
3	8	2
4	7	1
5	17	3
6	8	1
7	20	3
8	12	2
9	20	3
10	7	1
11	9	1
12	22	4
13	8	2
14	18	3
Missionary	7	1
Trader's son	12	1
Three men from Fort Good Hope	23	3
	224	36

Average number of dogs per team = 6.22

The census includes three men from Fort Good Hope who were trapping in the Colville area and were living with families from the band at the time the survey was taken.

number of domesticated animals supported by the members of the band (cf. Table 6). In a dog "census" conducted in the winter of 1967-68, the people of the community were found to be keeping approximately 224 dogs. This was a ratio of three dogs for every man, woman, and child in the village, and an average of one team for every two persons. The teams averaged out to 6.2 dogs apiece, and this corresponds to the number of dogs (i.e., six) which the people considered to be sufficient for adequate travelling. Four dogs was generally considered to be the minimum number required for a usable team. While the men of the community did most of the dogsled travelling, the women of the band were also adept at handling the animals, and several of the younger adult women regularly drove their own teams, set their own traps, and did some of the family's hunting and transporting.

2 EMOTIONAL EXPRESSION AND SOCIALIZATION

While the economic importance of dogs is evident from the nature of the people's ecology, there are several other respects in which dogs play an equally significant, if more subtle, role in the people's lives. In a community where dogs outnumber people by three to one, one would expect them to have some pervasive influences. Forms of emotional expression among band members constitute one area of life in which the animals play an intrinsic and important part. There are a limited number of circumstances under which direct emotional displays are permissible, and a significant proportion of these situations involve dogs and young children in focal roles.

People show a great deal of concern over their dogs, and the animals are one of their most frequent topics of conversation. The role of dogs as expressive outlets is especially evident in the people's relationship with young pups. The latter are spoiled, indulged, played with, given choice food and scraps, and sheltered from harsh weather (cf. also Sue, 1964, p.296 ff.). Fondling and handling occurs often, and dogs are rarely punished or scolded before they are several months old. They are sources and objects of pride which people talk about and display with great frequency. Members of the community constantly compare and comment on the care, condition, and growth of one another's animals, noting special qualities of size, strength, color, speed, and alertness. This affectionate and concerned treatment of young animals is participated in by people of all ages, and the nature of the relationship bears a striking resemblance to the way in which people treat young children. Pups and infants are, in essence, the only recipients of unreserved positive affect in the band's social life, all other relationships being tinged with varying degrees of restraint and/or negativism.

In every generation, however, both dogs and children must eventually be domesticated, and it is significant to note how much the Hare employ dogs and children to socialize one another, and how much consistency there is in the way that the young of both species are brought up.[2] The raising of pups plays an important and early part in the training of children, and, given the importance of dogs in the people's way of life, the animals are in appropriate medium for this purpose. Underlying the efficacy of this technique is the fact that the psychosocial development of domesticated humans and canines show many remarkable parallels in both sequence and process (Scott 1963, cited in Fox, 1965, p.116). Among the Hare, all dogs end up pulling in an adult team when they are grown, but as pups they are usually raised by young children. A child of four or five years of age will be made responsible for the care and feeding of a pup, and children from two years on will hold, play with, and treat young dogs as pets. Since pups and infants are often both placed in the care of slightly older children, they are frequently exposed to the same socializers.

Young children learn to handle dogs by observing the way in which their peers, older children, and adults deal with the animals. From infancy, they have travelled by dogsled with the parents, and these experiences enhance their familiarity with canines. Two or three-year-old children, for example, will tie up three and four-month-old pups to large paper boxes or fragments of wooden sleds, and then have the dogs pull them around the village or camp. In such play situations, the children will yell at and beat pups who disobey or frustrate them, imitating their elders in sudden displays of mock or real anger at the animals (cf. Sue, 1965, pp.36-37). Along with their familiarity, ease, and lack of fear of dogs, children also learn to respect their potential ferociousness. They learn which dogs are habitually vicious, and, from experience, they can tell when a dog is angry, as well as what kind of behavior will provoke a dog. They also learn never to walk or run through an area where another family's dogs are chained up, for their presence may excite the dogs to the point where one may break loose and attack them or another animal. A more experienced child or an adult will sometimes point out to a younger child that what he is doing will anger a dog and cause him to bite. Among the few instances in which parents feel that the spanking or smacking of a young child is warranted, is when the child repeatedly provokes dogs or exposes himself to danger in this way.

Children who are five years of age and older are given more responsible experience in handling dogs. They are often asked by their parents or older siblings to go along and help feed dogs, and, by the age of eight or nine years, this task will become an expected part of their household duties. During this same age period, children will often be given their own sled and harness to play with in conjunction with their pups, or they will be allowed to use their parents' spare equipment. A mother may sew a special harness or sled wrapper (*cariole*) for her child's "outfit," and a father will either make or adapt a backboard for it, as well as shorten the length of the sled itself in order to make it easier to handle. Children between the ages of five and ten thus often have a completely miniaturized dogsled outfit to play and experiment with while they are gaining experience in handling the dogs themselves. Mary Behdzi's six year old son Willy was actually allowed to travel with his own sled when his family moved from camp to camp during the winter. He stood behind the small sled while two nearly-grown pups pulled it directly behind his mother's team.

Having the use of their own sled and dogs is a matter of pride to young children, which is in turn reflected in their parents' pride for them. By the age of five or six, not only is children's play with dogs a close approximation of adult practice, but verbal behavior is also a close (if not perfect) imitation of what adults say and do. Children use the proper signals for "left" and "right," and they employ the same curse words and phrases (both in English and Athabascan) that their elders use in yelling at their dogs. People in the village or a camp encourage the children in their handling of dogteams, shouting to them as they ride by, and commenting to one another on both a child's ability, and on the strength and appearance of his dogs. Despite the high level of adult interest, however, there is little formal instruction given to children in the driving of dogsleds, and most of what they learn is gotten from direct experience or by observation around camps and while travelling.[3]

As children grow older, they take on increased responsibilities in regard to the care and use of dogs. Nine-year-old Daniel Yawileh (Fred and Thérèse's son) had the responsibility of supplying a good portion of his family's wood. He would harness up four of his father's dogs to a full-length sled, drive about a mile and a half to a good stand of timber, cut the wood, haul it back with the dogs, and then unharness them. He did this several times a week during the coldest part of the winter. Fourteen-year-old Suzanne Ratehne, who had two older and fully able brothers, was still expected to regularly drive dogs and bring in two or three loads of wood for her family every week. All young female adults were expected to be able to drive and handle a dogteam, and only the very young and old of either sex were exempted from this. Most of the women in the band between the ages of twenty and thirty-five cared for and periodically drove their own teams, and young men and women in their mid-teens were usually outfitted with a team, sled, and harness by their families. By their thirteenth or fourteenth year, most young people were fully contributing, economically productive members of their households, making dogsled travel an integral part of their everyday lives.

At the same time that young men and women get socialized to the care, handling, and use of dogs, the latter are, in turn, being domesticated to their tasks and roles by the children and young adolescents who train and raise them. By the age of six or seven months, a dog is strong enough to pull its own weight in a team of adult animals, and it is at this age that a pup will be harnessed up for the first time in a full team. While a dog has been prepared and partially trained for this eventuality by its experiences with children in the preceding months, this new role nevertheless marks an abrupt and radical transformation in its life. As in the education of a child, it receives almost no directed help or assistance from either driver or fellow dogs in learning its new tasks, and its adjustment can thus be a long, hazardous, and painful process. The affection and relative ease with which the dog has been treated are suddenly withdrawn and they are now replaced with new levels of discipline, authority, strenuous work, and dominance competition within the adult team.

The parallels to the socialization experiences of young children are striking and suggestive, for the relatively undisciplined, indulgent, and affection-laden early life of the child undergoes similar changes during an individual's fifth and sixth years. It is at this age that important tasks and responsibilities are first given to a child, including the hauling of wood and water, the feeding of dogs, and the time-consuming care of younger siblings. While parental shows of affection are by no means abruptly terminated, they are gradually reduced in frequency and warmth, slowly giving way to an increase in discipline, commands, and reprimands. Loss of parental attention may be aggravated by the birth of a younger sibling at this time, which also introduces factors of rivalry and dominance both for younger and older children. This constitutes a difficult period of adjustment for children, and the sharp discontinuities in this phase of socialization have been described and remarked upon in other Athabascan groups (cf. Honigmann, 1947, p.236, 1949, pp.306-315; Helm, 1961, 76-77; VanStone, 1965, pp.51, 57). This stage of life is marked by an undertone of rebellion and stubbornness, and the somewhat traumatic treatment that children experience in being "put in harness" resembles the difficulties faced by dogs in the corresponding phase of their own lives.

Adult responses to aggression among people and dogs extends the parallel still further. Mature, sober adults are never supposed to display hostility towards one another, and although dogs are not constrained by such cultural considerations, their owners are disturbed when canines also become aggressive. This is because dog fights frequently lead to the injury of at least one of the combatants, reducing the size of the working team, and making travelling that much more difficult. If such fights cannot be broken up swiftly — and this is a dangerous enterprise, since the peacemaker may get bitten in the process, just as drunken brawlers turn on neutral interlopers — a dog may be so severely hurt that it will have to be destroyed. The people say it is very difficult to control dogs "that have tasted blood in a fight." As Luke Bayjere explained,

they go on to tear one another to pieces and you can't stop them. Sometimes they rip open the neck or practically pull one another's guts out. Then there's nothing to do but get someone to shoot it.

In contrast to the distress which aggression among adult canines provokes, the people find amusement and enjoyment in the fighting, snapping, and barking of young pups. These animals are often set off against one another intentionally, in fact: people will take pups by the scruff of the neck, rub their heads in one another's faces, and set them to biting and wrestling with each other. Observers respond with laughter and shouts of encouragement, often re-engaging the pups repeatedly, even after the pups have lost interest or stopped fighting of their own accord.

The vicarious, aggressive pleasure that people experience with dogs in this way finds its parallel in the way that individuals react to the fighting of young boys. Youngsters who begin to quarrel and wrestle quickly attract an adult audience in the village, and bystanders respond with advice and amusement, encouraging first one fighter and then the other. As with pups, people comment on the strength and wiliness of the youngsters, showing their greatest approval for qualities of toughness and persistence, regardless of who the actual winner is. Young boys who are playing peacefully with one another may even be urged to fight by idle adults who enjoy watching them in combat. Older people thus manipulate both youngsters and pups to display emotional responses which they themselves are not permitted to indulge in: adults thereby enjoy vicarious affect and the stress-seeking of violence by recruiting the young of both species to perform as expressive actors for them. Both the canines and the children thus bear the burdens of other people's adult repression, just as they themselves will later undergo in their own adulthood, the stress of having to restrain the very aggressiveness which they have previously been encouraged to display.

There are thus a number of shared experiences in the domestication of children and dogs, and the parallels are further accentuated by the fact that socialization is itself a mutual and reciprocal process in which children and dogs educate each other for their ultimate confrontations with adults and adulthood. The upbringing of dogs can be viewed in its context, content and style as an extension of the education of children, just as children and their young dogs may be viewed collectively as constituting a single peer group. Their respective socialization processes are so intertwined and interrelated that one would be incomplete and inadequate with the other. Both children and dogs depend upon reciprocal feedback and information from one another in order to learn and complete their respective roles.[4]

Another factor which is also relevant to Hare socialization processes has been expressed in an argument made by William Laughlin, *viz.*, that a crucial element in developing effective hunters in a society is "the ethological training of children to be skilled observers of animal behavior, including (that of) other humans" (1968, p.304). He explains that:

Three indispensable parts of the hunting system are programmed into the child beginning early in life. These are the habits of observation, a systematic knowledge of animal behavior, and the interpretation and appropriate action for living with animals and for utilizing them for food and fabricational purposes . . . Appropriate behavior towards animals is prominently based upon familiarity with animal behavior and includes ways of living peacefully with animals, of maintaining a discourse with them, as well as the appropriate behaviors, the highly coordinated movements of the hunter proceeding toward a kill, and appropriate social behavior where other hunters are involved (1968, p.305).

One can suggest that, in the case of the Hare, childhood experience with dogs is an important first step in people's ethological training, being a type of programming which later pays off not only in their ability to handle dogs, but also in the hunter's capacity to understand, track, and relate to his prey. Here again, dogs would be the masters and teachers, people the pupils.

The way in which adults treat children bears additional resemblance to the upbringing and utilization of dogs. One basic distinction made in how children are reared hinges on the sex of the child, and the same criterion applies to the treatment of dogs. While all infants are ideally loved and indulged regardless of their sex, some perceptible differences in the treatment of boys and girls emerge at around the age of five or six. Males tend to be spoiled more and shown greater affection for a longer period of time than are females, and their introduction to responsibilities is often deferred for a year or two beyond the age at which such tasks begin for girls (cf. VanStone, 1965, pp.57-58; Honigmann, 1949, p.185). Furthermore, in the limited number of cases observed in the field, it appeared that, among other things, boys received somewhat better treatment than did girls in the quality and quantity of food and clothing given to the two sexes. Hurlbert (1962, p.39) recorded two cases among the Hare, occurring between 1956 and 1961, of female infants being neglected to the point where one child required hospitalization and the second one died.

These observations may indicate the persistence, in modified form, of some aboriginal attitudes towards selective infanticide and the relative desirability and economic worth of males and females, but the evidence at present is too scant to warrant any conclusions.[5] It is interesting to note, however, that there are, once again, some suggestive parallels between the treatment of children and the fate of dogs. Female pups are often killed at birth because they are potentially less valuable than males: they grow up to be smaller and weaker, and are thus less desirable as sled animals (cf. also Sue, 1964, pp.295-296). Bitches will occasionally be kept for breeding purposes, but according to informants their presence in a team, especially when they are in heat, is so disruptive, that they are of limited utility as draft animals. A taboo which is still adhered to by some of the more traditional families in the band forbids adult women to step over a dog harness lest the family's bitch have all female pups. In some respects, therefore, female canines and humans appear to be evaluated and treated in similar ways.

The correspondence between human and canine sex roles and attitudes are admittedly tenuous and incomplete, but they derive some indirect support from the strength of the other parallels we have illustrated. There are, in addition, some other facets of people's relationship with their animals which further reinforce the image of dogs as members and extensions of the social system. As they do with humans, people recognize distinctive identities and personalities among their dogs. This individuality is acknowledged and symbolized by extending to canines the human process of names and naming, and if

one of the owner's favorite dogs has recently died, the deceased dog's name may be given to a newborn one which resembles the former (see also Birket-Smith and deLaguna, 1938, p.57) (Sue, 1964, p.296).

Athabascan concepts of reincarnation (Slobodin, 1970; Sue, 1965, pp.12-13), which often involve naming a child after a recently deceased person whom it resembles or about whom the pregnant mother or the child has dreamed, thus apply to the canine as well as the human realm, underlining the bonds and continuities between the two species. Dogs are even included within human names themselves, for, in accordance with the Athabascan system of teknonymy, a childless adult, or one whose children are fully grown, may be referred to teknonymously by the name of his favorite or pet dog.[6]

Some people also stress the significance of what they regard as "kinship" bonds among the dogs. Several young men, for example, claim that they prefer to keep together sets of "brothers" in their teams because "they get along so well and work good together." They note with marked approval how, in a given dog fight, the canine brothers "stick together against the other dogs" and never turn on one another. In the words of Philip Ratehne, "that's the way brothers should be with one another." While these observations may not be totally accurate for the dogs in question, the model of social relations that they project is a clear reflection of how people themselves (i.e., siblings of the same sex) are ideally expected to behave towards one another (cf. Sue, 1964, p.277; Honigmann, 1949, p.126). People's perceptions and attitudes thus extend human kinship into the canine realm, incorporating the relations between dogs into familial and familiar patterns. Just as pups become the children's children (the child is father to the dog), man's best friend becomes his brother.

That dogs become members of the family through an extension of the corporate social bonds of the household is also evidenced by some deep-seated anxieties that people experience over the well-being of their animals. A lame or sick dog becomes a source of concern and worry for all family members, occupying their attention and efforts for many days. The members of a household or camp may spend hours discussing the conditions and treatment of their animals, and other people will often be consulted in the search for an effective cure. Special brush will be cut for the dog to rest on, its sleeping place and hair will be covered with ashes from the stove (which is "real Indian medicine" according to many of the people),[7] its sore limbs or paws will be rubbed with linament, and its diet will be varied and improved, including an increase in its portion of meat and the serving of a warm caribou or fish broth to it.

The health of their animals is a matter of concern to the people which goes beyond the economic value of the dogs. This deeper concern becomes especially evident when an animal becomes so sick or aged that it must be destroyed. People show an extreme reluctance to shoot their own dogs, and they will resort to numerous rationalizations, strategies and subterfuges in order to either postpone the inevitable or to induce someone else to perform the act for them. The dilemma becomes especially pronounced at the beginning of the summer period, for this is the only season of the year during which the dogs are relatively inactive, and the people do not care to feed any more non-working animals than they have to during the three-month interval. The anxiety over killing one's own dogs nevertheless persists. People may try to sell or give away dogs that they consider too old or too sick to be worth keeping for the following winter, but few are willing to take on new animals at this time of year. If this strategy fails, a person will usually try to get another individual to destroy the dog for him, but this is one of the few favors that people will often refuse to do, even for a close friend. As Peter Dehdele once explained.

Me, I just can't look at that dog and shoot it. It sure feels bad when you have to shoot a dog, especially when it's your own.

Statements like this, coming from people who hunt, trap, and even kill animals with their bare hands during the course of every year, clearly indicate an attitude towards dogs which places them in a category apart from other animals. The Hare share with other Athabascan Indians a deeply-felt set of traditional proscriptions on both the killing and eating of dogs, and they also surround their animals with a series of taboos, including a prohibition on allowing dogs to gnaw the bones or parts of certain animals lest the dog's owner incur bad luck in future hunting and trapping. It has been suggested by some scholars (e.g., Franklin, cited by Birket-Smith, 1930, pp.40, 106; Osgood, 1932, pp.82-83, 88) that the reverence, respect, and fear associated with canines in some Athabascan groups (e.g., the

Chipewyan, Satudene, and Dogrib) is related to the dog's role as one of the mythological ancestors of these people. Although all of the northern tribes do not share this specific belief, the basically supernatural attitude towards canines which can be derived from it is ubiquitous among them. If, indeed, the dog is reciprocally "father to the child" in the context of socialization, then perhaps there is more than meets the ear in the northern origin myths which give the Athabascans a canine forebear.[8]

As sub-human members of the human family, dogs thus provoke a pronounced ambivalence on the part of individuals who must dispose of them, and the problem of what to do with an animal may become a great source of stress. In their preoccupation with their dogs, the Hare alternately curse and commiserate with them. They complain of an animal's worthlessness and the trouble it has given them, and they then recall what a good worker it has been and how sick it must feel. The hostility and aggression which are usually displayed toward adult dogs (*infra*) are thus balanced with other "human" feelings at these moments. In the existential terms of Martin Buber (1968), dogs are neither an "It" nor a "Thou" to the people, they are beings of another order, perhaps somewhere in-between.

Due to the people's consequent ambivalence in the matter of unwanted dogs, an interval of several days or even weeks may elapse before action is finally taken on an animal. If the dog gets loose during this period, only half-hearted attempts will be made to catch it in the hope that some other person will eventually shoot it because of its troublesomeness. In some cases, rather than face up to the necessity of destroying their own animals, people have actually abandoned undesired dogs at their bush camps when returning to the community at the end of the spring.[9] Such an action was disapproved of by many of the villagers, however, who considered it harsh and cruel. Nevertheless, at this end point in the dog's life cycle, his fate again resembles one feature of man's treatment of his fellow man, recalling the current neglect — and aboriginal abandonment — of the infirm and aged by many northern groups.

There are a few remaining strategies which people employ to dispose of an unwanted animal. If the Royal Canadian Mounted Police are expected to visit the settlement soon, a dog may be intentionally turned loose so that the police, in fulfilling their responsibilities, will shoot it as a stray animal. A person may even offer to pay someone else to destroy the dog. This is a rare instance of direct payment being proffered for a service, for Colville Lake, being a kin-based community, is a village in which goods and services are generally exchanged on the basis of generosity and reciprocity rather than money. The offer of direct, cash payment underlines the exceptional and traumatic nature of the task, and it is only as a last resort that a man will kill his own animal.

The complex involvement of dogs in the people's emotional and social life also includes their role as outlets for aggressive and negative feelings. The burden of having to feed inactive dogs during the summer provokes resentment, and animals are often underfed and neglected during this period. During the winter, adult dogs are prime objects of verbal and physical abuse from their drivers, and although much of this treatment is the direct outcome of their misbehavior and disobedience, a good deal of what they experience is also the result of aggressive feelings which people have redirected from other areas of life. Men and women who set out from a bush camp in an angry mood are more prone to beat and yell at their dogs than a person who leaves in a tranquil frame of mind, and people who usually react mildly to the frustrations and stresses of dogsled travel tend to respond much more violently to the identical provocations when they have just left a tense social situation in the village or bush.

Drinking situations are culturally defined as permissible circumstances for emotional release, and drunken individuals occasionally direct a lot of their hostility towards their dogs, whether the animals are pulling in a team or are chained at a camp. There is considerable individual variation in the extent to which dogs are abused and mistreated under these and other circumstances, but most people indulge in such actions from time to time. The inclusion of dogs within the human, social and psychological order emerges dramatically in the development of the emotional "pecking order" which characterizes most bush camps. Patterns of emotional restraint among the Hare are thus made viable, in part, because the people can rechannel their aggression towards their dogs in a variety of ways. As noted above, children learn to relate to their animals in this manner at an early age, establishing an emotional precedent which will be followed throughout their adult lives.[10] Dogs are thus as crucial to these social processes as they are basic to economic tasks, and family life would be incomplete — and perhaps unbearable — without them.

Dogs, as social and psychological extensions of the human group, are important as an instrumental as well as an expressive medium for people. Consistent with the Indians' emphasis upon emotional containment, the Hare rely heavily upon physical mobility as a way of avoiding socially disruptive encounters. As we have seen, the people's annual cycle consists of a rhythmic alternation between periods of social dispersal and concentration, and emotional and psychological factors are as much a motivating force in this process as are ecological ones. Whenever possible, people will remove themselves from stressful situations rather than intensify or confront the source of tension. This mode of coping with stress may help to explain the great love of travel, and the dislike for, and inability to cope with, prolonged periods of sedentariness, which are traits manifested by many Athabascan peoples (Honigmann, 1949, pp.102, 156; Sue, 1964, p.421; Helm, 1961, pp.88, 111, 176; Welsh, 1970). Dogs, as a major means of movement, thus become an intrinsic and instrumental part of this process. Although neither the centrifugal nor the centripetal forces at work in Athabascan bands (Slobodin, 1960a) depend exclusively upon canines as a *modus operandi*, dogs certainly do facilitate these movements during much of every year.

3   DOGS AND THE PRESENTATION AND EXTENSION OF SELF

If dogs are social and emotional members of the Indian family, each with an identity, a name, and a set of roles and functions, then it is possible that dogs, like people, have public images. In addition, if dogs and people both derive and maintain their roles, in part, on the basis of their interaction with one another, then it is also possible that their public images are similarly a product of their mutual relationship. Furthermore, if dogs are physical, economic, social and psychological extensions of the human group, then it follows that their public image would be an extension of the individual and collective image of their extended family.

There are several respects in which family and individual identity among the Hare includes and incorporates the kind of public image projected by one's dogs.[11] Families and individuals are known, in part, by the quality, condition, and number of dogs that they keep, as well as by their ability to handle, train, and drive dogs. As noted previously, a minimal number of dogs is needed for adequate travel. People with very few dogs, just like people with very few kinsmen, are considered to be poor and hard-pressed (cf. Osgood 1932:54). When people tell hard-luck stories about others, or when they want to portray situations of distress and hardship that others have experienced, one of the first details seized upon is the number and condition of the victim's dogs: it will be related that they had few dogs to begin with, that some went lame, or that some got lost, sick, or injured in a fight. The drastic outcome is a portrait of a family who did not have enough animals to pull their sled effectively. As a consequence, they could not trap, or haul wood or caribou meat, and they may have had to walk all the way back to the settlement, pulling their own sled. There may then follow an account of the somewhat embarrassing act of their having to borrow dogs, or the economic hardship of their having to buy animals.

The ultimately destitute man is the one "who was so poor he had to sell all his dogs, his sled, and even his harness." Such a man's reputation and image suffer considerably, and most people become very *self*-conscious when the low number and poor condition of their dogs invites public comment and thinly-veiled mockery and derogation. It is noteworthy that in the many tales and pieces of folklore that were collected among the Hare, most of which dealt with aboriginal hardships and dangers confronting the people, none of the stories made the paucity or abundance of dogs a crucial element of the people's well-being during that period.

People are very aware of the movement of others by dogsled, and every trip into and out of the village receives at least perfunctory notice within the community. Large teams invite admiration and respect, and they may be the subject of comment for several days after their appearance. People will stand at the edge of the village, overlooking the large lake which borders the settlement, and they will be able to identify individuals and families at great distances simply by the size and appearance of their teams. People are very proud and self-conscious when setting off with a large number of animals, and from travelling with such persons on numerous occasions, I have seen how their enhanced self-image becomes evident in their comments, their bearing, their posturing, and their close attention to details of appearance. Since a large dogteam — one with nine or more animals — is often unwieldly, as well as being a strain on one's fish supply (and rarely an appreciable improvement in one's speed), the motive for travelling with so many animals clearly has more to do with self-image than with logistics.

The relationship between dogs and extended images of self also involves people's participation in cultural patterns of generosity, reciprocity, and economic interchange. At various times of the year, people find themselves in the position of either having to request or give fish and meat in order to feed, respectively, their own or someone else's dogs. Travellers who visit one's bush camp should be warmly received, and they and their dogs well fed. At the village, kinsmen and friends who, from either ill-fortune or inaction, are temporarily without fish, should similarly be assisted in feeding their animals.

Economic exchanges, involving the sale or trade of dogs, sleds, harnesses, and related pieces of equipment, also provide opportunities for the display of generosity, and young men sometimes give away good dogs to their girl friends in the hope of gaining their families' approval for marriage. The loan of dogs to a needy friend or kinsman is an especially praiseworthy act. In a community where the good man is the generous man, the unending series of goods and services which people supply and reciprocate with are central to a person's public and self-image. In a band whose life style revolves around dogs, one's responses to people's needs are often a response to those of their animals, and since the welfare of people and dogs are so inextricably bound up with one another, it is, in essence, often impossible and unnecessary to separate one source of action from the other. Among the Hare, as in our own society, anyone who is kind to children and dogs can't be all bad.

An even more direct presentation of one's self, as personal as your reputation for generosity but more expressive than the mere number of dogs that you possess, is the quality and appearance of your animals. A well-fed, good-looking team is an advertisement of one's concern, care, and industriousness. People are very attentive to the size, weight, coat, color, and over-all condition of dogs, and the collective image projected by a team is very much an extension of an individual's ego. Although the members of the band exercise little control over the breeding patterns of their animals, once a litter has been born they do attempt to weed out the weak and sickly pups, and several families made a concerted effort to raise only dogs of a certain color. They stated that they liked the appearance of a uniformly-colored team, and they traded and exchanged animals with other households just to get the kind of dogs that they wanted.

Public awareness and personal sensitivity to the appearance of dogs is reflected not only in conversations which center on the animals, but also in the content of some popular jokes and phrases which have had currency in the band. One family was notorious for the large number of scrawny, pathetic-looking dogs that it kept, and not only were this group's teams the object of invidious comparisons by other community members, but whenever a person encountered an underfed animal wandering around the village, the usual comment was: "Well, there goes another Yawileh dog looking for something to eat." Another family's dogs were so slow and out-of-condition that people used to joke about giving them "a three-hour headstart for a two-hour trip."

This concern with canine appearance and performance was

widespread both at Colville Lake and at the Hare community of Fort Good Hope. It became especially manifest when individuals were approaching the town or village with their team after having spent a long period in the bush. When there was only a mile or two left to the journey, a man would often stop his team so that his animals could rest for a while, and thus appear "fresh and strong" upon entering the community. People took advantage of this stop to tidy up the appearance of their sleds by readjusting and retying the load, and some men, who had painted the front and backboard of their toboggans, would wipe these areas clean of snow and mud so that they would show up better. A few men had fancy dog "blankets," i.e., specially hand-embroidered collars and harnesses, sometimes fixed with pom-poms and bells, and these would be put on the dogs in place of their regular trail harnesses at this time. Finally, before starting off again, a person might take off his everyday parka and mukluks that had been worn in the bush, and replace them with elegant, flower-embroidered garments reserved just for occasions like this. When a person enters a community, then, he does it not only in the company of his dogs, but — visually and aesthetically — in concert and in costume with them as well.

The unitary image projected by driver, sled, and dogs is not merely a static pose, it is also an image created by performance. The ability to train, drive, and handle animals well are prestigeful skills intrinsic to the social psychology of people's relationship with their dogs. Among the highest compliments that a man or woman can earn is to be considered a good hunter and "good with dogs." Capable children can earn such reputations by the time they reach their pre-adolescent years, and one of the most desirable qualities in a prospective husband or wife is that person's renown as a "good bush man" or "good bush woman." Young adult men frequently race their teams against one another, either in formally arranged competitions or, less directly, by comparing their travel times over standard bush routes. Status and respect go not only to the fastest but also the toughest man-and-dog-team. People take pride not merely in the speed of their animals, but the colder the weather, the longer the trip, the rougher the trail, and the fewer the number of stops and rests taken during the journey, all attest to the strength and toughness of driver and dogs. Travelling is thus a form of stress-seeking which offers rewards of pride as well as privacy.

These are not the only facts which receive publicity and affect a person's image, however, for dogs are potentially a source of embarrassment as well as prestige. The breaking-in of new animals into a team, and the toughening-up of dogs after a long summer of inactivity, provide situations in which a person's patience and abilities are put to an acid test. The recalcitrance, rawness, and inexperience of dogs at such times make it difficult to control a team, and a person's efforts and level of success in handling his animals are publicly displayed when he enters and leaves the village. Even a well-seasoned team can give a driver trouble, and it occasionally happens that a man or woman is thrown from the back of a sled by a balky or irritable group of dogs who then proceed to run away. When such an event is witnessed by other villagers, the driver's self-esteem suffers a sharp, though temporary, decline. The chagrin experienced by an individual at such times is manifested in the severe beatings usually administered to dogs following such an incident.

The best insurance against the occurrence of such incidents, and a key element in the successful presentation of self by means of one's dogs, lies in the quality and ability of one's lead dog. By late adolescence, most people have become experts in the area of canine psychology and behavior, and an individual can judge the worth of a dog, and pick out the hard workers and the potentially good leader. Qualities of strength, dominance, intelligence, sensitivity, and tractability are what make for a good lead animal, but these traits must first be recognized and then developed if an animal's potential is to be realized. Good lead dogs make for good teams, as the people say. They are objects of intense pride, and they may acquire village-wide reputations for their outstanding abilities. Their drivers, who put so much of themselves into the training of these animals, share in the prestige and become part of the collective image, for the owner's name is always linked to that of the dog when the latter is being discussed.

Some of the most frequently and excitedly told stories in the band center on the exploits which people have had with their animals. These tales usually relate dangerous adventures in which a person's dogs have been instrumental in avoiding tragedy and disaster. Several men tell stories about getting lost in a severe winter storm while crossing a large, frozen lake, and having to turn to their lead dog to rediscover the trail and guide them to shelter in the forest. While Indians share with Eskimos a high degree of environmental and spatial sensitivity, in both groups, as Carpenter points out for the Eskimo,

a good lead dog is apparently indoctrinated with some of this knowledge, or at least possessed of a remarkable ability of spatial orientation (1959).

A number of other men at Colville Lake have come within a few feet of possible death, only to be saved by their animals. Luke Bayjere, whose story is similar to those related by others, was travelling across a frozen lake on a windy, winter night. The swirling snows and lack of moonlight made for poor visibility, and he could barely make out his lead dog running some thirty feet ahead of him. Suddenly his dogs stopped, and he yelled at them to continue. When they failed to respond to a second and third command, Luke angrily grabbed his whip and ran up to where his lead dog stood. He raised the whip over his head, and was just about to bring it down on the animal's back, when he saw the huge, wide opening in the lake ice which had brought his team to a halt. The gaping hole lay some ten feet in front of his lead dog, and the animal had stopped just in time to prevent the team, the sled, and the driver all from plunging into the icy water.

Stories such as this illustrate an added dimension to the role of dogs in Hare culture. These animals are not simply economic, social, and psychological extensions of individuals and families, they are also, in McLuhan's (1966) terms, sensory extensions of the human central nervous system. Dogs can smell, hear, see, and feel under conditions where the corresponding human senses are inadequate to the situation. In some cases, canine sensory acuity is clearly superior to that of humans: dogs can smell or feel out a trail, and can sense the proximity of caribou and hear the approach of other dogteams much more rapidly and accurately than can their drivers. At other times, dogs are simply in a better physical position to acquire sensory data than are the people whom they serve: a dogteam is linear in form, and lead dogs are literally ten to thirteen yards ahead of their drivers. Their sensory apparatus spatially extends the human eye, ear, and nose, just as their legs and paws are extensions of the human foot.

It is especially significant that in a hunting style of life, such as the one led by the Hare, dogs play only a marginal role in the actual stalking and killing of game. This may have some important implications for interpreting the aboriginal significance of dogs in Athabascan cultures. Ecological factors and the type of game being hunted are key variables which have to be considered here. For example, while the men in southerly Hare bands, such as the ones at Fort Good Hope, occasionally employ dogs to chase moose, the people of Colville Lake, for whom caribou supersede moose as the major meat source, do not utilize dogs in this way. While dogs are more sensitive to the proximity of game than people are, they become extremely noisy and difficult to control when they come within sight, for example, of a herd of caribou. Their loud barking alerts the animals, and they generally scare the game away before a hunter can get close enough to get off a shot. When a herd of caribou inadvertently crosses a lake and approaches a bush camp, the greatest difficulty that the people have is to keep their dogs quiet enough so that a hunter can successfully stalk the animals without their being alarmed. Men who set off on a hunting trip by dogsled usually tie their teams up in the woods once they have reached an area where caribou signs are good, and they then proceed on snowshoes so that the noise and excitability of their dogs will not ruin their chances of a kill.

One implication of the way in which the Colville Lake Hare use and refrain from using their animals, then, is that dogs are good sensors but bad hunters. The people do not even utilize dogs to run down wounded game: if two caribou out of a herd of ten are shot, a hunter wants to get at the remaining eight animals, and a bunch of loose dogs may only serve to scare them off. The wounded caribou can always be recovered later by following their spoor, and, if they are initially left unpursued, they will travel a shorter distance than they would if immediately followed. During the interval they get progressively weaker and stiffer as they rest, making their ultimate capture easier (cf. Carpenter, 1961, pp.148-149).

On the other hand, the fact that people do appreciate and value the sensory capacities of their animals is evident from the stories related above. By extending human senses, dogs enhance human survival. With the exception of the sense of taste, the whole repertoire of human sensory abilities is amplified, intensified, and spatially magnified by man's special relationship with his domestic animals. If they can be kept quiet and at a safe distance, dogs can also serve to locate and point out game to hunters. The alert traveller is always aware of the direction in which his dogs' eyes, ears, and noses are pointed, for a sudden shift in their orientation often indicates the presence of other animals nearby. At a bush camp, dogs will suddenly stand up when they sense dogteams or caribou approaching, and here again the direction of their sensory organs points to the stimulus for their response. In the words of one man, the ears of the people's dogs constitute their "personal radar" and "warning system."[12] As in our own culture, then, the Hare enjoy the varied sensory services of "pointers," "watch dogs" and "seeing-eye dogs" who "see" with several senses.

4 DISCUSSION AND CONCLUSION

There is the possibility that if dogs can warn the people of the approach of game and kinsmen, then aboriginally they could have also warned people of the approach of enemies. On the other hand, by their noisy reactions, they could just as easily have tipped off the enemies to the presence of the people themselves. Since the Hare often made their traditional summer camps in isolated locations, their emphasis upon hiding from enemies during this season of warfare and raiding would indicate a strategy of inaccessibility and quietude which noisy dogs could have jeopardized. The value of dogs for either hunting or defense among the Hare is thus ambiguous and inconclusive, and the animals would appear to be, at best, a mixed blessing in both regards. In the nineteenth century, Richardson and Wentzel (cited by Sue, 1964, pp.179-180) reported that the Hare used small dogs to run down moose on the hardened, crusty spring snow, but no other mention of the Hare's use of dogs in connection with hunting is made in the post-contact literature. Their possible utility for taking caribou and other game does not materialize as a cultural technique. Currently, the use of dogs for direct stalking, tracking or chasing of either small or large game is rarely exploited in the Colville area. A more exhaustive analysis and pursuit of folklore and post-contact documents may ultimately help to resolve these historical issues, but at present they remain unclear. The extent to which the current utilization of dogs by the Hare reflects the aboriginal (and modern) significance of these animals among other Athabascan groups is also an open question, but this is a problem to which I think we can now attempt at least a partial answer.

If the Hare and certain other Athabascan groups did make only limited use of their dogs in the areas of hunting and defense, then observations which have been made on other hunting societies where dogs are also present, would indicate that the northwestern Indians are not alone in these respects. M. J. Meggitt, for example, after reviewing the literature on Australian Aboriginal use of tame dingoes, offered the following conclusion:

The available evidence, limited and uneven as it is, suggests that over wide areas of Australia the tame dingo was by no means an effective hunting dog and that it contributed relatively little to the Aborigines' larder. It seems that only in ecologically specialized regions where particular kinds of game were abundant (as in the tropical rain forest) was the dingo a significant economic adjunct to the family hunting unit (1965, p.24).

Edmund Carpenter has made observations that are even "closer to home" for the consideration of the Athabascans:

Canadian Indians, in my experience, prefer not to hunt with dogs. Could it be that their attitudes stem from an ancient hunting tradition?

We know that dogs were fairly common in many prehistoric camps in the Northeast, yet we know little of their role. Historic records more frequently refer to them as a source of food, or in connection with ceremonies, than as aides in hunting, and it may be that their hunting duties were slight.

Hunting with a bow is quiet work. The hunter must get in close to the game and here a dog could prove more troublesome than helpful. The Eskimo use dogs to locate seal-holes in the ice; Australian and Kalahari Bushmen dogs harass and keep at bay large game; Iban dogs tree game in the Borneo rain-forest. In the woodlands of the Northeast, however, where deer are the principal game, dogs can prove far less helpful.

One advantage the bow has over the rifle is silence. If the first arrow misses, the animal may fail to bolt and simply stand there, thus offering the bowman a second chance. A dog, however, would probably set the animal to flight.

Similarly, a wounded animal, if not pursued by dogs, often flees but a short distance, rests and stiffens up. Modern Indian hunters know this and generally, after wounding a deer, instead of racing after it, brew tea. Then they track down the animal which probably is but a short distance away (1961, pp.148-149).

I do not mean to imply by the above quotations that dogs are everywhere of marginal utility to hunters, for as Meggitt, Carpenter, and many others have noted, certain groups do make considerable use of these animals in taking game. In the North, the Eskimo employed dogs for hunting polar bear, seal, walrus, and musk-oxen, and the Tanaina used well-trained canines for pursuing or scenting several different kinds of animals, including porcupine, bear, caribou, sheep, and beaver. Dogs were also commonly used for hunting among the Great Bear Lake Indians, and the Kutchin in the Yukon and Alaska employed them to run down moose and caribou on the hard spring snow (or "crust"), as well as to chase wounded game. The Upper Tanana similarly used dogs for pursuing moose and bear, as well as for treeing lynx and wolverine. Elsewhere, the Tahltan raised a special breed of small dogs for driving bears out of their dens, and the Eyak of coastal Alaska employed canines to chase mountain goats, and also to scent out bear and porcupine. Other Northern Athabascan groups among whom the use of dogs for hunting is reported include the Han, Ahtena, Koyukon, Nahane and Slave.[13]

In contrast to the above cases, the Ingalik of interior Alaska only began to utilize dogs for pursuing game in historic times, and, with the exception of Richardson's account (1851ii, pp.26, 30), the Chipewyans to the east of the Mackenzie are generally reported not to have used dogs for hunting moose or any other game. To the south and west, the Kaska, while utilizing dogs to take porcupine, rarely employed them for pursuing moose, and their hunting dogs were actually purchased from the Tahltan. Furthermore, while some of the Tanaina in Alaska did use dogs for chasing caribou, other bands in the area captured them in surrounds without the aid of dogs, much like other Athabascan groups did.[14]

It should be evident from the foregoing that tribal and ecological variations thus have to be taken into account in order to evaluate the importance of dogs in specific Athabascan cultures. Domesticated canines play a large role in the hunting techniques of some groups, while in others their significance is minimal, marginal, or non-existent. Even in regions where their role is evident, the specific animals that dogs are used to pursue, and the type of pursuit for which they are employed, also show variation from area to area. To cite just one non-northern instance of this kind of phenomenon, Meggitt makes an observation for Australia that may be indicative of comparable situations in many parts of the world:

. . . there may have been significant differences among tribes or from region to region in the efficiency of the training and use of dingoes, or in the kinds, number and habits of the animals available for hunting (1965, p.18).

The Athabascan evidence would seem to bear out, in a general way, a similar observation made by Harold Driver in his discussion of the use of dogs for hunting in North America:

In general, it appears that dogs were of limited utility for large animals running in herds, which were easy for man to locate, but were of greater utility in hunting animals which were solitary or lived in small social groups and were, therefore, more difficult to find (1961, p.60).

This argument is especially pertinent for the Hare because of the contrasting dependence of different regional bands upon either migratory caribou herds, which are found mainly in the northeast, or more sedentary and solitary moose, which are concentrated primarily in the south and west. The argument concerning dogs and the type of game to be hunted is relevant historically as well as ecologically, because, in Richardson's (1851ii, p.26) estimation, the Hare were not successful in hunting moose, and according to modern informants,

. . . in the old days, there were mainly caribou in the area, and the moose were concentrated in the Rockies (Sue, 1964, p.175).

It was only recently (i.e., in the mid-nineteenth century), that "the moose started to come downhill and move all over the Fort Good Hope Game Area" (*idem*). A similar northward movement of moose has also occurred in parts of Chipewyan territory, as well as in other regions of the sub-Arctic (cf. McKennan, 1965, p.18; Rogers, 1969a, pp.28-29; Peterson, 1955, pp.36-45). There is, in fact, convincing evidence for the absence of moose as part of the aboriginal economy of specific Chipewyan bands, whose subsistence was focused mainly upon the taking of caribou (cf. the name "Caribou-Eaters"). In the case of certain northern Hare and Chipewyan groups, therefore, their traditionally greater dependence upon caribou herds rather than solitary moose as a major food source might have been a key factor in the limited role of dogs in their respective hunting techniques.

A major problem that we face in trying to determine the total cultural significance of dogs for the whole northern Athabascan area is that our historical sources are often silent or contradictory on certain aspects of the matter, while our contemporary material frequently neglects the wider dimensions of the issue. Comparisons and generalizations are thus difficult to come by. I have tried to show in this section that the modern role of dogs in Athabascan culture, especially in terms of their impact as extensions of man's senses, emotionality, and social structure, can provide a key to what the aboriginal importance of the animals may have been. The basic economic functions that we usually associate with dogs, particularly traction and hunting, would appear to be primarily either of recent vintage (traction) or of debatable or only regional validity (hunting). Perhaps there is an incompatibility between the use of dogs for traction and their employment as serious hunting aides. It may be that animals which have been trained and used in one capacity may be of limited utility in the other. If aboriginal Athabascans could not support enough dogs to make them significant as draft animals, it may have been more worthwhile for them to train the limited number of canines as silent stalkers and game chasers. This aspect of canine culture would perhaps have been superseded in some areas by the introduction of modern dogsled travel, with its focus upon different patterns of canine training and utilization.

As primary sources of food and clothing, domestic canines were probably resorted to only in extreme situations in the North, especially considering the strong and pervasive taboos on killing and eating dogs which continue to exist among almost all the Athabascans.[15] Their potential significance for packing and dragging, while undeniable, was probably limited by the small number of animals that the people were able to maintain in the past. That dogs may have also been used as a source of direct, bodily warmth during night-time sleep is also a possibility, but one for which I can find no substantial proof. It seems more likely that dogs, as extensions of man's senses, were more valuable as receptors, integrators, and conveyors of information for many groups rather than as executors of economically important tasks. Furthermore, by giving children and adults experience in relating to a non-human species, the presence of domesticated canines may have been an important aspect of sensitizing hunters to the ethological patterns of animals in general and their prey in particular, thereby making people more effective stalkers. The fact that some Athabascan groups aboriginally maintained various other types of animals as "pets" (including bear cubs, foxes, rabbits, wolf pups, minks, and several species of birds) may indicate a similar extension of human social bonds, which provided a set of relationships that indirectly allowed people to take advantage of these other species as teaching aides in the area of animal behavior. [16]

The process of extension, in the contemporary case of the Hare and their dogs, is ultimately an act of mutual incorporation and learning. People, in a sense, identify with and *become* their dogs while their dogs become members of society. Artists, photographers, and psychotherapists in Western cultures have poignantly (and therapeutically) shown how much people and their pet animals actually come to physically, psychologically, and behaviorally resemble one another over time (Szasz, 1969), and the same may be true within the cultural aesthetic and self-image of the Hare. People not only "become what they behold," as Carpenter (1970) and McLuhan (1966) have shown, but they are also domesticated by their domesticated animals. In such cultural traditions, projection, displacement, dominance, aggression, identification, nurturance, succorance, incorporation and other psychologically expressive processes accompany, or supersede, the more utilitarian aspects of dog ownership (cf. the psychoanalytic and experimental research on man-dog relationships summarized in Fox, 1965, pp.116-125). When thus viewed as "domesticated" members and extensions of the human social system, the dog's cultural significance takes on the added dimension of sociability and companionship. The social and psychological integration of the Athabascan band would then have to be viewed from this wider perspective: dogs serve as sources of emotional interest and anxiety, as well as outlets for affective displays of both a positive and a negative nature.

It is a short step, in the case of the Hare, from identifying people *by* their teams to identifying people *with* them. If one can do this for others, one can also do it for one's self, and people's animals thus become an inherent part of their identity. Dogs are thus a social, sensory and psychological, as well as an economic resource, and they are a self-reproducing resource at that. If one considers the various ways in which dogs are extensions of Hare social groups, then one must expand one's concept and definition of the band. At Colville Lake, for example, the band, in a corporate social, psychological, and economic sense, is no longer composed of just seventy-five people, but rather it consists of some 300 social beings, 224 of whom happen to be dogs.

I do not wish to stand Alexander Pope's dictum on its head (or tail) by suggesting that the proper study of mankind is the dog, but I think we can learn a great deal about certain groups of human beings by observing how they relate to domesticated canines. In an excellent essay on the role and position of dogs in Polynesian culture, Katherine Luomala (1960) has pointed out many of the same social and psychological factors which have been emphasized here, including processes of mutual identification and domestication between canines and humans. Similar insights have emerged from the work of Szasz (1969), Scott (1963), Fox (1965) and other scholars, who have looked at the social psychology of pet-keeping in Western societies. Evans-Pritchard's classic study of the Nuer (1940) long ago demonstrated how central domesticated cattle can be in the thoughts and social relations of pastoralists, and so by now we should be sensitive to the possibility of analogous situations in societies with different economies and ecologies.

My own observations on the Hare, while directed to just such an analysis, have two obvious limits to them. First, by arguing from the present to the past, there is the problem of their validity as historical arguments. Hopefully, future work in archaeology and ethnographic reconstruction will enable us to verify or reformulate our ideas on this and related problems. Secondly, my arguments are limited by the fact that they are derived primarily from the study of one community — a representative and crucial community, I would argue, but a single case nevertheless. Thus, it is difficult to judge the degree to which contemporary and historical statements about the Hare are applicable to other Athabascan groups. While I have tried to check my analysis by reference to published material on other northern peoples, the paucity of data on this problem makes comparison a tenuous proposition.[17] There has evidently been a great deal of regional diversity in the training, breeding, significance and use of dogs in the North, and this variety has undoubtedly had its social and psychological concomitants. Regional differences in modern trapping patterns and techniques may also be reflected in these ways (cf. VanStone, 1963; Leacock, 1954). The Hare indicate how complex and subtle man's relationship with his dogs can be, and if the ideas presented in this section have a wider applicability, then there are some important areas of Athabascan culture which demand a searching reappraisal.

PART 6

Conclusions

1 "THE EXALTED MELANCHOLY
OF OUR FATE"

The paradoxes of existence are often its deepest source of pain and revelation. Living with ambiguity can be dynamic and enriching as well as stressful if one can appreciate duality and cope with simultaneity. To the people of Colville Lake, existence is ambiguous in a multitude of ways, and we have seen this in their involvement with their environment, their kinsmen, their identity, their dogs, and their white neighbors. Each of these relationships shares in a basic paradox, namely, that the people are ambivalent about the very sources of their survival and being. The forest is variously bountiful or empty. Whites provide goods and services, but are also authoritarian and exploitative. Your own kinsmen are sometimes generous, and other times niggardly. Parents are warm and permissive in one's youth, but then become distant and more demanding as one grows older. Dogs are economically essential and emotionally valuable, but they are also vicious and frustrating. And to be an Indian is a source of pride, but when it is also the touchstone for discrimination, it then becomes a cause for self-doubt.

If, as Martin Buber (1958, p.11) declares, "all real living is meeting," then the case of Colville Lake reminds us that it is separation which makes relation possible. It is only by periodically leaving the people and the contexts of ambiguity that reunion with them becomes feasible and desirable. And it is only when we realize this dialectical rhythm in the existence of the community at Colville Lake that the villagers' mobility in time and space, and the stresses which they experience and seek, become intelligible and meaningful. Perhaps it is in this way that the people encounter what Buber (1958, p.16) has called "the exalted melancholy of our fate," the paradox "that every *Thou* in our world must become an *It*."

Among the people, as their relations with the trader and priest

194

revealed, stress could be as much a part of unity and identity as it was of disunity and depersonalization. The feud — like dogs and inanimate objects — was a means for redirecting energies and aggressions from within the group to outside sources. Trying to manipulate the whites was a clear instance of stress-seeking by the members of the band, and their participation in the conflict helped to define them as a people, and clarify their distinctiveness.[1] Identity, however, was not a matter of simple ethnicity for them, even though their relations with the whites often defined them in just these terms. Rather, there was a great deal more subtlety and substance involved in their Indianness than could be conveyed by skin color, language, and segregation. The people's involvement with their *sagot'ine* and their land, their sense of continuity with tradition, their celebration of self-sufficiency, and their self-image of freedom — these were all at the core of how they saw themselves.

Encountering the people again in 1971, several years after my first visit, I was reminded of how complex and vulnerable their lives could be. My wife and I flew into the village from Norman Wells, landing on a small air-strip which had been completed at the community shortly after my departure in 1968. We were flown in by the priest, who had recently obtained a small, single-engine plane. At Norman Wells, where he met us, the stark airport had seemed absorbed by the helicopters, cargo planes and ubiquitous crewmen of the oil and mineral companies, who were staging the most concerted invasion that the North had ever seen. As we flew the 124 miles to the village, the priest pointed out the naked seismic lines and abandoned camps of the geologists, who had spent the last few summers stripping and probing the land near the settlement with their unique economy of style. For all the miles of water-soaked, sunburnt, and uninhabited taiga we had just crossed, that landing strip, those scars on the land, and our own aircraft, suddenly made Colville seem less cut off and more exposed to the outside world than ever before.

In several ways, the "outside" had penetrated the community in some very visible forms during those three years. André Yawileh's family, and Yašeh and his grandmother Annie, were now living in new log cabins, the first buildings ever to be erected in the village as part of a government housing program. Luke Bayjere had become the first native person in the settlement to purchase a snowmobile, and several people who had spent their whole lives cutting wood with an axe, were now the owners of chain-saws. A number of households had also supplemented their transistor radios with battery-operated record players and cassette tape-recorders. Even the size, if not the number, of outboard motors had increased, for many of the young men were now visiting their fish nets with the aid of *klason* that were several horsepower stronger than the ones they had been using before.

The people of the village had also built their own boat dock at the foot of the embankment behind Wilfred Ratehne's house. There was even a new body of water just to the southeast of the settlement: the stream which drained the swamp behind the community had been dammed up by the game officer from Good Hope, who had planned to stock this artificially-created lake with muskrats. He had failed to trap any of them alive on his first few attempts, however, and since — characteristically enough for the government — he was transferred to another region before any muskrats could be introduced, the people now had a new lake without anything to harvest from it.

The changes which had occurred among the people themselves were more noteworthy, if less immediately visible, in some cases. There had been a number of marriages, births, and deaths which had altered the composition and life of the band. Old Joseph Tehgu had died at the age of ninety-one, breaking the strongest and most substantial link that the people had had with their folklore and oral history. A remarkably dramatic and energetic raconteur, Joseph had had no equal among his contemporaries for either knowledge or style, and two and a half years after his death, no one had replaced him as a source or a focus for narrative culture.

Marriage had also removed some people from the village. Suzanne Ratehne and her brother Adam had both found spouses from other communities, and Suzanne was now living in Fort Good Hope with her husband's family. Adam, after having tried unsuccessfully for several years to marry first Mary Behdzi and then Monique Yawileh, had finally gone all the way to Fort Franklin on Great Bear Lake to find a wife. He and his bride had alternated residences between Colville and Franklin for the last few years, and they were now back at the settlement to spend the summer months with his kinsmen.

Mary Behdzi had also finally married, having overcome her mother's opposition with a good measure of help from community opinion and public pressure. Unlike Suzanne and Adam, however, she had been able to marry within the village itself, her husband being Maurice Bayjere's eldest son Alfred. Many of the people had sympathized with Mary in her attempts to realize two previous proposals of marriage, but it was only in this third and most recent instance that she had felt confident enough to contravene her parents' wishes. Being an adult, as the priest had explained to her, she could marry without parental consent, and so torn between her personal wishes and her sense of filial respect — but bolstered by the consensus of the band — Mary had gone ahead with her decision.

Her father Yen and his wife Helen had nevertheless felt so strongly about the matter that, as a public but silent protest, they pulled out of the community on the eve of their daughter's marriage, and spent the next few days at a fish camp some ten miles away. Their symbolic mobility behind them, however, Yen and Helen eventually returned to the settlement, and gradually became reconciled to both Mary and her marriage. No small factor in the rapprochement was their close bond with Mary's son Willy, who, born out-of-wedlock to her six years previously, was himself very attached to his grandparents. During the next two years, Alfred and Mary had two more children, and these infants further helped to cement their ties to Yen and Helen. The elder Behdzis also wanted the help and company of the younger couple during their winter stays in the bush, something which could only be realized by this resolution of their differences.

The Behdzi's prolonged opposition to Mary's marriage, and their ultimate readjustment to it, highlighted one of the most stressful but infrequently discussed aspects of life among the people. At stake here — as well as in other cases of resistance to the marriage of sons and daughters — was not simply the issue of parental authority, but the more pressing dilemmas of security and aging. As people like Yen and Helen grow old, the vigor and resourcefulness which have earned them their survival and reputation over the years suffer a decline. Now, with age, they must look more and more to their adult children to aid and support them, a form of dependence which induces many parents to try to control their children's lives so as to be assured of their assistance. Marriage, which involves young adults in a wider range of family and kinship obligations, is often seen by parents as a threat to their influence over their children.

Even in their early years, youngsters are told, only half-jokingly by their parents, that when they grow up, they should remember how well their mother and father treated them, and that they should reciprocate by caring for their parents in their old age. A child will be given a piece of candy by his father and laughingly admonished to "remember how good I was to you when I'm an old man." Reflecting this indoctrination, adolescents often express their commitment "to take care of their parents when they are old, and not," as Philip Ratehne once said, "ignore them like other people do." To reinforce these feelings, people also try to publicize, both to their offspring and to others, how good and generous they are to their children, thereby proving their worthiness as parents, and hence their right to receive respect and good treatment from their progeny in later years. Food, clothing, and affection are publicly bestowed, and since young children roam the village freely — and are literally raised and socialized by the entire community — people can advertise their care and concern by their treatment of an entire generation, and not just of their own offspring.

The relationship between children and adults, by affecting the latter's public image, thereby influences their fate as elders. Despite attempts by older people to ingrain a sense of obligation in their children, however, the same adolescents who profess commitment are often the very people who later turn from their parents in proclaiming their own freedom. Three years after Philip had pledged his filial concern, his parents were actively blocking his intended marriage to a girl from Good Hope, and now, at the age of nineteen, he was talking about

leaving them, because all they care about is themselves. I'll go to town if I want and marry Dora, and when I bring her back here I'll build my own house. I'll show then that I don't need them and that they can't boss me.

The ambivalence surrounding the obligations at issue here draws its force from the people's emphasis on self-sufficiency and strength. In a culture where energy, resourcefulness and competence are highly regarded attributes, growing old is a stressful experience, mitigated only by the support that one can count on from others. The "old-age pensions" which are now given by the Canadian government make the elderly an important economic asset to a household, but people who are not productive in a direct physical or subsistence sense are more often tolerated than respected. The aged no longer face the abandonment which would have been their fate in aboriginal times, but the poor food, tattered clothing, and general neglect which is meted out to most of them makes their later years an anxious experience. People in the process of growing old, aware of how they often treated their own parents, and reminded of this by the state of the village's contemporary elders, react possessively to the possible loss of their children's presence. In their concern for their own security, they thus draw the next generation into the circle of their own stresses.

While some people in the settlement were growing old, others were growing up. The community contingent of infants and youngsters, commanding — as always — the attention and center of the village, was larger than before. Besides Mary's two children, Fred Yawileh's wife Therese had given birth once in each of the last three years, and Judy Alahfi had also had a little girl, purportedly fathered by a white government official who had spent several months in the village one winter writing a dictionary. The youthfulness of the band, over fifty percent of whose members were under thirty years of age when I had last visited, was thus being maintained. The pace of maturation was also a steady one. The young children whom I had known three years ago as expressive, uninhibited and aggressive individuals, free with both their laughter and their anger, were now shyer, more reserved, and emotionally less demonstrative as they entered adolescence. And it was their younger siblings, whom they now often had to care for, who exhibited the openness which had once been theirs.

A number of the children had also been to school for the first time, which had opened up both new opportunities and some old stresses for them and their parents. Adults at Colville have always been ambivalent about the value of education for their children because of the nature and content of schooling in the North. Because the community is too small to warrant its own facility, youngsters have had to go to the large residential schools in the Mackenzie delta, most recently the one at Inuvik. This has involved a lengthy, ten-month separation for them and their parents during each year of schooling, which compounds the anxiety of having to face a new life style in a strange environment. The barracks-like quality of the hostels in Inuvik, their lack of privacy — which exceeds even that of the people's own houses and tents — the uncustomary discipline and corporal punishment administered by school officials and the nuns who supervise the residence halls, and the compulsory and sudden switch from a monolingual to a bilingual existence, are among the most commonly lamented features which the people cite.

While on the one hand parents recognize the value of their children receiving some education, they regret the circumstances under which this must occur. The last week in August, just before the plane comes to the village to take the school children away, is consequently a trying one for many of the people. Parents must sign a release form if they want their youngsters to go, for without their signatures, no child can be compelled to attend school and leave the settlement. Parents are dealing here not only with their own ambivalence, but they are also confronted by the demands and pleas of their children, some of whom vehemently oppose a return to the scene of their former distress. In many cases adults yield to the wishes of their children, and I have seen parents who have signed the release forms several days previously, change their minds on the morning of the plane's arrival, and keep their children home for the year.

The ambiguous nature of schooling also derives from the content of the children's education. Almost all the people want to see their youngsters learn some English, attain a degree of literacy, and achieve some competence in dealing with whites. Beyond this, however, the value of schooling is debatable, and adults question the relevance of a protracted education. They feel, essentially, that a curriculum taken from the urbanized schools of the southern Canadian provinces bears little usefulness for the life of small Arctic communities.[2] They know from experience that education rarely prepares their children for secure, wage labor positions, most of which inevitably go to the better trained whites who are not only given job preference, but who are often especially recruited from the "outside."[3] A child who has had several years of schooling, therefore, cannot easily enter the "white" job market, which has a limited number of openings to begin with, and which has expanded very little over the years in proportion to a burgeoning native population. Most of the people feel that much of their children's future still lies in living off the land, and, as they argue, this requires the skills provided by experience rather than schooling. In Peter Dehdele's words,

Someone who's been to school so long can't even take care of himself in the bush, maybe he's never even lived one winter there. But that same guy can't even get a white man's job either. So him he's good for nothing. Too much school is no good. It's like those kids at Good Hope — they're spoiled and soft for the bush, and they can't do anything else. They just hang around and take rations from the government.

The people, then, solve the dilemma of education by using the schools in moderation. Children are most often sent away for two or three winters — not necessarily in succession — and are then kept home so that they can experience the rigors and training of the bush. They can thus deal with the "white" world when they have to, and can cope with survival and the forest as they must. The people have never tried to have a school built at Colville itself, for many of them are aware of what such a step has meant for other communities, including Good Hope (cf. Sue, 1964; Hurlbert, 1962; Van Stone, 1965; Welsh, 1970). Whereas the people at settlements without schools can remain mobile during the year and live off the land, native populations at other forts become more sedentary since parents stay in town to look after and be with their children. Even the construction of local hostels, or the placement of school children in other native homes, has not reversed this trend towards sedentariness and dependency, and it has usually spelled the end of a bush way of life for the people affected. The families of Colville, however, by keeping schooling at both a distance and a minimum, have maintained their ability to adapt to the modern culture of the North without losing their heritage.

The Western presence in the village itself has changed considerably in the last few years. In the fall of 1968, the community's fur trader suddenly died, and with his passing, and the departure of his family, the long-standing feud with the priest was finally laid to rest. The settlement's trading post was initially taken over by the government, but it has since been turned into a publicly sponsored co-operative, managed and operated by a young and very capable native couple from Good Hope. The missionary, with his rival removed from the scene, has closed down his own small store, and so the people once again have a single commercial outlet available to them.

The villagers have been pleased with the new situation, not only because the feud's termination has reduced the level of tension within the community, but also because Batiste Sašo, the new store manager, has held down the level of their debts. Furthermore, Batiste draws his salary from the government rather than from the trading post's profits, thus giving people a larger percentage of the auction value of their furs since a key middleman in the marketing process has been eliminated.[4] Band members have also been encouraged to produce and sell handicrafts through the co-op, and so their bone knives, model dogsleds, fish-skin boats, and finely-sewn mukluks have brought them in some additional income.

Relationships with the priest have also been redefined, not only as a result of changes in personnel at the store, but because of some actions by the missionary himself. His acquisition of an aircraft has made travel more convenient and reliable for people who want to visit other settlements, but the villagers remain ambivalent about the man and his motives. Since the priest does not have a commercial flying license, he is technically not allowed to charge people for his services — except for the cost of fuel. Yet he has been requiring local people to pay a mileage fee for every trip that he takes them on. Although his cost is still lower than that of most commercial pilots in the area, this policy provokes the same kind of resentment as the people experienced over the financial strategies of the old feud.

Also reminiscent of that earlier conflict have been some of the recent transactions between the missionary and the new co-op manager. In the beginning, the priest welcomed the idea of a village co-operative, and praised Batiste and his wife for their efforts at the store. In what now seems a spirit of *déjà vu*, however, he has taken to criticizing some of their policies, using a vocabulary of "inefficiency" and "exploitation" which he once reserved for the trader. According to some of the people, the priest has also used his influence in government circles to get co-op funds diverted to projects from which he himself has personally benefited. For example, a large percentage of the profits from the store's first year of operation were used to repair the village's caterpillar tractor so that the air-strip could be cleared of snow . . . and made usable to the priest for his own aircraft. The missionary counters these innuendos by arguing that both the strip and the aircraft are really there for the benefit of all the people, and so the project was in actuality a community one. Wherever truth may lie in this matter, and regardless of the persons involved, one begins to feel a sense of repetition about it, a reminder that in the village, as in the world outside, *plus ça change, plus c'est la même chose.*

Finally, identities as well as relationships have been redefined in the community. The missionary has literally ceased to be a priest, having recently resigned from his position within the Church after gaining a release from his vows. Though the people continue to call him "Father," he no longer performs any priestly offices, and the villagers, instead, conduct their own rosaries each week, using either the community church, or one of their own homes. The priest has also announced his intention to marry a woman from outside the settlement, making his new role a radical one indeed, and giving rise to a good deal of gossip and sexual punning within the band. While on the one hand the people remain puzzled by these sudden changes in the priest's status — he gave them no explanation or advance warning of his decisions — they continue nevertheless in their sincere commitment to Catholic belief. As in the past, they derive a deep sense of peace and satisfaction — both as individuals and as a community — from a collective and ritualized relationship with god, and their communal ceremonies thus persist as a meaningful and cohesive element in their lives. In a world-view that comfortably accommodates both Christian dogma and aboriginal taboos, the frailties of men are no barrier to belief.

Among the people themselves, the nature of identity has undergone some subtler changes. In the summer of 1971, the area administrator from Good Hope gave the members of the band a supply of building materials to repair and improve their homes. Doors were replaced, roofs were re-shingled, floors were re-laid . . . but most striking of all were the new partitions that went up in many of the houses. In a privacy-sparse village, where all but two families were living in single-room structures in 1968, there were six multi-room dwellings by the start of August 1971. The instigators of these changes were primarily young adults, people like Judy Alahfi, Gabyel Behdzi and Philip Ratehne, who explained the alterations that they had made in their houses quite explicitly in terms of privacy. They wanted their "own rooms," they did not want to "be bothered by their parents," they each wanted to create their "own place." Just as seating arrangements at public occasions — like Church services (Figure 19) — reflect the voluntary segregation of the community by sex, age, ethnicity, and acculturation level, internal living space was now being divided as an expression of the needs and self-image of a new generation.

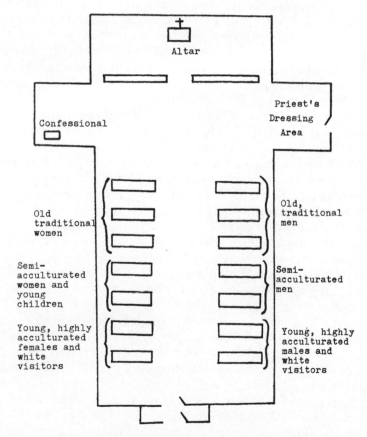

FIGURE 19   Seating arrangement at church services.

Young adults were also both redefining and re-affirming their ethnic identities. Recent years had witnessed the development of a nascent "red power" movement in the Northwest, focusing primarily upon native rights and economic opportunities. It had begun in response to a massive influx of white personnel and oil company capital, whose ultimate goal of monopolizing most Territorial resources was being pursued without consideration or regard for aboriginal claims and interests in the land.

The native movement confronting these challenges, involving both Indians and Eskimos, had made itself felt even in Colville Lake, where some new styles and painful questions were much in evidence. When Susan and I arrived in the village, we were greeted by the novel sight of several young men with flowing, shoulder-length hair and bright red headbands, looking for all the world like their distant Apache kinsmen to the south. This pan-Indian appearance — so clearly a borrowed part of their identity — was a mask as well as a display, however, for we found that the people were harboring some deep resentments about their fate and their situation. Administrators, the police, the game department, and other agencies were constantly being criticized for their ineffectual role in the community, and many people felt that Colville was being ignored both administratively and financially in preference to larger settlements. Despite the construction of a still-unstaffed nursing station in the village, for example, the ex-priest continued to be responsible for the community's only medical supplies, and — rather than interrupt his painting or his chess games — he often kept people waiting for over an hour before giving them the medication that they had come to him for. There was also the condescending, impatient, and paternal attitude of the summer tourists and fishermen, whose behavior was ridiculed by the people at the same that they felt debased by it.

In the last few years, Philip and some of his age-mates had found seasonal employment outside the community as well, and their intensified contact with whites, while working for oil and exploration companies, and as fire-fighters, had heightened their ethnic self-consciousness. While on the one hand they externalized their Indianness in dress and hair styles, they also betrayed some deeper confusions about their image and their own worth. Since whites were simultaneously admired as well as disliked by these young people, being "put down" by them was having its cumulative effect in the form of ethnic and self-denigration. Ambiguously troubled and amused by their experiences, some individuals expressed their feelings by scrawling their doubts on the plywood partitions in their homes. As the graffiti in the Ratehne's house declared:

What am I, nothing
but a crazy Indian

I'm nothing but
a dark Indian

I'm too much
of a crazy Indian

These people here
are all stupid
just like old Indians

If younger people were becoming ambivalent about their identity, they were quickly fossilizing their culture with electricity. Within a brief span of years, native music had become a sometimes substitute for the radio and the phonograph, and traditional gambling had turned into an almost forgotten pastime. Whereas the summer, even just a short time ago, had been a season for renewal and performance, the power of batteries now seemed stronger than the motives of tradition. People were capturing their parties on cassette tape-recorders, and preserving the rare drum dance or *udzi* session in the same way. One evening of drinking and dancing thus furnished the substance for hours of future listening, so that — in three years' time — recreation had literally given way to re-creation. It often seemed that people would rather re-play than perform their culture, and remember rather than participate in it. For a group which had always been concerned with its identity, content had suddenly become a very disposable commodity for some of its younger members.

2 MODELS AND METAPHORS

The style and structure of a culture are often more permanent than its content. In adapting and defining themselves, the techniques that people use may be more important than the materials they manipulate. Along with the changes they have experienced in recent years, the Hare have shown that movement can coexist with diverse economies, and that flexibility can supersede the confinement of rules and architecture. Old values can have contemporary relevance if they are malleable ones, and if people think enough of them to redefine their applicability. The aboriginal and historical exposure of the Hare to a diversity of social and ecological stresses has promoted an existential commitment to adaptability on their part, rendering stress a simultaneously challenging and sensitizing force in their lives. Present and future changes in the North will often be met in ways that have deep roots in such a past, and planners and participants will have to recognize and build upon this reality.

Two keys to the present are the stresses of life which confront people, and the basic ways in which individuals create and respond to their tensions. Taking Colville Lake both as a microcosm and as an end in itself, we have considered these problems by examining them not only in their cultural and psychological dimensions, but in their historical and ecological ones as well. Our efforts can be summarized, in part, by taking inventory of the primary stress sources and coping styles which concern the people of this community, an overview which is provided by Tables 7 and 8.

TABLE 7
Stress sources

Scarcity of environmental resources: this includes cyclical and seasonal features of meat, fish, and fur sources; there is an unstable income from fur trapping.

Harshness of bush life and working conditions: these include cold, wetness, hard physical labor, dangers, and the difficulties posed by weather and animals.

Isolation during bush living: this generates interpersonal stresses from relations within families, and from those between partners and co-workers; isolation is itself a serious form of deprivation.

Dogs and travelling: the sources of concern include the behavior, health, and appearance of dogs, the supply of dog food, and the hardships and dangers of winter and spring dogsled travel (e.g., snowblindness). For some people, travelling under dangerous or challenging conditions is a form of stress-seeking.

Interdependence, cooperation, and helpfulness; and generosity, hospitality, and reciprocity: these themes involve the provision of goods, food resources, and services; jealousies arise over hunting, trapping, and fishing luck, as well as over invitations to brew parties. There is a strong consciousness of the balance of generosity in conjunction with kinship and friendship obligations; this is accentuated by the diffuseness of expectations and the lack of specificity in relations among extended kinsmen; interdependence is thus stressful in conjunction with interrelatedness. People show anxiety over owing things to others. These types of behavior relate to an individual's status and reputation in the village.

Population concentration: there are interpersonal, aggregate, and psychological stresses during village ingatherings and visits to Fort Good Hope.

Drinking behavior and aggression: disruptive and abusive drinking behavior generates conflicts and tensions.

Gossip, and sexual and other jealousies: these occasion, or are occasioned by, extra-marital affairs and illegitimate children, rumors, criticisms, accusations, relative generosity, and feud tensions and allegiances.

Limited privacy: village and bush living conditions have few readily available "back" regions; interaction and observability are often at a high level. People become conscious of and irritated by the surveillance of others; this heightens the extreme distress felt by individuals when they are in embarrassing situations.

Old-age insecurity: there is a loss of respect, authority, and economic usefulness that comes with advanced age; there is consequently poor treatment of the elderly which is related to their inability to live up to the themes of generosity and self-reliance.

Generational and acculturative differences in outlook and orientation: acculturation levels affect attitudes and participations in most areas of life; there is ambivalence shown by some people over Colville Lake versus Fort Good Hope as a place of residence, and trapping versus wage labor as a way of life; some individuals show cultural disorientation, and acculturative differences have been aggravated by feud allegiances. There are conflicts and/or misunderstandings between some parents and their grown children because of subcultural differences in life style.

Sex and age composition of the village: these accentuate the generational split, and aggravate frustrations over blocked marriages and the level of village social life. The interrelatedness of band members also restricts sexual and marital possibilities.

Family authority structure: this involves some parental controls over the mobility and activities of younger family members; there are several cases of parents blocking the marriages of young adults.

Socialization processes: there is a shift around five or six years of age from indulgent and affectionate treatment of children to increased responsibilities for them and a lesser show of warmth; favoritism is shown towards boys. Young children often receive rough treatment in their play and peer groups, and they learn to respond in kind; later, however, they must adjust to the more emotionally restrained behavior of adult life.

Emphases on individualism, individual competence, self-reliance, and non-interference with others: these contrast with the generosity ethic and its implications; people feel a loss of pride in having to ask others for help.

Emotional restraint: it masks, defers, redirects, and intensifies reactions to stresses from various sources; people continually strive to inhibit both their own hostile outbreaks, as well as actions which would provoke such displays in others; a basic, underlying factor is the knowledge of, and need for, one's interdependence with others.

The feud between the missionary and the fur trader: it involves various pressures for alliance and compliance which capitalize on the people's reliance upon the goods and services of these men. Major pressures and strategies focus on the people's fur catch, their government assistance checks, and their symbolic acts of support.

High debts and loss of credit at the trading post: this involves severely limited access to the Western foods and items upon which the people depend.

Number of children in the household: a large number can create economic difficulties and great hardships for the mother. In very small family units, adults may be lonely for children, and they may also lack sufficient help in the division of labor. Lack of children can also mean lack of security in one's old age. Illegitimate children are a serious cause of tension among married couples.

Schooling: the prolonged periods of separation between children and their families, necessitated by the current educational situation in the area, is a source of psychological stress for both students and parents.

Health and disease: tuberculosis has largely been brought under control, but cases occasionally become reactivated; minor injuries and illnesses persist, several of which are derived from bush activities. People must often depend upon the local priest and the village's limited supply of medicine for medical aid. For operations, major types of treatment and birth deliveries, band members are flown to a hospital or nursing station.

Belief in ghosts, medicine men, magicians, "bad medicine," magic, and predictive or manipulative superstitions: there is little evidence for active belief in these ideas, and there are no hostilities or accusations derived from them; they are not of great consequence in the current context, although certain taboos are observed in hunting, fishing, and trapping.

Belief in "bush men" and fear of isolation in the bush: "bush man" ideas are not taken too seriously by most adults, but they are used as a scaring technique in socialization. People dislike the idea of themselves or others being isolated for protracted periods because of the personal and psychological dangers involved. People generally do not like to trap far from the village or in unknown areas.

TABLE 8
Coping techniques

Caching and storage of meat and fish for times of shortages: this is done for both human and dog food.

Native and Western-derived technologies for coping with conditions of bush life: these include the use of moss and snow for insulation, snowshoes, bone hide-scrapers, steel axes, rifles, nets, canvas tents, etc.

Isolation during bush living: this affords privacy and relieves stresses from population concentration.

Treatment of dogs: this involves beating, kicking, whipping and cursing when people are both drunk and sober; it is a sanctioned and frequently used outlet for aggression, and it is also participated in by children. Travelling by dogsled is also a major form of stress-seeking in the band, especially among young adult males; in addition, dogs are a source of pride, a part of individual self-image, a mode of self-presentation, and an emotional and sensory extension of people.

Population concentrations: these relieve isolation tensions and include ingatherings at Colville and Good Hope, trips from the bush to the village and the town, and visits between different bush camps; in the village, a few houses, and the mission and trading post, serve as primary social centers.

Friendships, warm ties, formation of partnerships, and camping and work alliances:

warm ties are found between parents and young children, grandparents and grandchildren, some husbands and wives, and some siblings. Partnerships and alliances make work easier, and they relieve the loneliness and the fear of bush isolation and its dangers; these arrangements stem from kinship ties and friendships.

Camping in familiar areas that are not far from the village: this relieves anxieties about the hazards of bush life, lessens feelings of isolation, and eases travelling hardships.

Listening to radios, and sending and receiving letters and parcels: these relieve feelings of isolation and help maintain contacts with physically distant kin and friends; economic interchanges also provide the people with certain scarce and needed materials, such as moose hide.

Preference of some people for seasonal wage labor over trapping: the former provides greater security of income and permits one to avoid some or all of the hardships of bush life.

Governmental family allowances and old-age pensions: these provide steady income for families, permit the coverage of debts, and provide economic and social security for the elderly.

Generosity, hospitality and reciprocity; and interdependence, cooperation, and helpfulness: these expectations and obligations between kinsmen and friends provide security and help in times of need and shortages.

Emphases on individualism, individual competence, self-reliance, and non-interference with others: these afford people pride in their work and accomplishments in the face of hardships with which they must contend. The focus on non-interference provides some insulation against bothersome, "bossy" and nosy concern by others in one's personal affairs.

Limited privacy: a few opportunities for relative privacy exist, including family and personal property and caches, "personal territory" within houses and tents, the use of outhouses, the locking of doors at certain times, limited withdrawal from interaction, travelling, and periods of bush life. On the other hand, access to information about others is facilitated by the limited availability of means to privacy.

Drinking: this overcomes restraints on emotional expression due to the cultural definition of the drinking situation and drinking behavior. This permits release of stress in verbal, aggressive, and disruptive modes of interaction.

Gossiping, sexual adventures, gambling, and other forms of leisure: these provide both relaxation and opportunities for retaliation and indirect hostility against people. Along with drinking, they constitute both direct and vicarious means of stress-seeking.

Humor and joking: these are prevalent modes of tension release, and they are often thinly veiled expressions of hostility, jealousy, and similar emotions.

High mobility: this occurs in various forms, on an individual, household, and village level. Tensions from isolation, population concentration, drinking encounters, family arguments, feud pressures, bush hardships, ambivalent and acculturative orientations, and other sources, all find release in this way.

Emotional restraint: this restricts and channels outbursts to expected and culturally sanctioned times and places.

Conciliatory actions to please the missionary and fur trader within the context of the feud: the people's interactions with these men relieve tensions surrounding the conflict. Their use of the mission and store as social centers also provides the people with opportunities for relaxing and releasing other stresses of life: included in this is the projection by the people of some of their non-feud stresses and dissatisfactions onto the feud and its principal characters. In addition to the sale of their fur, the people sell resources (meat, fish, wood), engage in wage labor, and sign over their government assistance checks to the whites, in order to prevent the loss of their credit and to cover their debts. Feud involvements also serve as a source of identity for the band as a whole.

Giving or taking children for adoption or for care for a period of time: these means relieve stresses for families with too many children or too few children. Illegitimate children produced by a member of a married couple are usually given away to lessen tensions within the family.

Schooling: the values and the dilemmas presented by the current educational system in the North are balanced by the people through their limited use of schooling opportunities; they thereby insure their children of a modicum of education, as well as appropriate types of experience in learning more traditional skills and life styles.

Medical aid and assistance: they are provided both by the village's missionary and by government personnel and facilities from outside the community.

Participation in Catholic beliefs and services: religious involvement provides psychological and social release from a variety of stresses in the people's lives, and affords the members of the band an opportunity to enjoy a sense of communality and communication with God.

While an inventory is a useful device, it is nevertheless a static picture, and the preceding chapters have therefore emphasized the dynamics of stress-coping as an on-going process. The tables which summarize stress sources and coping techniques are highly redundant, for many of the same cultural features appear on both inventories. Yet these tables have been constructed in a purposeful and intentional manner: the redundancy derives from the fact that many of the people's modes for dealing with tension and anxiety become, in their turn, sources of further stress. In addition, while in some cases a specific form of tension release can be connected with a particular stress, more often such one-to-one relations are impossible to make: a given stress may simultaneously or sequentially be responded to in a variety of modes, just as a specific response pattern may simultaneously operate as a way of handling a number of tensions. A man releases hostility by beating a dog that misbehaves, but the tension created by the dog's behavior is only part (and usually only a small part) of the total motivation for the man's aggression. Emotional restraint and repression thus often obscure the links between stresses and their specific releases. The stress process is thus subtle and dialectical in nature, and it affects social life and individual existence on a number of levels and through a range of dimensions.

There are a number of insights about the human condition that can be gained from the people of Colville Lake, but these are only forthcoming when the community's experiences are considered from this active and dynamic perspective. It is for this reason too that particular emphasis has been placed upon time, space, and relationship in our analyses, for these factors have made it possible to identify and describe the adaptive procedures that the band participates in. We can, however, go beyond this level of comprehension as well. If we consider the people's existence both as a system and as a process, then their encounter with stress also suggests some broader understandings about the nature of life and its experience. While the content of the people's adaptations may be particular for their own culture, one can discern certain general features to their life style as well, some of which may be relevant to the existence of other human groups. I would therefore propose that the following characteristics of the situation at Colville Lake be considered as possible elements in the stress patterns of any society.

1) *Process*   First, and to reiterate a previous point, it is suggested that one cannot understand the stresses of existence if one looks at them statically, taking them simply in terms of their basic sources and the kinds of responses that they typically evoke. Rather, one must seek to understand stress and coping as a process, involving thought, perception, emotion, action and pattern, as well as the individual nuances of the people concerned.

2) *Specificity*   The experience of the Colville band demonstrate that there is no one-to-one relationship between specific stresses and particular coping techniques. Each stress may be met with a diverse repertoire of responses, and one coping style may be operative in dealing with a range of problems. Furthermore, specific aspects of the coping process may not be equally relevant for dealing with all situations. In the case of Colville, for example, mobility is utilized for dealing with ecological scarcity and population densities, but it is less germane for coping with white men. One can minimize one's dependence upon whites by living off the land as much as possible, but there are certain goods and services — ranging from matches to medical care — that can only be gotten at their hands. Hence, one has

to ultimately confront and deal with them, and so strategies that are more "political" than mobility must eventually be brought into play.

3) *Sensory Context*   Thirdly, the dynamic aspects of the stress process become meaningful only when they are considered within their cultural context. Relevant variables include not only the cultural definitions of what constitute stressful circumstances and appropriate modes of response, but also the subtler patterns of perception and cognition, involving both the interpretation of environmental stimuli and situations, and one's ability to cope with them.[5] Cultural styles of appraisal may involve the differential use of sensory modalities, such as the utilization of touch and sound — as well as sight — in spatial orientation. Senses may also be extended through the use of electronic media or, as at Colville, through a relationship with domesticated animals. The over-all level of sensitivity to the environment should similarly be evaluated, along with the ways in which memory is trained and utilized. All major psychological parameters should thus be examined for their role in the coping process, one dividend of which would be a fuller appreciation of the acquisition, use, storage and retrieval of knowledge in the group being studied.

4) *Emotional Context*   The types of emotional expressiveness which people are allowed, and the cultural definition of the appropriate contexts in which affect can be displayed, channel both the experience of stress and its creation. Emotional modalities may not only be defined in terms of their range and context, but certain enhancers or inhibitors of affectivity, such as alcohol, may have special cultural significance, as well as elaborate patterns surrounding their use. The rhythms of constraint and release among the members of the Colville band suggest that comparable cycles may be found in other groups, and that these periodicities may be related to the pervasive biological rhythms which govern the human organism.[6] The fact that young people in the community must change and constrict their emotional repertoire as they grow older also highlights both the stresses of socialization itself, and the process by which response patterns are learned — and restructured — during an individual's life cycle.

5) *History*   The cognitive and emotional roots of a society's stress patterns can often be illuminated by an examination of their history. Previous circumstances may have been conducive not only to the formation of types of social structure, but to the establishment of behavioral and coping styles as well. Among the Hare and neighboring peoples, for example, chronic environmental threats

during aboriginal and post-contact times would appear to be related to the bilaterality, individual autonomy, self-reliance, emotional restraint, and kinds of cognitive sensitivity which characterize these groups. The continued presence of historically relevant coping patterns may, of course, simply be a cultural artifact; on the other hand, it may indicate the persistence of earlier stresses into contemporary times, and/or the applicability of established behavior to more recent problems. Each of these possibilities deserves investigation.

6) *Socialization* It is necessary to translate "historical" time into "life"-time in order to grasp the existential quality of a culture. The patterning of an individual's experience of stress, as part of the process of socialization, includes his training in the treatment and perception of threat, challenge, anxiety and tension. The acquisition of a broad spectrum of social and technological skills is essential for coping with interpersonal and survival problems. Competence and success thus constitute the outcome of one's ability to mobilize effort, expertise, support, and the appropriate materials to confront a specific challenge (cf. Pepitone, 1967, pp.201-202). Training and experience may also involve exposure to, and acquired tolerance for, certain levels of stress (Naroll, 1962, p.72), whether these be — as in the case of Colville — the tensions of drinking, or the deprivations of isolation. Socialization often includes the patterned induction of anxiety as well (such as the fear of "bush men"), plus the learning of an emotional repertoire, as illustrated by the band's inculcation of restraint and displacement techniques in young children.

7) *Environment* The context of living must be broadly construed to include the physical, social, and psychological environments. Stress should be viewed as an organism-environment transaction (McGrath, 1970b, p.14). Natural elements and processes, wild and domesticated species, social and ethnic groups, ambience and architecture, and supernatural beings, are all significant ecological features that affect the creation, experience and handling of stress. Just as witchcraft beliefs have been shown by anthropologists to be both a symptom and a cause of tension (Naroll, 1962, pp.65-66), ancestral cults, Christianity, "bush man" beliefs, and related spiritual concepts may constitute a projection and a personification of cultural anxieties. Other "environmental" relationships may involve similar ambiguities, and reveal the subtler contours of the coping process. Affective displacement among the Hare, for example, involving physical aggression towards dogs, trees and inanimate objects, and the verbal

abuse of kinsmen and white men through gossip and humor, clarifies the dimensions of the people's total ecology.

8) *Identity* Stressful experiences may promote unity and identity among a people by defining their corporate boundaries and their ethnicity (Klausner, 1968). Confrontations with the bush and with white men have affected the Hare in these ways, although the former involvement has also divided the community in terms of life style, just as the latter involvement has recently led to a questioning of ethnicity itself.

9) *Population* The distribution of people in time and space is one parameter of their subsistence needs, but the densities and durations of their groups also influence, and are in turn a function of, their styles and rates of interaction. Certain contexts may involve social and sensory deprivation or information overload as stressful circumstances.[7] There may be corporate and individual limits to how long extremes of isolation and concentration can be endured by the members of a community. Architecture, and the social uses of living space, may reflect these thresholds, as well as contribute to the very conditions which eventually violate the tolerance levels possessed by a people. Cultural and situational limits on privacy, and on the control which people have over the flow of information about themselves, can aggravate stresses pertaining to public and self-image. Programmatic statements about the desired nature of social groups and interaction, such as the enthusiastic way in which the people of Colville alternately speak of the bush and the village, should be compared with the actual behavior of individuals under these same conditions.

10) *Mobility* Physical movement can be a way of simultaneously readjusting a population both to the distribution of ecological resources and to the limits and demands of sociability. Either one of these functions may take precedence over the other as the prime cause of a given move, although the actual motives for mobility may be consciously unrecognized or publicly unacknowledged by the participants. In groups where patterned movement is of adaptive significance, it will usually be part of a larger coping repertoire: technological procedures and materials will be relevant for dealing with economic problems, communications media may temper the rigors of isolation, and institutionalized forms of separation — as in seclusion or the use of veils — may augment privacy (Gregor, 1970; Murphy, 1964). It is therefore not sufficient to simply choreograph the movements of a people, for mobility must be related to the other techniques which complement it.

11) *Values*   Social orientations include values which bear upon the experience of stress. Cultural themes may prescribe the seeking or avoidance of stressful circumstances, such as the way in which the people of Colville anticipate the challenges of bush life but avoid confrontations with whites. Values may also embody generic response patterns to tension and anxiety, such as in an ethos which emphasizes self-reliance, affective containment, individual autonomy, and personal competence. Themes which relate to the handling of stress may, however, be a source of stress themselves, if — as in "interdependence" and "independence" — they are contradictory, or if the behavior and role conflicts they promote cannot be realized or resolved much of the time. The latter situations may be a pre-condition for anomie, and would, at the least, be productive of frustration.[8]

12) *Individuality*   Different segments of a population may have distinctive susceptibilities to types of stress, and these may be accompanied by characteristic coping styles. Culturally defined life patterns for age and sex groups, for example, including their participation in the division of labor, may crystallize some of these key variations in the experience of stress, as well as promote role conflicts for individuals and sub-groupings. Acculturative differences in the Colville band had similar consequences and correlates. Other societies may have correspondingly distinctive stress patterns for ethnic, racial, religious, and socio-economic sub-groups.[9] Furthermore, and beyond these cultural and subcultural differences, individuals in a population will also have idiosyncratic tolerance levels and response patterns, a feature which complicates but enriches the dynamics of the coping process.

13) *Ambiguity*   Relationships and processes often incorporate ambiguities which promote stress. Certain involvements may be simultaneously disparaged and esteemed by people, or sequentially reacted to by them in contrasting ways. Environmental, inter-generational, inter-specific, and inter-ethnic ties at Colville each illustrate these qualities. Cultural and social changes over time may also create or intensify contradictions in value orientations, as well as prompt the redefinition of individual and group identity.

14) *Dialectics*   A basic feature of the coping process is that solutions or responses to a given stress usually create other stresses in their turn. As one anthropologist has expressed this:

man's physical, social and cultural environments are so closely interwoven that stresses which accompany them should be viewed as interdependent. The resolution of stress in one sphere not infrequently promotes additional stress in another (Chance, 1968, p.572).

It is therefore a measure of completeness rather than redundancy that most of the factors presented in Tables 7 and 8 appear as both producers *and* reducers of stress. The duality of these elements contributes to the ambiguous and dynamic aspects of existence: the alternation between involvement and disengagement, as part of the coping process, imparts a dialectical quality to life as people experience its rhythms in time and space.

15) *Creativity* The degree to which stress-seeking is emphasized in a culture may affect the amount of innovation and individuality which people participate in (Selye, 1956, pp.269, 277). The pursuit of challenge, and the experience of stimulation, may also enhance competence, as well as the satisfactions which can be derived from it. Furthermore, direct and vicarious stress-seeking, such as in sports, exploration, gambling, humor, intoxication, and narrative drama, may rechannel energies from more destructive outlets (Bernard, 1968, p.17), and heighten a people's sense of their own creative capacities.

Anthropology, as a pursuit, is a form of stress-seeking in its own right, as are most attempts to "get close to strangers" (Marshall, 1968, p.64). Its satisfactions derive from the experience of stress itself, and from the sense of understanding that one ultimately hopes to achieve. Living with the people of Colville Lake, and trying to grasp the essence of their problems, their senses, and their own satisfactions, has been at times a difficult encounter, because it forces us to confront our own strengths and frailties. It has, however, also suggested to us a dynamic and multi-dimensional approach to stress as a quality of life. The holistic model of coping that has been developed exposes the inadequacy of some of our own cultural metaphors for existence. The engineer's notion of "stress and strain" may be appropriate for solid materials of limited plasticity, but it scarcely encompasses the subtlety and flexibility of human behavior. An hydraulic analogy may be more germane, for at least fluids adapt readily to the forces of stress and the contours of their environment, and then return to their previous state after a period of "release" and "relaxation" (Blum, 1972).

Equilibrium models of stress, however, are also deficient in one important regard, for in emphasizing homeostasis, i.e., the continual return of a system to a prior and undisturbed condition, they either overlook or minimize the dynamic and dialectical quality of human existence. Stabilizing mechanisms are, indeed, operative in all social systems, and one could, for example, classify the handling of stressful emotions at Colville into techniques for release and displacement, mobility and avoidance, or inhibition and containment. Situations also repeat themselves, and people must periodically — or even cyclically — re-confront a previous challenge. A static perspective, however, not only misses the entire dimension of stress-seeking, but the nature of growth, change and maturation as well. Individual and cultural development are processes rooted in the experience of stress, and they should be appreciated for their sources as well as their outcomes.

If metaphors are not always as useful as models, then the latter are only as good as the descriptions upon which they are based. Besides the data presented in the preceding sections, our arguments concerning the people of Colville Lake derive support from the nature of other hunting-fishing-and-gathering groups, many of which — as shown in Parts II and III — share with the Hare an emphasis upon flexibility, restraint, generosity, mobility, and bilaterality. These cross-cultural similarities, which include many non-northern societies as well, do not constitute a case for the universality of any of these coping techniques, but they do highlight the ecological utility of a broad spectrum of adaptive procedures.

Even where coping styles are similar in different groups, cultures vary in the amount and types of stress that they impose upon people (Honigmann, 1967, p.86). While some scholars have tried to characterize entire systems as being either "tough" or "easy" on their members (Arsenian and Arsenian, 1948), there are no well-established indicators that one can use to measure the over-all level of stress in a given society. Some anthropologists (Naroll, 1962; Nadel, 1952) have tried to compare cultures by using such stress symptoms as homicide, suicide, witchcraft accusations, and drunken assault, but such analyses are necessarily limited to those groups in which these reaction patterns are already institutionalized. Of the four variables cited, for example, only the last one would be applicable to the people of Colville Lake.

It is also difficult to measure or determine whether the general level of stress within a social system is more than the members of that society can bear, or whether the stress level is more than the social system as a whole can deal with. One gross index of generalized stress is the incidence and nature of mental illness in a population, with a high incidence of psychopathology (as defined by members of the society themselves) being indicative of severe strain. In one Western culture, for example, the pioneering Midtown Manhattan Study in New York has shown an extremely high rate of neurotic and psychotic disturbance among urban dwellers, a situation which the study's inter-disciplinary research team attributed to wide variety of stress sources (Langner and Michael, 1963). Since we have also been dealing with stress, tension and anxiety in the case of Colville Lake, it is noteworthy that only one individual in the entire band has been defined as mentally unbalanced by the people themselves, and this particular woman has only periodically exhibited symptoms severe enough to warrant that community members intercede and request her hospitalization.

Although it is patently unfruitful to compare this one isolated case with the figures for urban New Yorkers, it is significant and relevant to contrast it with the stress and mental instability levels in a place like Fort Good Hope.[10] There, in the settlement that is physically, culturally, historically and even genetically closest to Colville, several dozen people have been hospitalized for mental disorders in the last decade, and a number of the fort's inhabitants can live in the town only with the aid of regularly-administered tranquilizers and sedatives from the nursing station. While no one has ever systematically (or even cursorally) investigated the etiology of mental disorders at Good Hope, the contrast between this fort town and the bush community at Colville does suggest a number of possible interpretations which might make these differences comprehensible.

First of all, as we have seen, the people of Colville do experience a large variety of stresses in their lives, but they have also developed a number of specific and "broad spectrum" techniques for coping with these problems. Their relatively low incidence of mental disorders would seem to indicate, in a crude fashion, that these techniques are adaptive and serviceable enough to allow almost all villagers to lead normal lives. This is worth emphasizing here since this book's focus upon stress may have fostered the impression, among some readers, of an unusually strife-torn existence that is dysfunctional or pathological. On the contrary, I think it is true, as I stated in the Preface, that the Arctic does amplify many of life's stresses, but I also think that a comparable array of tensions and threats could be found in any social system in the world; and, rather than the situation at Colville being pathological, I have tried to demonstrate that the people's coping techniques are efficacious and well-suited to their particular circumstances.

This situation may be contrasted with the one at Good Hope, where, to again take mental disorders as a rough index, we apparently have a discrepancy between the townspeople's exposure to stresses and their ability to handle them. In simplistic terms, one can suggest at least three possible developments which would yield such an outcome. One is that either the magnitude or variety of stresses has been appreciably increased over time, with no corresponding amplification or broadening of coping strategies. Secondly, with or without an increase in stress, traditional coping techniques may have become ineffectual, inoperable, or unrealizable under contemporary circumstances. The third and most likely possibility is that both of these processes have been occurring simultaneously, i.e., that stresses have been augmented and diversified at the same time that traditional modes of coping have become insufficient or unworkable.

At nascent urban centers like Good Hope, for example, the last several decades have witnessed a number of developments of this nature, including a collapse of the traditional trapping economy; a growth in unemployment and welfare; an increasingly sedentary and concentrated population, with even less access to privacy than before; a related decline in the pride and sense of competence that once came from living off the land; and an increased dependence upon whites for livelihood and survival, as well as for leadership, decision-making and direction.[11] The latter situation may have created a strong conflict with traditional Indian values of autonomy and self-reliance, and hence promoted a diminished sense of identity. To these stresses have been added the loss, or decline in value, of a number of coping techniques, including the use of mobility to change environments and achieve privacy; the weakening of kinship bonds in the social support system; a decrease in personal effort and ability as a source of status, esteem, and validation; and the disruption of the generosity ethic because of a growing commitment to contradictory Western values.

This interpretation is a highly speculative one, and I offer it with that *caveat* because I do not know the situation in forts like Good Hope well enough to write about them definitively. An analysis of how, in a psychogenetic sense, the factors and processes suggested would actually operate to produce an increase in mental disorders is also beyond my competence, but I think the variables that I have indicated are very relevant to this phenomenon, and would have to be considered in any attempt to explain it. If I have correctly estimated the value of mobility as a stress-reducing device, then the loss of this technique may be especially damaging to the people's psychic economy. Moving into a large town completes the process of diminishing mobility that began over 150 years ago with a dependence upon Western goods. In moving to a fort, in fact, you abdicate

mobility as a life style, and commit yourself instead to the sedentary
establishment which has since grown up around the early trading
post.

The problem then becomes, as Welsh (1970, p.28) has suggested,
one of whether native people can develop social mechanisms to deal
with a constant, year-round residence pattern and its high rates of
interaction. Whereas at Colville, sociability was often seen as a reward
and an end in itself, living in town may provide too much of what —
under other circumstances — was indeed a good thing. At the fort,
however, people must simultaneously create a new life-way, a new
support system, and new means to privacy, as well as develop new
leadership patterns to deal with an increasingly influential white
power structure.

In these regards, the people of Colville Lake stand out as a
community whose members have adopted and adapted a set of coping
techniques which, taken as a whole, have so far proven effective in
dealing with a mélange of stress sources. Whether this will continue to
be the case in years to come depends upon the continuation or
alteration of basic features in their style of life. This is indeed
problematical, for the changing and ambiguous qualities of the
people's current situation also contain the elements of an impending
existential dilemma: how to create meaning from the chaos of change,
from the sense of loss, and from the loss of sense. Life in this part of
the North has not yet become the "fear and trembling" of which
Kierkegaard spoke, nor are decisions so stark as the "either/or"
encounters which he described Yet it does not seem that, in the future,
the people will be able to move between town and village, between the
forest and the band, and between *societas* and *communitas*, with the
ease that they have enjoyed in the past. While the physical distances
will remain constant, the psychological space of that middle ground
will broaden and deepen. If Fort Good Hope is the wave of the future,
many people may well drown in it unless the process of change is
redefined. Though it may be quixotic, I would enter a plea here not
only for new economic opportunities in the North, but for preventive
community mental health programs as well, so that people can learn
to deal with situations like this before — rather than after — they
have developed.

The experience at Colville Lake also highlights some
misconceptions and stereotypes about Athabascan Indians, especially
their undeserved reputation as aloof, cold and taciturn individuals.
People who have spoken of them in these terms have failed to
appreciate the social ecology of their lives, and its impact upon their

psychic economy and emotional repertoire. The people clearly possess psychological and affective outlets . . . though some are more subtle, and others more violent, than those which Westerners are wont to experience. This should sensitize us to a basic problem in inter-cultural relations, viz., the need to discover and appreciate the emotional styles which people employ in a society, be they direct, manifest, subtle, or vicarious ones. We would then be in a better position to realize the dimensions of their psychic economy, and could perhaps improve upon the pioneering but simplistic cultural personality labels that have been suggested in the past, such as the concepts of "tough," "easy," "Dionysian," "Apollonian," and "shame" and "guilt" cultures (Arsenian and Arsenian, 1948; Benedict, 1934; Piers and Singer, 1953).

If the above request for preventive community mental health programs in the North sounds painfully contemporary, then perhaps it is because it reminds us of how pressing and similar some of our own problems are. The fact that we experience a totally different environment from the people of Colville Lake may be a deceptive screen which masks the common features of our respective fates. In what one critic (Canby, 1971) has called our "see-through civilization," there are few places left for us to hide, either from ourselves or from the outside. We have abdicated our privacy for the sake of efficiency, and display our neuroses like red badges of urban courage. With the partial (and sometimes total) collapse of extended families in urban settings, people who want to escape personal stresses often have no one to turn to. Friends may replace kinsmen as a means of retreat, but unless friendship has attained a level of commitment comparable to deep family ties, joint reesidence may prove to be more of a strain than a release to the people involved. A communal home away from "hell" may eventually become a "hell" away from home, destroying these non-kinship ties, and leaving a person with few other alternatives.

All too often, nomadism, drugs, avarice, religion, or psycho-analysis fill an existential vacuum by defining a life style for people who cannot define themselves. Crisis cults have come to play as large a part in the Western stress experience as revitalization and nativistic movements do in the rest of the world (cf. LaBarre, 1971, p.22ff). One urban scholar (Doxiadis, 1963, pp.38-39) has even suggested that Westerners travel so much in order to escape the horrid architecture that their cities envelop them with. We are certainly more mobile, as a society, than ever before, but it is a moot question whether movement alone will be sufficient to relieve the anxieties of crowding, deprivatization, and depersonalization we are exposed to. The fact that some ethnic and economic segments of our population are financially better off and less visibly stressed than others should not obscure the fact that we all pay the cost of inequity in terms of the quality of the human environment in which we must live. If some people can afford a richer coping repertoire than others, and if some groups appear to enjoy a monopoly over the more satisfying and creative stresses of life, then we are all impoverished either by our delusions, or by the narrowness of our opportunities. It is not a paradox that cities are simultaneously among the most stressful and the most creative of settings, for these two qualities are really complementary. In most cases, however, we have yet to realize the full dimensions of our human potential, for we have not learned to control our stresses or cope with their possibilities. Until we confront that reality, both as individuals and as a society, we will not achieve the kind of freedom and creativity that a true level of awareness would allow.

Notes

PREFACE

1. Though I recorded and learned a great many Hare words while in the field, I did not attempt to make my transcriptions in a rigorous, phonetic manner. In reproducing Hare words in the text of this book, I have tried to adapt my notes to the phonemic schemes presented by Sue (1964) and Hoijer (1966), both of which derive from the fieldwork done by Fang-Kwei Li in 1929. My adaptation omits tones and is undoubtedly inaccurate in other respects, but it nevertheless seemed both proper and necessary to utilize native words for concepts and relationships that had no English equivalent. My usage of vowel sounds is as follows:

   a as in mock (English);   Hare, *ason* = "grandmother"
   e as in bet (English);   Hare, *bele* = "wolf"
   ie as in pièta (Italian);   Hare, *bie* = "knife"
   i as in meet (English);   Hare, *ni* = "moss"
   o as in wrote (English);   Hare, *dzo* = "marten"
   u as in food (English);   Hare, *uyalele* = "spring" (the season)
   a^n, e^n, i^n, o^n, u^n are nasalized vowels.

2. Although I have used pseudonyms in the text, the names employed reflect the kind of naming patterns actually followed by the people. In real life, family names — which are a Western introduction — are in most cases derived from a native word for an object or an animal species, or they are taken from a European family name. Hence, among the pseudonyms, one finds such names as Limertu ("hammer"), Tahso ("crow"), Behdzi ("owl"), Godanto ("door"), Nota ("lynx"), Bayjere ("navel"), Ratehne ("storm), Alahfi ("canoe head"), Yawileh ("duck"), Dehdele ("pike"), Tehgu ("hawk"), and Sašo ("grizzly bear"). Surnames are most often of European origin, with the actual range of choice being influenced by the French-speaking priests of the area. This is reflected in the use of such names as Leon, Jean-Marie, Michèle, André, Monique, and Thérèse. Among themselves, the people also use nicknames, as well as their own unique pronunciation of certain European names: thus, Joshua becomes Yašeh, Germaine becomes Yerimen, John appears as Yen, and Bernadette is transformed into Berona.

PART I: ECOLOGY AND COMMUNITY

1. Recent archaeological investigations by Noble (1971) indicate an occupation of the central taiga-tundra zone of northern Canada since at least 5,000 B.C.
2. It is difficult to specify with accurary the territorial range of any of the Northern Athabascan groups. There were no corporate tribes or boundaries in aboriginal and early contact times, and all of the regional bands were highly nomadic. Historical sources, however, delineate the general area which the people's ancestors occupied.

223

In the nineteenth century, the missionary-explorer Petitot placed the Hare along the lower Mackenzie River from Fort Norman to the Arctic Coast, extending eastward to the area of Great Bear Lake and down northward along the route of the Anderson River (1876, p.xx; 1891, p.362). Other early accounts of the Hare largely agree with this description. Osgood, writing in 1936, described their traditional range in the following terms: "Northwest of Great Bear Lake, a section of the Lower Mackenzie River and its drainage, Northwest Territories" (1936a, p.11).

3. Descriptions of contemporary Fort Good Hope can be found in the works of Cohen (1962), Balikci and Cohen (1963), Hurlbert (1962), and Sue (1964, 1965).

4. Work on a landing strip for the community was finally finished in the autumn of 1968, allowing wheeled aircraft to land there for the first time. By 1971, there had been a small but noticeable increase in the amount of air traffic into the village.

5. In 1970 the village's missionary purchased a single-engine aircraft, and this, like the presence of the air-strip, somewhat reduced the settlement's isolation and relative inaccessibility. The control over air traffic was still a "white" monopoly, however, and this was so direct and more manifest than before, that the people's resentment was intensified.

6. See the estimates and percentages cited by Kelsall (1968, pp.47, 56) and Symington (1965, pp.21, 66).

7. Descriptions of aboriginal clothing styles among the Northern Athabascans can be found in early historical sources and more recent ethnographies, including Hearne (1795), Mackenzie (1801), Richardson (1851ii, pp.8-11), Jenness (1967, pp.67-76), Oswalt (1966, pp.25-26), Hatt (1969), Osgood (1936b, 1937, 1940, 1971), and Honigmann (1946, 1954).

8. Symington (1965, p.39) and Kelsall (1968, pp.269-274) provide both pictures and detailed accounts of the warble fly infestation of caribou.

9. Cf. Symington (1965, p.52) and Kelsall (1968, p.276). Native band names for many of these groups reflected their geographic and ecological position. Helm (1965), for example, mentions "edge-of-the-woods" Dogrib bands, and the people of Colville Lake are descended, in part, from a nineteenth century Hare group called the *Nne-lla-gottine* (Petitot, 1875, 1876, 1891) or *ne la go t'ine* (Osgood 1932), the "end of the earth people" (cf. Sue, 1964, p.30a). The taiga-tundra ecology of the Chipewyans is summarized by Oswalt (1966, pp.30-32).

10. Indians and Eskimos who utilized caribou for clothing preferred different types and parts of hides for different items of apparel. Symington (1965, p.53) notes that: "Calf skins were favoured for undergarments, and summer or autumn skins for outer parkas. Leg skins (which the people of Colville stressed as being especially tough and long-lasting) were used for mittens, for mukluk legs, and for the soles in the absence of the superior moose or seal skin" (cf. Kelsall 1968, p.211, and Hatt, 1969, for further descriptive material).

11. Kelsall (1968) contains excellent maps showing the limits of the winter migrations by caribou herds. Fort Good Hope is clearly beyond the western border of the Barren Ground caribou's winter range, but it is in the midst of a forest ecosystem (a willow, poplar and birch succession area) favored by the moose. As noted, the caribou generally restrict their movements to the climax spruce-lichen forest, which typifies the ecology of the Colville area (cf. Kelsall 1968, p.53, which draws upon the forest region classification given in Rowe, 1959).

12. Some of the names which have been applied to regional groups, either individually or collectively, are Hare Indians, Hareskins, Harefoot Indians, Rabbitskins, *Peaux-de-Lièvres, Dene Peaux-de-Lièvre, Kā-cho-'dtinne, Kah-cho-tinne* ('Arctic hare people'), *Kat'a-gottinẽ, Kha-t'a-ottinẽ, K'a-t'a-gottinẽ* ('people among the

hares'), *Kawchodinneh* ('people of the great hares'), *Khatǫa-Gottine* ('people among the rabbits'), and *Kawchogottine* ('dwellers among the large hares') (cf. *BAE*, 1907, **30**, pp.667-668, which gives an extensive listing of names which have been used and recognized). Savishinsky and Hara (In Press) reconsider the problem of Hare identity.

13. Additional data on the population cycle of the snowshoe hare and other rabbit species is provided by Chitty (1971).

14. A daily temperature chart was kept from August 1967 to August 1968 by means of an indoor-outdoor thermometer. While this was not a precision instrument, I believe that the readings I obtained were accurate to within a few degrees. I periodically checked my data against the readings on the thermometers kept by the priest and fur trader.

15. "Windchill is a measure of dry atmospheric cooling, or heat loss, in terms of temperature and wind . . . The higher the wind and the lower the temperature, the greater the loss of heat. Although a temperature of -30 °F with no wind may not be uncomfortable, the same temperature in conjunction with a 32-mile-per-hour wind will freeze exposed human flesh within one-half minute" (Kelsall, 1968, p.49).

16. Other examples of Athabascan lunar calendars can be found in the monographs by Honigmann, McKennan, Osgood, and Sue listed in the bibliography.

17. In aboriginal times the Hare may have also eaten the contents of caribou stomachs as a source of vegetable food, as did other regional groups such as the Chipewyans (Oswalt, 1966, pp.28, 33).

18. The unpredictable nature of certain caribou movements is documented by Kelsall (1968, pp.106 ff., 231) and Symington (1965, pp.35-36, 45).

19. Kelsall summarizes much of the evidence on the sporadic availability of caribou to many northern Indian groups, including the Hare. For example:

Fort Franklin, populated largely by Hare Indians, probably did not have caribou even in early times. It is on the northwestern range extremities for the species. Anthropological evidence (Jenness 1932) suggests that rabbits, moose, and fish supplied the basic necessities of life . . .

The large fluctuation in number of caribou taken at Fort Rae (affecting the Dogribs on the north arm of Great Slave Lake) appears common to virtually all points on the caribou range. Nor were such fluctuations uncommon when the caribou population was high. Russell (1898) documented the near absence of caribou in the Fort Rae area in 1893-94 and preceding winters, and Anderson (1937) recorded such scarcity that Eskimos starved at Padlei in 1926-27, continued scarcity in 1927-28, and abundance in the following 2 years (1968, p.231).

20. Estimates of the number of caribou needed by families living off the land are based upon data cited by Kelsall (1968, p.207).

21. The inconclusive evidence for caribou population cycles is given by Kelsall (1968, pp.147-148, 205).

PART II: KINSHIP AND HISTORY

1. Representative studies and summaries of social organization from these areas can be found in the writings of Osgood (1936b, 1937, 1958, 1959, 1971), McKennan (1959, 1965), Slobodin (1962), Birket-Smith and deLaguna (1938), Pehrson (1964), Whitaker (1955), and Forde (1963).

2. Cf. Jenness (1967, pp.385-399), Helm and Leacock (1971), and Cohen and Osterreich (1967, pp.4-5) for brief summaries of seasonal patterns among the

aboriginal Hare and other Northern Athabascans. Helm (1965a, 1968a) discusses the demographic and ecological factors which would have promoted regional ties among bands.

3 The maps and descriptions in Osgood (1936a) and Jenness (1967) place the Hare in relation to these neighboring peoples. Jenness (1967, pp.392-396) provides a brief summary of aboriginal Hare culture, stressing its basic similarity to that of other Mackenzie drainage groups.

4. This pattern of Indian intermediaries characterized the expansion of the fur trade into most areas of North America. In eastern Canada, for example, it had been the Algonkian tribes and the Iroquois who had acquired and fought over this highly profitable, monopolistic position (Innis, 1962; Rich, 1967, pp.1-23).

5. There is evidence that the Hare and other lower Mackenzie groups had already felt the impact of white men and the fur trade prior to Mackenzie's trip. European goods had been spreading westward from the trading forts on Hudson's Bay since the early eighteenth century (Rich, 1967, pp.102-103), and Hearne (1795) reports trading activity by the Dogribs and Copper Indians (Yellowknives) at Fort Prince of Wales (on Hudson's Bay) in the 1760's and 1770's. Mackenzie states in his journal that he interviewed Copper Indians and Slaves along his northern route, and that these people attested to their being plundered by the Cree and Chipewyans for furs (1801, pp.3, 18, 20). The fact that all the groups in the vicinity of the Hare were already involved in the fur trade by 1789 implies that the Hare were probably trading furs with peoples to the south and east of them by that time as well. Mackenzie urged the Hare to trade their pelts to the Dogribs, a group which was already being supplied with iron and goods by the men of his company (1801, p.83).

6. Mackenzie noted the contempt in which the Kutchin held the Hare (1801, p.50), and cited instances of hostility between the Hare and the Eskimo (1801, p.83). In the nineteenth century, Richardson emphasized the Hare's great fear of the Eskimo, even though the former had possession of firearms by the time he wrote (1851i, pp.212, 352-353). He also dwelt upon the Hare's reputation for timidity and cowardice, stating that: "unless . . . they are assembled in large numbers, as we found them at the Ramparts (on the Mackenzie River), they seldom pitch a tent on the banks of the river, but skulk under the branches of a tree cut down so as to appear to have fallen naturally from the brow of a cliff; they do not venture to make a smoke, or rear any object that can be seen from a distance. On the first appearance of a canoe or boat, they hide themselves with their wives and children, in the woods, until they have reconnoitered, and ascertained the character of the object of their fears" (1851i; p.212).

7. As MacNeish has described this situation: "The following set of conditions are all that investigators have to work with when staking out tribes or other major divisions of the Northeastern Athabascans . . . .: a set of peoples living in physical contiguity (but not together), speaking a mutually intelligible tongue (though often with regional dialectical variations), sharing a common culture (though not necessarily one distinct in essentials from neighboring tribes), and having at least a vague sense of common identity which may be based in whole or in part on the foregoing conditions" (1956, p.133).

8. Helm (1968a) makes a related point in her discussion of the three major types of socioterritorial groups found among the Dogribs. She distinguishes between regional bands, local bands, and task groups, and goes on to point out that: "Membership in these three kinds of socioterritorial entities is in no wise mutually exclusive. An individual may at the same time have social identity as a member of a

regional band and of a local band, and, by the simple fact of his presence, also be a member of a task group" (1968a, p.118).

9. Rogers (1969a, p.36) documents the fact that the confusion in band names for the Cree and Ojibwa of the eastern subarctic stems from a similar set of ecological, historical, and cultural features.

10. McKennan has documented the fact that the Chandalar Kutchin owe their name to a similar derivation: "From the time of the first white trader-explorers, the least known of the various Kutchin groups trading at Fort Yukon were the people inhabiting the mountain fastness to the north. The voyageurs of the Hudson's Bay Company called them *gens du large*, a name that stressed their highly nomadic existence in the wide expanses between Fort Yukon and the Arctic Ocean . . . This term was easily corrupted into Chandalar, and came to be applied to both the natives and the principal river that flows through their territory . . . (1965, p.14).

11. The latter estimate is based upon Helm's kinship chart of the band for the period 1956-1957 (Helm, 1965a, p.365).

12. The complex history of post-marital residence choices among Colville Lake's married couples has been summarized in another work (Savishinsky 1970a, pp.57-65), which shows a trend towards the solidarity of sibling sets, and a slightly higher incidence of virilocal over uxorilocal unions (cf. also Helm, 1965a, 1969b).

13. In earlier times, young husbands among the Northern Athabascans lived for a period with the family of their new spouse (i.e., uxorilocal residence), providing a year of "bride service" for these people. As Helm states: this "makes possible a flexibility in residence. A man thus makes a contact in his wife's area and then returns to his own band where he is already acquainted with the people and locales. Manoeuverability is possible between the two regions" (1969d, p.238). McClellan carries the implications of this one step further: "I had thought that I found a functional correlate in this as well. Although the Southern Tutchone and Atna (Athabascan groups to the southwest of the Hare) did not know what they were doing, their initial uxorilocality really insured that in times of starvation and famine they could quickly mobilize their forces, for the adult males would be familiar with two hunting territories" (1969, p.238).

14. Some of the key features of the social system can be delineated as follows. Six of the community's fourteen native households (numbers 1 through 6 in Figure 6) are composed of families with the same surname, i.e., Behdzi. Four of these six units (numbers 1, 3, 4, and 5) are headed, respectively, by Leon, Yen, Pierre, and Paul Behdzi, a set of four brothers. Charlie Behdzi, the married stepson of Pierre, heads a separate household (number 6), and Yašeh, the son of Yen, maintains his own residence (number 2) with his maternal grandmother, Annie Kayšene. Furthermore, two of the four Behdzi brothers, Leon and Pierre, were married to a pair of sisters, and Yen's wife Helen is a parallen cousin to two other married adults in the community.

Two other brothers, Wilfred and George Ratehne, head households 7 and 8, and they have established marital ties with several band families. Another set of family units (numbers 12 and 13) are headed, respectively, by André Yawileh and his married son Fred. The male heads of ten of the fourteen native households, therefore, show a series of primary, patrilineal linkages among themselves. Historically, it was the cluster of Behdzi households, along with the elder Yawileh family, which formed the nucleus of the band in the 1950's. This core population thus centered around a set of male siblings and the elderly, patriarchal Joseph Tehgu, André's father-in-law, who was a dominant or focusing figure for the

Yawilehs. It was on the basis of the kinship links extending outward from this nodal group of older people that the Colville community was ultimately re-formed.

Beyond the linkages already noted, ties within the settlement can be — and are — traced bilaterally and affinally as well as patrilineally. Of the four households not considered above (numbers 9, 10, 11, and 14), two (number 9 and 14) include wives from one of the aforementioned patrilineally-linked families: Albert Limertu's wife Paula (number 9) is a Ratehne, and Maurice Bayjere's wife Dora (number 14) is the daughter of André and Berona Yawileh. A former marriage of Dora's husband Maurice involved a case of sister-exchange with a man from a different family in the band, Wilfred Ratehne. Nora Godanto and Lena Dehdele, the wives of the men who head the remaining two households in the village (numbers 10 and 11), are sisters. Lena's husband Peter is a parallel cousin of the male head of another community household, Albert Limertu. Through his deceased brothers, Peter is also related to the wives in two of the settlement's other families. Adoptions, out-of-wedlock children, ties through additional ascending and lateral kin, and the previous marriages of some of the community's older men and women, further expand the picture of band interrelatedness. Sister-exchange unions, and pairs of brothers marrying pairs of sisters, are some of the traditional marriage arrangements still illustrated by the current community, and they constitute marital forms which would have intensified ties within and between bands in earlier times as well.

The possibility that cross-cousin marriages were once a significant practice among the Hare was raised by MacNeish (1960) and Sue (1964), but a recent statistical study of Hare marriages by Helm (1968b) has not borne this out. MacNeish (1960, pp.288-289) cites evidence for polygamy, polyandry, sister-exchange, wife-exchange, and sororate and levirate unions among the Mackenzie Dene in the past.

15. Slobodin points out (1969, p.75) that the ambivalence surrounding the brother-in-law relationship among the Kutchin, which combines elements of closeness and distrust and hostility, is reflected in the variable way in which people use and extend the term for "brother-in-law."

16. Cf. Sue (1964, pp.412-413) for a full explanation of these kinship norms.

17. Cf. the accounts of Richardson (1851l, p.211), Hooper (1853, pp.268-282, 303-305), McLean (1932, p.343), Petitot (1889, pp.39-44), Wentzel (1889, pp.106-107), Keith (1890, pp.118-119), Hurlbert (1962, pp.11-12), Sue (1964, pp.21, 53, 172, 231), Jenness (1967, p.394), BAE (1907, p.667), Osgood (1932, pp.37, 42), Back (1836, p.209), Hearne (1795, pp.33-34, 74, 294-295, 331), and King (1836, pp.170-171, quoted in Helm, 1965a).

18. Descriptions of shamanistic curing in the nineteenth century are given by Keith (1890, pp.118, 127). Curing of ghost sickness or illness entailed singing over the afflicted person, with blowing, sucking, and the laying on of hands onto the ailing part of the body being involved in cases of disease. The curer extracted a small piece of wood, a sliver of bone, or some other tiny object, and then displayed this as the cause of the sickness.

19. In terms of the actual number of people who are still living off the land in the Colville-Good Hope-Bear Lake region (i.e., excluding the sedentary individuals living permanently in fort towns), the present population density of this area is probably comparable to what it was in earlier periods.

20. This phrase is taken from Goodenough (1962, p.11).

21. For an analysis of how stress is produced and coped with by the people of the

Colville band, see Savishinsky (1971a) and the detailed material in the following three sections.

22. Cf. the discussion of envy by Foster, and the comment on Foster's analysis by Savishinsky (1972b). Slobodin (1969) describes a similar pattern of distributing a moose-kill among the Kutchin.

23. Helm (1965b) notes the same procedure among the Dogrib, and describes the patterns of allocation which operate among these people.

24. Some of the contemporary studies which deal with the advantages and problems derived from the persistence of these values include those of Chance (1966, 1968), Ervin (1968, 1969), Lubart (1969), Sindell (1968), Smith (1968), Vallee (1967), and VanStone (1965).

25. In one study the authors compared early twentieth century Chipewyan tales with stories told by contemporary Chipewyan children (Cohen and VanStone 1962). In a subsequent study, a group of tales recorded by a Loucheux (Kutchin) man, Paul Voudrach, who has lived most of his life among the Hare at Fort Good Hope, were similarly analyzed for themes of dependency and self-sufficiency (Cohen and Osterreich, 1967). In comparing the results of these two studies, Cohen and Osterreich concluded:

In both the children's stories and the contemporary adult's material there is a substantial rise in the percentage of scores devoted to dependency. Although dependency is somewhat higher than self-sufficiency for early twentieth century Chipewyan tales, it is on balance more nearly equal to self-sufficiency than in the contemporary material. We have therefore obtained further substantiation for the hypothesis that the contact period, especially that part that includes government welfare programs, tends to stimulate the dependency motivations at the expense of desires for self-sufficiency (1967, p.50)

PART III: STRESS AND MOBILITY

1. The inhibiting influence of Western materials upon native mobility has been documented in several areas of the North: see, for example, VanStone (1965), Helm (1965b), Graburn (1969).

2. The numbers identifying the camps in the maps and figures refer to households discussed in Part II. Several of the early and mid-winter encampments included men from Fort Good Hope, who spent part of the winter trapping with Colville families: these include, in Figure 12, Billy Gafee (Camp 1, 7), Antoine Tahso and his family (Camp 6), Jack Eddee (Camp 8), Jonas Tahso (Camp 9, 10), and Batiste Sašo (Camp 11). Jack Eddee and Jonas Tahso were also members of Camp 8, 9 (Figure 13) during the mid-winter dispersal. Thomas Godanto (Camp 11, Figure 12), whose parents left Colville Lake just before the trapping season in order to take government wage jobs, spent the first part of the winter with Batiste Sašo. After these two men quarreled and split up during the Christmas ingathering, Batiste returned to Good Hope, and Thomas left to rejoin his parents. Hence there is no Camp 11 on Figure 13.

3. Indians have resisted the establishment of family trapping areas in most parts of the Northwest Territories. The Chipewyans at Snowdrift on Great Slave Lake, for example, opposed it, "saying that it would limit their mobility" (Oswalt, 1966, p.48).

4. Turnbull (1968a, 1968b) and Woodburn (1968) cite instances of African hunting groups, the Mbuti and the Hadza, who also employ ecological arguments to explain

socially motivated separations.
5. This set of values and attitudes concerning travelling has also been noted by Slobodin (1969, p.84) for the Kutchin.
6. The relationship between impression management, privacy, and public and self-image is discussed by Goffman (1959), Schwartz (1968), and Gregor (1970). Helm and Lurie (1966) provide an excellent description of how *udzi* is played among the Athabascans.
7. Bernard (1968) points out the eustress-seeking qualities of gambling, sports, and such dramatic forms as folk and fairy tales, novels, and theatre. As Bernard notes,
8. intoxication is also a form of stress-seeking. VanStone (1965) documents a similar problem, with comparable statistics, in a contemporary Chipewyan community. Some of the major demographic features of
9. Colville Lake, besides the preponderance of unmarried males, can be summarized as follows:

Composition of Population by Sex and Age

	Age Range	Number of People	Percentage of Males		Number of People	Percentage of Females
	0-15	12	29.2%		9	30.0%
	16-30	9	22.0%		6	20.0%
	31-45	9	22.0%		5	$16.6^{2}/_{3}\%$
Males	46-60	5	12.2%	Females	2	$6.6^{2}/_{3}\%$
	61-75	5	12.2%		6	20.0%
	76-90	1	2.4%		2	$6.6^{2}/_{3}\%$
	Totals	41	100.0%		30	100.0%

10. Data on mobility as a tension-reducing device for other hunters-and-gatherers are presented in Lee and DeVore (eds., 1968). The way in which residence arrangements reflect stress patterns has been noted by anthropologists in many groups from diverse ecologies: see, for example, Gluckman's comments on the Zulu (1967, pp.99-100), Gregor's observations on the Mehinacu (1970: 241), and Mead's description of the Samoans (1968, pp.42-43, 122, 158, 198).

PART IV:　THE MISSIONARY AND THE FUR TRADER

1. It should be noted that although the settlement's priest belongs to a missionary order, the Indian people of the region had been fully converted to Catholicism by the early years of the twentieth century. Hence, the local feud and its strategies did not directly stem from religious or "missionizing" activities *per se*.
2. Welsh (1970) provides an analysis of how patterns of ethnic segregation have developed in a larger northern community in the Yukon. See also Honigmann's (1952) work on Great Whale River.
3. In the dramaturgical framework suggested by Goffman (1959), the living quarters of the store and mission were "backstage" areas in which the trader and priest could meet with native allies and white visitors. The ability to penetrate these

private spaces was thus a mark of status for people (cf. also Schwartz 1968, p.743; Sommer 1969, pp.18-19).

4. In structural terms, I occupied the position of "high-status friend" that Morris Freilich denotes in his discussion of the "natural triad" (1964). A high-status friend is someone who, "though superior in status to ego, frequently plays the role of intimate friend, adviser and helper" (1964, p.530). "In many field work situations anthropologists (and at times sociologists) are the (high-status friend) to their informants (the low-status subordinates), whose activities are directed by various people (i.e., high-status authority figures)" (1964, p.531).

Within the context of Colville Lake, the geometry of the situation was somewhat more complex than this, for one could speak analytically, of at least four triads, all of which involved me in the role of high-status friend, viz.,

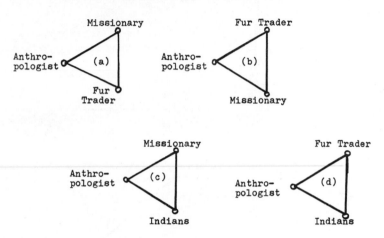

Triads (a) and (b) materialized under those conditions where the priest or trader recognized that his antagonist possessed certain specific advantages over him, advantages which they assumed I could be instrumentally helpful in overcoming.

If one were to further differentiate among the native people of the village, and consider the patron-client relationships established between the whites and selected Indians, then the latter also occupied "high-status friend" roles for the less committed natives; viz.,

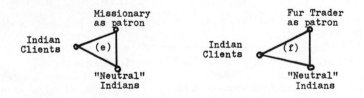

In other words, as Balikci (1960) and others have argued, native populations in small northern settlements are really not completely undifferentiated, and problems of social structure should be approached with these subtleties in mind.

The number of triads or triangles (natural or otherwise) which could be delineated within the community would thus depend upon how many distinctions one wanted to make within the village's population. Furthermore, additional geometric models could be utilized if the above triads were combined in various ways. As Homans notes in his discussion of triangular situations, a rule applicable to one triad "can be extended to any number of persons, and thus a matrix or system of relationships is formed" (1950, p.248). Possible combinations and permutations at Colville Lake would include the following:

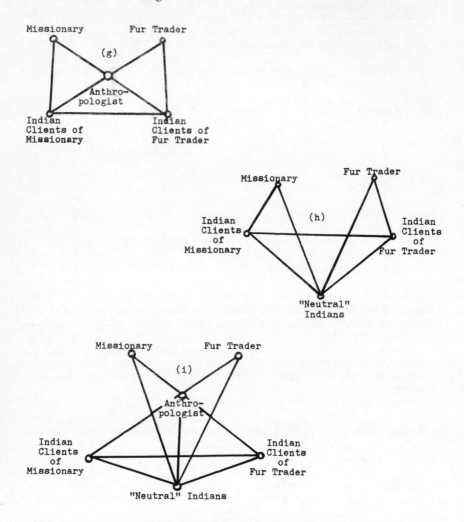

I. C. Jarvie, in discussing the problems confronting a fieldworker, has observed that ". . . it is his lack of a fixed and defined role, or his shifting about among the various roles, that enables him to get at information which would otherwise be inaccessible" (1969, p.508). Jarvie also notes that "... to some extent the success of the method of participant observation *derives from* exploiting the role clashes insider/outsider, stranger/friend, pupil/teacher" (1969, p.505).

6. Since the priest's strongest supporters come from among the village's most traditional and religious families, Kluckhohn and Leighton's observations on the Navaho is suggestive of the type of situation which developed at Colville:

   Of those who practice the Christian religion exclusively, it is merely factual to point out that a higher proportion are directly or indirectly dependent on the missionaries for their livelihood (1962, p.133).

7. The effect of the feud upon the people's ecological involvement was really quite complex. Some of the more traditional men actually increased their fishing in the spring and summer, selling their surplus fish to the trader in order to clear up part of their debt. Most of this fish was later resold by the trader to more acculturated, heavy-drinking families for use as dog food during the following winter. Caribou hunting was also increased by some people in the village and the surplus meat was similarly sold by them to the trader to pay off their debts. In general, however, if one considers the activities of all band members, their subsistence pursuits have declined over the years as people have come to rely more and more upon Western commodities and new techniques for obtaining them. Van Stone (1963) has documented the fact that increased wage labor opportunities and sedentariness, unpredictable and sometimes incomprehensible fluctuations in fur prices, and related social, economic, and ecological factors, have reduced and restricted Indian trapping throughout the eastern and western sub-Arctic (cf. also Usher, 1971).

8. Dunning (1959, pp.119-121), for example, in discussing the strategies used by whites to win favor and power among native persons, notes the following features in the communities he considers: the spatial segregation of ethnic groups and the carefully controlled access of natives to "white" areas; the manipulation of wage labor, store prices, and assistance funds by whites; and the white monopoly over communication channels. Honigmann, in describing the situation at the northern settlement of Great Whale River, also points out the position of power enjoyed by the trader there because of his control over radio contact with the outside (1952, pp.515-516).

9. Freilich notes that the high-status friend often functions as a major tension-reducer within the triadic social situation by providing people with a safe outlet for the expression of their feelings (1964, pp.532-533).

10. Cf. Honigmann (1952) for a discussion of symbiotic interdependence between ethnic groups in the North.

PART V: THE HARE AND THE DOG

1. Weyer (1969, pp.100-101), Graburn (1969, p.44), Birket-Smith (1929i, p.170), Sue (1964, pp.293-294, 297), and others have commented on the periodic, epidemic diseases which have wiped out large numbers of dogs in the North, and this may have also been a factor in keeping down the size of the aboriginal dog population among sub-Arctic Indians. Franklin described a unique occurrence among the Chipewyans in the early nineteenth century which adds a religious dimension to the scarcity and limited utility of dogs: "The Northern Indians suppose that they originally sprang from a dog; and, about five years ago, a superstitious fanatic so strongly pressed upon their minds the impropriety of employing these animals, to

which they were related, for purposes of labour, that they universally resolved against using them any more, and, strange as it may seem, destroyed them. They now have to drag everything themselves on sledges. This laborious task falls most heavily on the women . . ." (1824, pp.160-161). The relevance of Athabascan mythology and religion to their treatment of dogs, as indicated here in the case of the Chipewyans, is more fully considered later in this section.

2. Cf. the same parallel described among the Kaska by Honigmann (1949, pp.55, 185).

3. Cf. also Sue (1964, pp.471-472), Helm (no date), and Honigmann's (1949, p.185) observations on the unstructured nature of childhood learning in Athabascan culture.

4. The raising of young dogs as pets by children is a common feature in other Athabascan groups. The same process is noted by Driver among the Eskimo: "Puppies were even turned over to children who harnessed them to toy sleds: both the pups and the children were supposed to learn something of value from this experience" (1961, pp.466-467). Robert Flaherty captures just such a relationship on film in one of the segments of "Nanook of the North."

5. A nineteenth century observer of the Hare, Bernard Ross, wrote that: "Male children are invariably more cherished and cared for than females. The latter are mere drudges, and obliged on all occasions to concede to their brother; and though female infanticide, formerly so prevalent, is now unknown, still in seasons of starvation or times of danger, girls invariably fall the first sacrifices to the exigencies of the case" (this 1866 source is quoted in Sue, 1964, p.445). Sue gives population figures for the contemporary Hare in the Fort Good Hope-Colville Lake area which show "that today (c. 1963) more males of ages 10 to 30 have survived than females. The same reason as mentioned by Ross may be partly responsible for this fact" (1964, p.445). Osgood (1932, p.76) supplies additional historical documentation concerning the prevalence of female infanticide in the region.

6. Names are given by the Hare in both English and Athabascan: examples of the former are Gray, Buck, Aces, Horse, and Blacky. The English equivalents of some dog names in *deneké*, "the people's language," are Butter, Skinny One, and Sharp Ears. The practice of naming dogs is, of course, not unique with the Hare: see for example Osgood (1937, p.161) on the Tanaina and (1959, p.28) the Ingalik; McKennan (1965, p.58) on the Kutchin; and Honigmann (1949, p.56) on the Kaska. As part of the Tanaina system of teknonymy, Osgood notes that: "Before a man marries, people call him by his own name and if he marries and has no children, they substitute the name of his dog" (1937, p.161). McKennan points out a parallel process among the Chandalar Kutchin, among whom a childless man "might be known as the father of his dog" (1965, p.58).

7. Ashes are used especially for treating a dog who has lice, a practice which Honigmann also describes among the Kaska (1949, p.56). Osgood (1940, p.187; 1958, p.230) notes that the Ingalik used charcoal and ashes to treat themselves, employing these substances both internally, in the form of a drink, for stomach aches, and externally for wounds, but he does not refer to their use for treating dogs.

8. Birket-Smith and deLaguna, in their monograph on the Eyak (1938, pp.57, 427-429, 492), and McKennan, in his work on the Upper Tanana (1959, pp.92, 162-163), have summarized much of the relevant literature on Athabascan attitudes towards dogs. McKennan's statement is as follows: "The Upper Tanana hold the dog in peculiar reverence, and they will neither kill nor eat it although they have no rationalized explanation for this taboo.

"Such a regard for the dog is widespread among the Northern Athapaskans. The Hare, Dog-rib, and other Mackenzie groups will not kill this animal, and the Chipewyan explain a similar taboo by claiming descent from the dog. This belief in canine descent is not found among the Alaskan Athapaskans, but the Han, Kutchin, Eyak, and Tanaina all hold the dog in such reverence that they will neither kill nor eat one. Many of these groups extend this taboo to forbid the eating of wolves also, but among the Upper Tanana the latter animal is occasionally eaten in times of famine" (1959, pp.162-163; the references cited by McKennan are omitted).

Birket-Smith and deLaguna provide additional information on related beliefs among other Athabascan and Eskimo groups, suggesting that: "It is probable that this attitude (of reverence) towards both dog and wolf should be seen in a far wider connection, i.e., the typical circum-Pacific mythology to which Koppers has called attention" (1938, p.492). Other pertinent data relating to native beliefs and attitudes concerning dogs among the sub-Arctic Indians is given in Savishinsky (In Press).

9. An observer of the Tanaina (cited by Osgood, 1937, p.37) has written of their recourse to a similar strategy.

10. Helm writes as follows concerning the Slave utilization of dogs as an emotional outlet: "The fact that any display of anger is so severely checked in the interpersonal situation gives special interest to the observations on the treatment of dogs. Toward dogs, all, but the men especially, give free vent to angry actions, shouting, swearing, and belabouring them. More than one man spoke, almost with pride, of a flaring rage toward a loafing sled-dog that was released by sending a bullet or an axe into the animal's skull. The excited, angry actions of the men towards their dogs are startling to the observer accustomed to their usual quiet, controlled behaviour. By the age of two, children begin practicing the raging and beating techniques of their fathers on any amenable dog" (1961,pp.89-90).

11. Many of the points in this section have benefited from the writings of Szasz (1969) and Goffman (1959).

12. The imagery resembles a point made by McLuhan, who speaks of art as a "radar environment" and the arts as "radar feedback" (1966, p.xi).

13. Cf. Birket-Smith (1929i, pp.112, 119); Birket-Smith and deLaguna (1938, pp.241, 427-429); Weyer (1969, p.100); Osgood (1932, p.40; 1936b, p.27; 1937, pp.32-33); McKennan (1959, p.49; 1965, pp.32, 42).

14. Cf. Osgood (1937, p.33; 1940, p.451); Richardson (1851ii, pp.26, 30); Birket-Smith (1930, pp.19-26); Hearne (1795, p.284); Honigmann (1949, pp.54, 56, 64).

15 See the summary of the Athabascan evidence given in note 8. Jenness states that dogs were "of little value for either food or clothing" among Canadian Indians (1967, p.29). Brief summaries of the use of dogs for food by native Americans are provided by Wissler (1957, p.36) and Driver (1961, p.34), who stress its rareness outside of certain geographic regions, and its general restriction to ceremonial and religious occasions.

16. Cf. Osgood (1940, pp.185-186; 1958, pp.259-260); Honigmann (1949, pp.187-188); Sue (1964, p.297); Helm (1961, p.74); and deLaguna (1969/1970, p.26), who notes a taboo on non-canine pets among the Atna.

Laughlin, in his analysis of hunting as a process, mentions "pets" (i.e., captured wild animals) as a source of feedback for hunters, providing them with information about the nature of the game that they pursue. He adds that these "pets" are also a useful means for instructing children about animal behavior (1968, pp.310, 320).

Although Laughlin does not discuss domesticated dogs from the cybernetic-feedback viewpoint suggested here, his analysis could be extended to include this aspect of their use.

17. Additional material relating to the points raised in this chapter is provided in Savishinsky (In Press), where extensive documentation is given concerning the scarcity and limited use of dogs in aboriginal northern cultures.

PART VI: CONCLUSIONS

1. On the role of conflict in promoting unity and identity, see the work of Simmel (1964).
2. Serious attempts are underway in the Northwest Territories now to reform school curricula and bring them into line with the needs and backgrounds of the region's population. Problems of staffing, finances, and over-all educational philosophy persist however.
3. One recent attempt to make educational programs more valuable to native people in the Territories has been the introduction of vocational training in such areas as nursing, mechanics, and heavy-duty equipment operation.
4. When the store was under private ownership, the people sold their pelts to the local trader, who then shipped them out to one of the large fur auction centers in the southern Canadian provinces. Except for a small percentage retained by the auction company, the trader earned close to the full auction value of the furs, which was anywhere from ten to one hundred percent more than what the trappers at the village received for the same skins.
5. On perceptual and cognitive aspects of stress, see Opler (1967a), Lazarus (1966, 1967), and Klausner (1968).
6. The relation of biological and social rhythms to stress and release is discussed by Aginsky (1939), Chapple (1970), and Wallace (1970, p.236).
7. Cf. the summary of the literature on stress resulting from "underload" and "overload" in McGrath (1970a).
8. These points have been elaborated by Merton (1957), Honigmann (1967, p.351 ff.), and Wallace (1970, pp.230-232).
9. Cultural data from a number of settings which illustrate this point may be found in the works of Opler (1967a, 1967b), Langner and Michael (1963), Honigmann (1967), and Torrance (1968).
10. My information on Fort Good Hope comes from conversations with many residents of the town, both native and white, and from a brief period of residence there during my first field trip. The staff of the community's nursing station was especially helpful and informative, and they allowed me to examine medical records and histories for both Colville and Good Hope.
11. One native community which stands out as an exception to the general decline of fur trapping as a viable economy is the Eskimo settlement of Banks Island, where the annual harvesting of white foxes continues to be of prime importance (Usher 1971). Villiers (1967) presents income statistics for an array of Mackenzie River towns, documenting the other trends which are mentioned. The constriction of environmental mobility in the North has led to a congruency between what Chang (1967) calls "settlement patterns" and "community patterns."

Acknowledgments

I would like to thank the authors, editors and publishers of the following works for permission to quote from their publications:

Edmund S. Carpenter: "Ethnological clues for the interpretation of certain northeastern archaeological data." *Pennsylvania Archaeologist* **31**, pp.148-150 (1961).

June Helm: *The Lynx Point People: The Dynanics Of A Northern Athapaskan Band*. Bulletin No. 176. Ottawa: National Museum of Canada (1961). Reproduction authorized by Information Canada.

June Helm: "Bilaterality in the socio-territorial organization of the arctic drainage Dene." *Ethnology* **4**, pp.361-385 (1965).

John P. Kelsall: *The Migratory Barren-Ground Caribou Of Canada*. Canadian Wildlife Service. Ottawa: Department of Indian Affairs and Northern Development (1968).

Robert McKennan: *The Upper Tanana Indians*. Yale University Publications in Anthropology No. 55. New Haven: Yale University Press (1959).

J.S.S.

References

Adams, William Y. *Shonto: a study of the role of the trader in a modern Navaho community.* Smithsonian Institution: Bureau of American Ethnology, Bulletin 188. Washington: U.S. Government Printing Office, 1963.

Aginsky, B. W. "Psychopathic trends in culture," *Culture and Personality* 7, pp. 331-343, 1939.

Appley, Mortimer H. and Richard Trumbull. (Eds.) *Psychological stress, issues in research.* New York: Appleton-Century-Crofts, 1967a.

"On the concept of psychological stress." *In* Appley and Trumbull (Eds., 1967a), 1967b.

Arsenian, John and Jean M. Arsenian. "Tough and easy cultures." *Psychiatry* 11, pp.377-385, 1948.

Back, George. *Narrative of the arctic land expedition . . . in the years 1833, 1834, and 1835.* London: John Murray, 1836.

BAE (Bureau of American Ethnology). "Kawchodinne." (Anonymous). *In* Frederick Webb Hodge, Ed. *Handbook of American Indians north of Mexico,* I. Bureau of American Ethnology, Bulletin 30, Part 1. Washington: U.S. Government Printing Office, 1907.

Bakan, David. *Disease, pain, and sacrifice.* Boston: Beacon Press, 1971.

Balikci, Asen. "Ethnic relations and the marginal man in Canada: a comment." *Human Organization* 19, pp.170-171, 1960-61.

"The Netsilik Eskimos." *In* Lee and DeVore (Eds.), 1968.

Balikci, Asen and Ronald Cohen. "Community patterning in two northern trading posts." *Anthropologica N.S.* 5 pp.33-45, 1963.

Barnouw, Victor. "Acculturation and personality among the Wisconsin Chippewa." *American Anthropologist* 52, pp.19-27, 1950.

Benedict, Ruth. *Patterns of Culture.* Boston: Houghton Mifflin Co., 1934.

Bernard, Jessie. "The eudaemonists." *In* Samuel Z. Klausner, Ed. *Why man takes chances: studies in stress-seeking.* Garden City: Doubleday and Co., Inc., 1968.

Birdsell, Joseph B. "Comment on population control factors: infanticide, disease, nutrition, and food." *In* Lee and DeVore (Eds.), 1968.

Birket-Smith, Kaj. "The Caribou Eskimos." *Report of the Fifth Thule Expedition 1921-1924,* 5, 2 volumes. Copenhagen: Gyldendalske Boghandel, Nordiske Forlag, 1929.

"Contributions to Chipewyan ethnology." *Report of the Fifth Thule Expedition 1921-1924,* 6, No. 3. Copenhagen: Gyldendalske Boghandel, Nordisk Forlag, 1930.

Birket-Smith, Kaj and Frederica de Laguna. *The Eyak Indians of the Copper River Delta, Alaska.* Kobenhavn: Levin and Munksgaard, 1938.

Blum, David. "Axial pressure profiles in non-Newtonian flow." Unpublished doctoral dissertation. The City University of New York, 1972.

Buber, Martin. *I and Thou.* 2nd edition. Ronald Gregor Smith, translator. New York: Charles Scribner's Sons, 1958.

Burt, William H. and Richard P. Grossenheider. *A field guide to the mammals.* 2nd, revised and enlarged edition. Boston: Houghton Mifflin Co., 1952.

Canby, Vincent. "Film: two parallel love stories with one object (review of *Sunday Bloody Sunday*)." *New York Times*, September 22, 1971, p.56, 1971.

Carpenter, Edmund S. *Eskimo.* With Frederick Varley and Robert Flaherty. Toronto: University of Toronto Press, 1959.
"Ethnological clues for the interpretation of certain northeastern archaeological data." *Pennsylvania Archaeologist* **31**, pp.148-150, 1961.
They became what they beheld. New York: Outerbridge and Dienstfrey, 1970.

Chance, Norman A. *The Eskimo of North Alaska.* New York: Holt, Rinehart and Winston, Inc., 1966.
"Implications of environmental stress: strategies of developmental change in the North." *Archives of Environmental Health* **17**, pp.571-577, 1968.

Chang, K. C. *Rethinking archaeology.* New York: Random House, 1967.

Chapple, Eliot D. *Culture and biological man.* New York: Holt, Rinehart and Winston, Inc., 1970.

Chitty, Dennis. "The natural selection of self-regulatory behavior in animal populations." *In* Ian A. McLaren, Ed. *Natural regulation of animal populations.* New York: Atherton Press, 1971.

Cofer, C. N. and M. H. Appley. *Motivation: theory and research.* New York: John Wiley and Sons, Inc., 1964.

Cohen, Ronald. *An anthropological survey of communities in the Mackenzie-Slave Lake region of Canada.* Northern Co-ordination and Research Centre. Ottawa: Department of Northern Affairs and National Resources, 1962.

Cohen, Ronald and Helgi Osterreich. "Analysis of 'Good Hope Tales' by Paul Voudrach." *In Contributions to Ethnology* **V**. Bulletin No. 228. Ottawa: National Museum of Canada, 1967.

Cohen, Ronald and James W. VanStone. "Dependency and self-sufficiency in Chipewyan stories." *In Contributions to Anthropology* 1961-1962, Part II. Bulletin No. 194. Ottawa: National Museum of Canada, 1963.

Damas, David. *Igluligmiut kinship and local groupings: a structural approach.* Bulletin No. 196. Ottawa: National Museum of Canada, 1963.
"The diversity of Eskimo societies." *In* Lee and Devore (Eds.), 1968.
(Ed.) *Contributions to anthropology: band societies. Proceedings of the 1965 Conference on Band Organization.* Bulletin No. 228. Ottawa: National Museums of Canada, 1969a.
(Ed.) *Contributions to anthropology: ecological essays. Proceedings of the 1966 Conference on Cultural Ecology.* Bulletin No. 230. Ottawa: National Museums of Canada, 1969b.

Deevey, Edward, Jr. "Comments on the magic numbers '25' and '500': determinants of group size in modern and pleistocene hunters." *In* Lee and DeVore (Eds.), 1968.

de Laguna, Frederica. "The Atna of the Copper River, Alaska: the world of men and animals." *Folk* **11/12**, pp.17-26, 1969/70.

Dostoyevsky, Fyodor. *Notes from a dead house.* Moscow: Foreign Languages Publishing House (no date).

Doxiadis, Constantinos A. *Architecture in transition.* London: Hutchinson and Co., 1963.

Driver, Harold. *Indians of North America.* Chicago: University of Chicago Press, 1961.

Dunning, R. W. "Ethnic relations and the marginal man in Canada." *Human Organization* **19**, pp.117-12, 1959.

Ervin, A. M. "New northern townsmen in Inuvik." *Mackenzie Delta Research Project*, Report No. 5. Northern Science Research Group. Ottawa: Department of Indian Affairs and Northern Development, 1968.
"Conflicting styles of life in a northern Canadian town." *Arctic* **22**, pp.90-105, 1969.

Evans-Pritchard, E. E. *The Nuer*. Oxford: The Clarendon Press, 1940.

Forde, C. Daryll. *Habitat, economy and society*. New York: E.P. Dutton and Co., 1963.

Fox, M. W. *Canine behavior*. Springfield, Ill.: Charles C. Thomas, 1965.

Franklin, John. *Narrative of a journey to the shores of the polar sea in the years 1819-20-21-22*. 2nd edition, 2 volumes. London: John Murray, 1824.

Freeman, J. D. "On the concept of the kindred." *Journal of the Royal Anthropological Institute* **91**, pp.192-220, 1961.

Freilich, Morris. "The natural triad in kinship and complex systems." *American Sociological Review* **29**, pp.529-540, 1964.

Gluckman, Max. "Gossip and scandal." *Current Anthropology* **4**, pp.307-316, 1963.
Custom and conflict in Africa. New York: Barnes and Noble, Inc., 1967.

Goffman, Erving. *The presentation of self in everyday life*. Garden City: Doubleday and Co., Inc., 1959.

Goodenough, Ward. "Kindred and hamlet in Lakalai, New Britain". *Ethnology* **1**, pp.5-12, 1962.

Graburn, Nelson H. H. *Eskimos without igloos*. Boston: Little, Brown and Co., 1969.

Gregor, Thomas. "Exposure and seclusion: a study of institutionalized isolation among the Mehinacu Indians of Brazil." *Ethnology* **9**, pp.234-50, 1970.

Hall, Edward T. *The hidden dimension*. Garden City:Doubleday and Co., Inc., 1969.

Hallowell, A. Irving. "The social function of anxiety in a primitive society." *American Sociological Review* **7**, pp.869-881, 1941.
"Some psychological characteristics of the northeastern Indians." *In* Frederick Johnson, Ed. *Man in northeastern North America*. Andover: Papers of the Robert S. Peabody Foundation for Archaeology, No. III, 1946.

Hatt, Gudmund. "Arctic skin clothing in Eurasia and America: an ethnographic study." *Arctic Anthropology* **5**, pp.3-132, 1969.

Hearne, Samuel. *A journey from Prince of Wales's Fort in Hudson's Bay, to the Northern Ocean . . . in the years 1769, 1770, 1771, and 1772*. London: A. Strahan and T. Cadell, 1795.

Heidegger, Martin. *Being and time*. John Macquarrie and Edward Robinson, translators. New York: Harper and Brothers, 1962.

Helm, June. "The Dogrib Indians." Unpublished manuscript" (no date).
The Lynx Point people: the dynamics of a northern Athapaskan band. Bulletin No. 176. Ottawa: National Museum of Canada, 1961.
"Bilaterality in the socio-territorial organization of the arctic drainage Dene." *Ethnology* **4**, pp.361-385, 1965a.
"Patterns of allocation among the arctic drainage Dene." *In* June Helm, ed. *Essays in economic anthropology. Proceedings of the 1965 Annual Spring Meeting of the American Ethnological Society*. Seattle: University of Washington Press, 1965b.
"The nature of Dogrib socioterritorial groups." *In* Lee and DeVore (Eds., 1968), 1968a.
"The statistics of kin marriage: a non-Australian example." *In* Lee and DeVore (Eds., 1968), 1968b.

"Remarks on the methodology of band composition analysis." *In* Damas (Ed., 1969a), 1969b.

"A method of statistical analysis of primary relative bonds in community composition." *In* Damas (Ed., 1969a), 1969b.

"Relationship between settlement pattern and community pattern." *In* Damas (Ed., 1969b), 1969c.

"Discussion." *In* Damas (Ed., 1969a), 1969d.

Helm, June and David Damas. "The contact-traditional all-native community of the Canadian North: the Upper Mackenzie 'bush' Athapaskans and the Igluligmiut." *Anthropologica N.S.* **5**, pp.9-21, 1963.

Helm, June and Eleanor Burke Leacock. "The hunting tribes of subarctic Canada." *In* Eleanor Burke Leacock and Nancy Oestreich Lurie, Eds. *North American Indians in historical perspective*. New York: Random House, 1971.

Helm, June and Nancy O. Lurie. *The subsistence economy of the Dogrib Indians of Lac La Martre in the Mackenzie District of the Northwest Territories*. Northern Co-ordination and Research Centre. Ottawa: Department of Northern Affairs and National Resources, 1961.

The Dogrib handgame. Bulletin No. 205. Ottawa: National Museum of Canada, 1966.

Hiatt, L. R. "Ownership and use of land among the Australian Aborigines." *In* Lee and DeVore (Eds.), 1968.

Hoijer, Harry. "Hare phonology: an historical study." *Language* **42**, pp.499-507, 1966.

Homans, George C. *The human group*. New York: Harcourt, Brace and Co., 1950.

Honigmann, John J. "Ethnography and acculturation of the Fort Nelson Slave." *Yale University Publications in Anthropology* No. 33. New Haven: Yale University Press, 1946.

"Witch-fear in post-contact Kaska society." *American Anthropologist* **49**, pp.222-243, 1947.

"Culture and ethos of Kaska society." *Yale University Publications in Anthropology* No. 40. New Haven: Yale University Press, 1949.

"Intercultural relations at Great Whale River." *American Anthropologist* **54**, pp.510-522, 1952.

"The Kaska Indians: an ethnographic reconstruction." *Yale University Publications in Anthropology* No. 51. New Haven: Yale University Press, 1954.

Personality in culture. New York: Harper and Row, 1967.

"Interpersonal relations in atomistic communities." *Human Organization* **27**, pp.220-229, 1968.

Honigmann, John J. and Irma Honigmann. *Eskimo townsmen*. Canadian Research Centre for Anthropology. Ottawa: University of Ottawa, 1965.

Hooper, W. H. *Ten months among the tents of the Tuski*. London: John Murray, 1853.

Hurlbert, Janice. *Age as a factor in the social organization of the Hare Indians of Fort Good Hope, N.W.T.* Northern Co-ordination and Research Centre. Ottawa: Department of Northern Affairs and National Resources, 1962.

Innis, Harold A. *The fur trade in Canada*. Revised edition. New Haven: Yale University Press, 1962.

James, Preston E. *A geography of man*. Boton: Ginn and Company, 1957.

Jarvie, I. C. "The problem of ethical integrity in participant observation." *Current Anthropology* **10**, pp.505-508, 1969.

Jenness, Diamond. *The Indians of Canada.* 6th edition. Bulletin No. 65. Ottawa: National Museum of Canada, 1967.

Keats, John. "To George and Thomas Keats." *In* John Keats, *Selected poems and letters* (1959). Douglas Bush, Ed. Boston: Houghton Mifflin Co., 1817.

Keith, George. "Letters to the Hon. Roderic McKenzie, 1807-1817." *In* L. R. Masson, Ed. *Les bourgeois de la Compagnie du Nord-Ouest.* Deuxième Série. Quebec: A. Coté, 1890.

Kelsall, John P. *The migratory barren-ground caribou of Canada.* Canadian Wildlife Service. Ottawa: Department of Indian Affairs and Northern Development, 1968.

Kelsall, John P., Vernon D. Hawley and Donald C. Thomas. "Distribution and abundance of muskoxen north of Great Bear Lake." *Arctic* **24**, pp.157-161, 1971.

King, Richard. *Narrative of a journey to the shores of the Arctic Ocean in 1833, 1834, and 1835.* 2 volumes. London: R. Bentley, 1836.

Klausner, Samuel Z. "The intermingling of pain and pleasure: the stress-seeking personality in its social context." *In* Samuel Z. Klausner, Ed. *Why man takes chances: studies in stress-seeking.* Garden City: Doubleday and Co., Inc., 1968.

Kluckhohn, Clyde and Dorothea Leighton. *The Navaho.* Revised edition. Garden City: Doubleday and Co., Inc., 1962.

Kroeber, A. L. "Cultural and natural areas of native North America." *University of California Publications in American Archaeology and Ethnology* 38. Berkeley: University of California Press, 1939.

La Barre, Weston. "Materials for a history of studies of crisis cults: a bibliographic essay." *Current Anthropology* **12**, pp.3-44, 1971.

Landes, Ruth. "The Ojibwa of Canada." *In* Margaret Mead, Ed. *Cooperation and competition among primitive peoples.* New York: McGraw-Hill, 1937a.
"The personality of the Ojibwa." *Character and Personality* **6**, pp. 51-60, 1937b.

Langner, Thomas S. and Stanley T. Michael. *Life stress and mental health. The Midtown Manhattan Study*, Volume II. New York: The Free Press of Glencoe, 1963.

Laughlin, William S. "Hunting: an integrating biobehavior system and its evolutionary importance." *In* Lee and DeVore (Eds.), 1968.

Lazarus, Richard S. *Psychological stress and the coping process.* New York: McGraw-Hill, 1966.
"Cognitive and personality factors underlying threat and coping." *In* Appley and Trumbull (Eds., 1967a), 1967.

Leacock, Eleanor. "The Montagnais 'hunting territory' and the fur trade." *American Anthropological Association Memoir* No. 78, 56, *No. 5, Part 2, 1954.*
"The Montagnais-Naskapi Band." In Damas (Ed., 1969a), 1969.

Lee, Richard B. "What hunters do for a living, or, how to make out on scarce resources." *In* Lee and DeVore (Eds.), 1968.
"!Kung Bushman subsistence: an input-output analysis." *In* Damas (Ed., 1969b), 1969.

Lee, Richard B. and Irven DeVore (Eds.). *Man the hunter.* Chicago: Aldine Publishing Co., 1968.

Lee, Richard B. and Irven DeVore. "Problems in the study of hunters and gatherers." *In* Lee and DeVore (Eds.), 1968.

Lefroy, John Henry. "Sir Henry Lefroy's journey to the North-West in 1843-4." W. S. Wallace, Ed. *Transactions of the Royal Society of Canada*, Section II, 1938.

Levi-Strauss, Claude. *Structural anthropology.* Claire Jacobson and Brooke

Grundfest Schoepf, translators. New York: Basic Books, Inc., 1963.

Lips, Julius E. "Public opinion and mutual assistance among the Montagnais-Naskapi." *American Anthropologist* **39**, pp.222-228, 1937.

Lubart, J. M. "Psychodynamic problems of adaptation — Mackenzie Delta Eskimos." *Mackenzie Delta Research Project*, Report No. 7. Northern Science Research Group. Ottawa: Department of Indian Affairs and Northern Development, 1969.

Luomala, Katherine. "The native dog in the Polynesian system of values." *In* Stanley Diamond, Ed. *Culture in history: essays in honor of Paul Radin.* New York: Columbia University Press, 1960.

Mackenzie, Alexander. *Voyages from Montreal on the River St. Laurence, through the continent of North America, to the Frozen and Pacific Oceans; in the years 1789 and 1793.* London: R. Noble, 1801.

MacNeish, June Helm. "Leadership among the northeastern Athabascans." *Anthropologica* **2**, pp.131-164, 1956.

"Kin terms of the arctic drainage Dene: Hare, Slavey, Chipewyan." *American Anthropologist* **62**, pp.279-295, 1960.

Marshall, S. L. A. "The better part of man's nature." *In* Samuel Z. Klausner, Ed. *Why man takes chances: studies in stress-seeking.* Garden City: Doubleday and Co., Inc., 1968.

Mauss, Marcel. "Essai sur les variations saisonnières des sociétés eskimos. Essai de morphologie sociale." *L'Année Sociologique* **9**, pp.39-132, 1904-1905.

May, Rollo. *Existential psychotherapy.* Canadian Broadcasting Corporation. Toronto: CBC Publications, 1967.

McClellan, Catherine. "Discussion." *In* Damas (Ed., 1969a), 1969.

McGrath, Joseph E. (Ed.) *Social and psychological factors in stress.* New York: Holt, Rinehart and Winston, Inc., 1970a.

"A conceptual formulation for research on stress." *In* McGrath (Ed., 1970a), 1970b.

McKennan, Robert. "The Upper Tanana Indians." *Yale University Publications in Anthropology* No. 55. New Haven: Yale University Press, 1959.

"The Chandalar Kutchin." *Arctic Institute of North America, Technical Paper* No. 17. Montreal, Washington, New York, 1965.

McLean, John. *Notes of a twenty-five years' service in the Hudson's Bay Territory.* W. S. Wallace, Ed. Toronto: The Champlain Society. 1932.

McLuhan, Marshall. *Understanding media: the extensions of man.* New York: The New American Library, 1966.

Mead, Margaret. *Coming of age in Samoa.* New York: William Morrow and Co., 1968.

Meggitt, M. J. "The association between Australian Aborigines and dingoes." *In* Anthony Leeds and Andrew P. Vayda, Eds., *Man, culture, and animals.* American Association for the Advancement of Science, Publication No. 78. Washington, D.C., 1965.

Merton, Robert K. *Social theory and social structure.* Revised edition. Glencoe, Ill.: The Free Press, 1957.

Mooney, James. "The aboriginal population of America north of Mexico." *Smithsonian Miscellaneous Collections* **80**, No. 7. Washington, D.C.: Smithsonian Institution, 1928.

Murdock, George Peter. *Social structure.* New York: Macmillan, 1949.

"The current status of the world's hunting and gathering peoples." *In* Lee and

DeVore (Eds.), 1968.

Murphy, Robert F. "Social distance and the veil." *American Anthropologist* **66**, pp.1257-1274, 1964.

Murphy, Robert F. and Julian H. Steward. "Tappers and trappers: parallel process in acculturation." *Economic Development and Cultural Change* **4**, pp.335-355, 1956.

Nadel, S. F. "Witchcraft in four African societies: an essay in comparison." *American Anthropologist* **54**, pp.18-29, 1952.

Naroll, Raoul. *Data quality control — a new research technique: prolegomena to a cross-cultural study of culture stress.* New York: The Free Press of Glencoe, 1962.

Netting, Robert McC. "Beer as a locus of value among the West African Kofyar." *American Anthropologist* **66**, pp.375-384, 1964.
"The ecological approach in cultural study." *McCaleb Modules in Anthropology.* Reading, Mass.: Addison-Wesley Publishing Co., 1971.

Noble, William C. "Archaeological surveys and sequences in Central District Mackenzie, N.W.T." *Arctic Anthropology* **8**, pp.102-135, 1971.

Opler, Marvin. *Culture and social psychiatry.* New York: Atherton Books, 1967a.
"Cultural induction of stress." *In* Appley and Trumbull (Eds., 1967a), 1967b.

Opler, Morris E. "Themes as dynamic forces in culture." *American Journal of Sociology* **51** pp.198-206, 1945.
"An application of the theory of themes in culture." *Journal of the Washington Academy of Sciences* **36**, pp.137-166, 1946.
An Apache life-way. New York: Cooper Square Publishers, Inc., 1965.

Osgood, Cornelius. *The ethnography of the Great Bear Lake Indians.* Bulletin No. 70. Ottawa: National Museum of Canada, 1932.
"The distribution of the northern Athapaskan Indians." *Yale University Publications in Anthropology* No. 7. New Haven: Yale University Press, 1936a.
"Contributions to the ethnography of the Kutchin." *Yale University Publications in Anthropology* No. 14. New Haven: Yale University Press, 1936b.
"The ethnography of the Tanaina." *Yale University Publications in Anthropology* No. 16. New Haven: Yale University Press, 1937.
"Ingalik material culture." *Yale University Publications in Anthropology* No. 22. New Haven: Yale University Press, 1940.
"Ingalik social culture." *Yale University Publications in Anthropology* No. 53. New Haven: Yale University Press, 1958.
"Ingalik mental culture." *Yale University Publications in Anthropology* No. 56. New Haven: Yale University Press, 1959.
"The Han Indians." *Yale University Publications in Anthropology* No. 74. New Haven: Department of Anthropology, Yale University, 1971.

Oswalt, Wendell H. *This land was theirs.* New York: John Wiley and Sons, Inc., 1966.

Pascal, Gerald R. "Psychological deficit as a function of stress and constitution." *Journal of Personality* **20**, pp.175-187, 1951.

Pehrson, Robert N. *The bilateral network of social relations in Konkama Lapp District.* Samiske Samlinger, Bind VII. Oslo: Utgitt av Norsk Folkemuseum, Universitetsforlaget, 1964.

Pepitone, Albert. "Self, social environment and stress." *In* Appley and Trumbull (Eds., 1967a), 1967.

Peterson, R. *North American moose.* Toronto: University of Toronto Press, 1955.

Petitot, Emile. "Géographie de L'Athabaskaw-Mackenzie et des Grands Lacs du Basin Arctique." Bulletin, *Société de Géographie, 6me Série* **10**, pp.5-42, 126-183, 242-290, 1875.
Dictionnaire de la langue Dènè-Dindjië . . . précédé d'une monographie de Dènè-Dindjië. Paris: Ernest Leroux, 1876.
Quinze ans sous le cercle polaire. Paris: E. Dentu, 1889.
Autour du Grand Lac des Esclaves. Nouvelle Librairie Parisienne. Paris: Albert Savine, 1891.
Phillips, R. A. J. *Canada's North.* Toronto: The Macmillan Company of Canada, 1967.
Piers, Gerhart, and Milton B. Singer. *Shame and guilt: a psychoanalytic and a cultural study.* Springfield, Ill.: Charles C. Thomas, 1953.
Rand, A. L. *Mammals of Yukon, Canada.* Bulletin No. 100. Ottawa: National Museum of Canada, 1945.
Rich, E. E. *The fur trade and the Northwest to 1857.* Toronto: McClelland and Stewart Limited, 1967.
Richardson, John. *Arctic searching expedition.* 2 volumes. London: Longman, Brown, Green, and Longmans, 1851.
Rogers, Edward S. "Band organization among the Indians of eastern subarctic Canada." *In* Damas (Ed. 1969a), 1969a.
"Natural environment — social organization — witchcraft: Cree versus Ojibwa — a test case." *In* Damas (Ed., 1969b), 1969b.
Rowe, J. S. *Forest regions of Canada.* Bulletin No. 123. Ottawa: Forestry Branch, Department of Northern Affairs and Natural Resources, 1959.
Sahlins, Marshall. "Notes on the original affluent society." *In* Lee and DeVore (Eds.), 1968.
Saum, Lewis O. *The fur trader and the Indian.* Seattle: University of Washington Press, 1965.
Savishinsky, Joel S. "Stress and mobility in an arctic community: the Hare Indians of Colville Lake, Northwest Territories." Unpublished doctoral dissertation. Cornell University, 1970a.
"Kinship and the expression of values in an Athabascan bush community." *Western Canadian Journal of Anthropology* **2**, pp.31-59, 1970b.
"Mobility as an aspect of stress in an arctic community." *American Anthropologist* **73**, pp.604-618, 1971a.
"Comment on 'Southwestern studies: a view to the future' by M. Estellie Smith." *Human Organization* **30**: p.434, 1971b.
"Coping with feuding: the missionary, the fur trader, and the ethnographer." *Human Organization* **31**, pp.281-290, 1972a.
"Comment on 'The anatomy of envy' " by George Foster. *Current Anthropology* **13**, p.195, 1927b.
"The dog and the Hare: canine culture in an Athabaskan band." *Proceedings of the 1971 Conference on Athabaskan Studies.* Publications in Ethnology, National Museum of Man, Ottawa: National Museums of Canada (in Press).
Savishinsky, Joel S. and Susan B. Frimmer. *The middle ground: social change in an arctic community, 1967-1971.* Mercury Publications, No.7, National Museum of Man. Ottawa: National Museums of Canada, 1973.
Savishinsky, Joel S., and Hiroko Sue Hara. "The Hare Indians." *In* June Helm, Ed. *The subarctic.* Vol. VI of The Handbook of North American Indians. Washington, D.C.: Smithsonian Institution, Center for The Study of Man (in

press).

Schwartz, Barry. "The social psychology of privacy." *American Journal of Sociology* **73**, pp.741-752, 1968.

Scott, J. P. "The process of primary socialization in canine and human infants." *Monographs of the Society for Research in Child Development*, Serial No. 85, **28**, No. 1, 1963.

Selye, Hans. *The stress of life*. New York: McGraw-Hill, 1956.

Service, Elman R. *The hunters*. Englewood Cliffs, N.J.: Prentice-Hall, Inc., 1966.

Simmel, Georg. *Conflict and the web of group-affiliations*. Kurt H. Wolff and Reinhard Bendix, translators. New York: The Free Press, 1964.

Sindcell, Peter S. "Some discontinuities in the enculturation of Mistassini Cree children." *In* Norman A. Chance, Ed. *Conflict in culture: problems of developmental change among the Cree*. Canadian Research Centre for Anthropology. Ottawa: Saint Paul University, 1968.

Slobodin, Richard. "Some social functions of Kutchin anxiety." *American Anthropologist* **62**, pp.122-133, 1960a.

"Eastern Kutchin warfare." *Anthropologica* **2**, pp.76-94, 1960b.

Band organization of the Peel River Kutchin. Bulletin No. 179. Ottawa: National Museum of Canada, 1962.

"Leadership and participation in a Kutchin trapping party." *In* Damas (Ed., 1969a), 1969.

"Kutchin concepts of reincarnation." *Western Canadian Journal of Anthropology* **2**, pp.67-79, 1970.

Smith, D. G. "The Mackenzie Delta — domestic economy of the native peoples. A preliminary study." *Mackenzie Delta Research Project*, Report No. 3. Northern Co-ordination and Research Centre. Ottawa: Department of Indian Affairs and Northern Development, 1968.

Sommer, Robert. "Studies in personal space." *Sociometry* **22**, pp.247-260, 1959.

Personal space: the behavioral basis of design. Englewood Cliffs, N.J.: Prentice-Hall, Inc., 1969.

Steiner, Ivan D. "Strategies for controlling stress in interpersonal situations." *In* McGrath (Ed., 1970a), 1970.

Sue, Hiroko. "Hare Indians and their world." Unpublished doctoral dissertation. Bryn Mawr College, 1964.

Pre-school children of the Hare Indians. Northern Co-ordination and Research Centre. Ottawa: Department of Northern Affairs and National Resources, 1965.

Symington, Fraser. *Tuktu, the caribou of the northern mainland*. Canadian Wildlife Service. Ottawa: Department of Northern Affairs and National Resources, 1965.

Szasz, Kathleen. *Petishism: pets and their people in the Western world*. New York: Holt, Rinehart and Winston, Inc., 1969.

Torrance, E. Paul. "Comparative studies of stress-seeking in the imaginative stories of preadolescents in twelve different subcultures." *In* Samuel Z. Klausner, Ed. *Why man takes chances: studies in stress-seeking*. Garden City: Doubleday and Co., Inc., 1968.

Turnbull, Colin M. *The forest people*. New York: Simon and Schuster, 1961.

"The importance of flux in two hunting societies." *In* Lee and DeVore (Eds., 1968), 1968a.

"Discussion of resolving conflicts by fission." *In* Lee and DeVore (Eds., 1968), 1968b.

Usher, Peter . *The Bankslanders.* 3 volumes. Northern Science Research Group. Ottawa: Department of Indian Affairs and Northern Development, 1971.

Valentine, Victor F. and Frank G. Vallee (Eds.). *Eskimo of the Canadian Arctic.* The Carleton Library No. 41. Toronto: McClelland and Stewart Limited, 1968.

Vallee, Frank G. *Kabloona and Eskimo in the Central Keewatin.* The Canadian Research Centre for Anthropology. Ottawa: Saint Paul University, 1967.

Van Stone, James W. "Changing patterns of Indian trapping in the Canadian subarctic." *Arctic* 16, pp.159-174, 1963.
The changing culture of the Snowdrift Chipewyan. Bulletin No. 209. Ottawa: National Museum of Canada, 1965.

Villiers, Desmé. *Central Mackenzie: an area economic survey.* Industrial Division. Ottawa: Department of Indian Affairs and Northern Development, 1967.

Wallace, Anthony F. C. *Culture and personality.* 2nd edition. New York: Random House, 1970.

Welsh, Ann. "Community pattern and settlement pattern in the development of Old Crow Village, Yukon Territory." *Western Canadian Journal of Anthropology* 2, pp.17-30, 1970.

Wentzel, W. F. "Letters to the Hon. Roderic McKenzie, 1807-1824." *In* L. R. Masson, Ed. *Les bourgeois de la Compagnie du Nord-Ouest.* Première Série. Quebec: A. Coté, 1889.

Weyer, Edward Moffat. *The Eskimos.* Hamden, Conn.: Archon Books, 1969.

Whitaker, Ian. *Social relations in a nomadic Lappish community.* Samiske Samlinger, Bind II. Oslo: Utgitt av Norsk Folkemuseum, 1955.

Willmott, W. E. "The flexibility of Eskimo social organization." *Anthropologica* 2, pp.48-59, 1960.

Wissler, Clark. *The American Indian.* 3rd edition. Gloucester, Mass.: Peter Smith, 1957.

Woodburn, James. "Stability and flexibility in Hadza residential groupings." *In* Lee and DeVore (Eds.), 1968.

Index